Author's Note

This book is the fruit of nearly 20 years of listening to the Gospel of John — and you can listen to it, too. To learn how, make sure you read the Introduction. There you'll discover a free gift that will allow you to hear the same dramatic presentation of this beautiful Gospel that I myself have enjoyed for so many years.

33 Days
to
Greater
Glory

A Total Consecration to the Father through Jesus
Based on the Gospel of John

Fr. Michael E. Gaitley, MIC

MARIAN PRESS
STOCKBRIDGE MA 01263

PRO CHRISTO ET ECCLESIA

2019

Available from:
Marian Helpers Center
Stockbridge, MA 01263

Prayerline: 1-800-804-3823
marian.org
Orderline: 1-800-462-7426
shopmercy.org

IMPRIMI POTEST:
Very Rev. Kazimierz Chwalek, MIC
Provincial Superior
The Blessed Virgin Mary, Mother of Mercy Province
December 12, 2019

Library of Congress Control Number: 2019957986
ISBN: 978-1-59614-513-9

Cover Art: "The Crucifixion" by Leon Bonnat (public domain)

Stained glass images were chosen to divide the weeks of this retreat because Jesus tells us in the Gospel of John, "I am the light of the world" (8:12).

Printed in the United States of America

To my dad

I love the Father.

~ Jesus

Contents

In Gratitude

I've written nearly all of my books while at my parents' house during my annual vacation. This one was no exception — although it almost was. When it came time to write, I knew my dad would be undergoing cancer treatment. Not wanting to be a burden, I found an alternative location to work. When my parents heard, they would have none of it and insisted I come home. I obeyed, and as usual, they were as generous and loving as they've always been. Thank you, Mom and Dad, for putting up with me during a time when you were both going through so much.

I am also grateful to my sister, Heather, and to Sarah Chichester, both of whom offered many helpful comments and suggestions while I was writing. When you read the Introduction, you'll see why I certainly can't omit the Marian Missionaries of Divine Mercy and Leonardo Defilippis from my list of thanks. Finally, I am grateful to my many faithful friends who have prayed for me during this intense month of writing. I am well aware that if a book is to bless others, it must be the fruit of prayer. I pray I've not wasted too many of the graces that others have obtained for it. I hope it truly will be a blessing and help us come to better know and love our Father in Heaven.

Fr. Michael Gaitley, MIC
Ascension of the Lord, 2019

INTRODUCTION
A Time of Turmoil

I'm writing this book from a place of great turmoil. Based on what I'm hearing, I'm not the only one experiencing it, which comes as no surprise. After all, the turmoil is everywhere. It's in the world, in the Church, and so also, in ourselves.

This 33-day retreat aims to help us overcome our turmoil with the peace and joy that the world cannot give. Before we can get to that peace and joy, however, we first need to face the turmoil.

TURMOIL IN THE WORLD: TIME TO TUNE OUT. I used to be a news junkie. No more. At least I want to say no more. The tenor of public discourse has gotten to the point where I'm trying to tune out to keep my sanity and recover some sanctity.

"Oh, but you've got to stay up on current events."

Yes, I suppose that's true, especially for a priest. But there's got to be another way. The current mode of getting information about the world (and one another, if we're on social media) often fills one with the world in the worst possible way.

Now, of course, there are great things about the digital age and our amazing devices that connect us with just about everything. But that's part of the problem: They connect us with *everything*, which often includes an overwhelming dose of darkness. I say "overwhelming" because there's no possible way our spirits can filter through the massive stream of information into which most of us are daily immersed. In view of that, unless we do some form of "tuning out," the subtle and not-so-subtle innuendo, violence, gossip, and vanity will dig into our hearts and souls, making us into selfish and petty people. If we're not careful, we'll find ourselves not just *in* the world but *of* it. If we're not vigilant, we'll certainly become worldly.

Worldly. That old word should come back into fashion, because worldliness is our problem. It's the worldliness of Christians who should be a light in the darkness but who hardly shine at all. It's the worldliness of believers who are barely different in opinion from their political party or source of daily news. It's the worldliness of clergy who should have shepherded the flock but, rather, shepherded themselves and even preyed on the sheep.

Let's start with the latter.

*T*URMOIL IN THE CHURCH: TIME TO WAKE UP. I was a seminarian in Boston during the "Long Lent of 2002."[1] That was when a clergy sex abuse scandal rocked the Archdiocese and then the whole Church — and it lasted well past Lent.

I know that because every morning for the better part of a year, I'd pick up a copy of *The Boston Globe*, and right there on the front page was yet another story announcing the unthinkable things a priest had done to God's innocents (some 700 stories on the topic in one year). To cope with the unbelievable horror of it all, we seminarians would say things like, "Terrible as that is, it's old news. Those are all cases from decades ago." Some even talked about it as a persecution of the Church, because Catholic clergy on average committed fewer cases of abuse than teachers and ministers of other faiths did.

Despite such rationalizations, I think we all knew deep inside that there were no excuses. We all knew, but maybe didn't admit, that the Catholic Church should be held to a higher standard, as we've been entrusted with more. We all knew, but maybe didn't say, that we were witnesses to the reality of an unthinkable tragedy and a betrayal of outrageous proportions.[2]

One particular narrative attempted to console us. It went like this: The problem is really with those darn liberals, the "bad guys," who were letting all the homosexuals into the seminaries and condoning immoral behavior. The solution, we were told, would come from the "good guys," that is, the conservative bishops and cardinals appointed by Pope John Paul II who were going to clean things up and save the Church.

Apparently, the promoters of that narrative hadn't read the newspapers.

One of the supposed "good guys," Cardinal Bernard Law of Boston, turned out to be a big part of the problem.[3]

Without reporting the sex abuse crimes of his priests to civil authorities, he repeatedly oversaw the transfer of those sick men to various parishes, where they continued their predatory practices on countless children.

The Cardinal resigned in December of 2002, and with that, I hoped and prayed that the scandals of that terrible year were over and that the Boston Church could begin to heal. I further hoped that the situation in Boston, including the actions of the Cardinal, was an outlier. Others did, too. And so, the "good guys" versus "bad guys" blame game I often heard continued, with conservatives as "the good guys" and liberals as "the bad guys."

Fast forward to 2009.

Late that year, I was getting ready to publish my first book, *Consoling the Heart of Jesus*, which I intended as a sort of belated response to the clergy sex abuse scandal.[4] Living in Boston that tragic year of 2002, I'd had a deep sense of the Lord's sorrow and how the scandal was breaking his Heart. I figured one small thing I could do was to try to console Jesus, and with my book, I wanted to inspire others to do so as well.

As I was getting ready to publish the book, I thought it would be great to have an endorsement from a bishop or, better yet, a cardinal.

Fortunately (or so I thought), I had just met one the year before.

His name was Cardinal Theodore McCarrick, and we first met when he arrived at the National Shrine of Divine Mercy in Stockbridge, Massachusetts, to celebrate our Divine Mercy Sunday celebration. At the time, I was a seminarian, assigned to hospitality, specifically to the Cardinal. I recall that McCarrick was very kind and personable and that when someone mentioned I was working on a book, he had encouraged me to keep at it. Well, a year later, when I needed an endorsement, I thought of the Cardinal, reached out to his secretary, and boldly requested not only that he consider endorsing my book but that he be the main celebrant at my upcoming priestly ordination.

To my great joy, he agreed to both!

That joy would later turn to sorrow ... and anger.

Fast forward to the summer of 2018.

At the time, I was already reeling from the discovery of a vicious and cowardly conspiracy of lies sparked by the jealousy of certain brother priests. Then came horrific details from a grand jury report on a clergy sex abuse scandal in Pennsylvania. Finally, all summer long, there was the steady stream of news headlines featuring the predatory actions of the very same cardinal pictured in my ordination photos — yes, McCarrick — followed by allegations of cover-ups by high-ranking Church officials in Rome.

Suddenly, it felt like 2002 all over again, and I'd had enough. In my anger, I kept asking myself, "What the heck is wrong with the Church?!" And as I asked that, any remaining vestiges of the simple narrative I'd heard in my seminary days were thoroughly wiped from my mind and heart. I became convinced that the problems in the Church were not the result of a battle between the "good guys" and the "bad guys." (That was way too simplistic.) Rather, the problems clearly were much deeper, more complex, and thoroughly widespread. Yes, the so-called "bad guys" had sometimes been loose on sexual ethics and dissented against Church teaching. But also, yes, some of the so-called "good guys" demonstrated glaring arrogance, cowardice, and a slap-you-on-the-back, protect-your-own, good-ol'-boy mentality.

So as I began to calm down in the fall and into the winter, I thought to myself, *It's time to wake up and face the real problem.*

And what's the real problem?

Again, I suggest it's the sin of worldliness. It's the sin of being no different in our actions from the larger society. It's the sin of claiming to be set apart for God but of being just like "the pagans" (or worse than the pagans, because of self-righteousness). It's the sin of professing one thing but actually living the opposite.

The real problem, then, is the worst kind of worldliness: the worldliness of those who claim to be otherworldly, the worldliness that stinks with the rot of hypocrisy.

So, what's the solution?

It's a hard one, at least in this day and age. It's authentic Christianity. It's giving up worldliness to follow Christ more radically. It's a complete commitment to the Gospel — which brings me to my own personal turmoil.

Let me back up a bit and tell more of the story.

TURMOIL IN ME: TIME TO WRITE. After my priestly ordination in 2010, I was assigned to run an office with about 80 employees. I had no business background, was the only priest there, and faced a mountain of financial and fundraising challenges that I was supposed to fix.

Confronted with that complex situation, I settled on a simple strategy: evangelization. I believed (hoped) that if our organization didn't just seem to be asking people for money but put greater emphasis on feeding souls with such things as more books, programs, and religious art, then the Lord would provide for us through those very same people.

Armed with that belief, I threw myself into writing books, creating programs, and engaging in other evangelization ventures. I got into marketing and promotion. I started speaking at conferences and various events and experienced a lot of worldly success in a religious context. Meanwhile, as I faced a myriad of battles and life-sapping betrayals, I grew hard-hearted and probably thought of myself as more important than the nothing that I am (apart from Christ).

Thanks be to God, in his great mercy, he broke me down. (Rather, he let me break myself down.) I lost a ton of weight and was sick all the time. I also felt powerless to deal with my growing anger and resentment over injustices both perceived and real. Clearly, there was something wrong, and so I became more open to listening to the voice of the Lord, calling me to conversion and renewal.

That voice came in 2014. Specifically, I heard it through a small group of extraordinary and generous young people who basically showed up at the National Shrine of Divine Mercy with the desire to dedicate themselves to putting mercy into action by serving the poor — and they wanted my help. Actually, they *needed* my help. That is, they needed not a CEO or a "Catholic celebrity" but rather the very things I actually wanted to be: a priest and a father.

Still, at first, I resisted. I'm an impatient introvert, and I wasn't sure how I'd handle having to be constantly present to young people amid work that on the surface and to the ego, frankly, didn't seem as important as running an office. I'm also a worrywart, and so, such a brand new, uncertain project for the poor had nowhere near the appeal of my relatively stable office job, even with all its craziness.

One day, I summoned the courage to speak with my superior, who had assigned me to my position in the office. Specifically, I opened up to him, telling him of the growing hardness of my heart and of how I felt the Lord might be asking me to make a change. My superior listened attentively, confirmed what I felt God was saying, and shifted my assignment from running the whole office to serving those young people who wanted to help the poor, the Marian Missionaries of Divine Mercy.[5]

Thank God for obedience. My work with the Missionaries has become one of the greatest joys of my life. Also, I believe it has not only saved my vocation but has helped me to discover something very important: Christianity is so much more than a profession of faith and the upkeep of buildings. It's about love. It's about loving our enemies, loving the poor, and loving our neighbor.

Believe me, I know all that sounds cliché, but during these last five years with the Missionaries, I've discovered it to be something very real. I've also painfully discovered how very much I fall short. My joy, however, is in the mercy of the good Lord and in the clarity of knowing exactly what kind of priest, what kind of Christian, I really do want to become for Christ and the Church.

Because writing helps me to "own" what I believe, this book is kind of selfish: Through it, I want to own becoming an authentic Christian right at a time when we badly need the witness of such Christianity. I also hope it might help you, too, and I invite you to join me in this process of owning it, this process of overcoming the widespread turmoil in the world, in the Church, and in ourselves, through the peace and joy that the Lord's love brings.

Before getting right down to it, however, I need to tell you some good news that will help show us the way forward in this book.

A Time of Mercy

A powerful insight of St. John Paul II is the source of some great hope for me. It's the good news that *now is the time of mercy*.[6] Essentially, this comes down to Romans 5:20, which says, "Where sin abounded, grace abounded all the more." Applied to today, that's the Lord saying, "In the time of great evil and turmoil you're facing, I'm giving you even greater grace and mercy to overcome it."

Here in part two of this Introduction, I'd like to share one of the greatest graces I've personally received in this time of mercy, a grace that will serve as the basis of this book. Before getting to that, however, let's first turn our attention to something that marks the beginning of the current time of mercy, something that St. John Paul II called "the great grace of the 20th century,"[7] something that gives us a clear blueprint for the renewal of the Church in the modern world.

I'm talking about the Second Vatican Council.

Now, if you're rolling your eyes, please bear with me.

MERCY FOR THE CHURCH: VATICAN II. Why is Vatican II so great? In addition to it being an Ecumenical Council of the Catholic Church, which carries the highest level of teaching authority of the Magisterium, Vatican II in fact gets right to the heart of our problem.

And what's the problem?

Again, it's hypocrisy. It's the scandalous split between faith and life, the problem of the widespread worldliness of believers.

Thankfully, for us, Vatican II was a council of mercy, a pastoral council that sought not to condemn us in our hypocrisy but to help us get out of it. As St. John XXIII put it when he inaugurated the Council: "Nowadays ... [the Church] prefers to make use of the medicine of mercy rather than that of severity."[8]

And how does Vatican II apply that merciful medicine? How does it aim to help us overcome our hypocrisy? I've written about that at length in another book,[9] so here I'll just cut to the chase: It does so by helping us bring the truths of the faith *from our heads to our hearts to our lives.* In other words, its strategy is to help us better understand, love, and live the faith. One way it does this can be found in the very style of the Council documents themselves.

Unlike previous Church Councils, which used technical language intended for the experts, Vatican II aimed to put the ancient truths of our faith in a language and a context that modern Catholics, including the laity, could better understand. It recognized that the faith needs to be communicated in a way that regular people in the pews can easily grasp. Following on this idea, the bishops made one of the most recognizable and important decisions of the Council: The new rite of the Mass, the *Novus Ordo*, would be said primarily in the language of the people where the Mass would be offered. (Here in America, for instance, the Mass went from Latin to English.)

Now, I know a lot of people, fed up with the scandals in the Church and the worldliness of Christians, have rediscovered and love the old rite Latin Mass. It's a Liturgy that certainly has a more otherworldly feel, and its beauty can help people get away from the turmoil of modern society and experience the sublimity and glory of God in an atmosphere of pronounced reverence. I know it's a great blessing to many, and I don't want to take anything away from that. However, in this book, I intend to share something about the logic of the liturgical renewal of Vatican II, something that, unfortunately, is not very well known. I believe that if it were better known, the renewal called for by the Council would catch fire, and people would more fully discover and embrace the *Novus Ordo* liturgical celebration of the Eucharist for what it truly is: like the Latin rite, "the source and summit of the Christian life."[10]

I'll get into the specifics of all that later in the book. For now, I'll just say that part of the purpose of this writing is to help people own the liturgical renewal in such a way that they always feel "fed" at every Mass, no matter how platitudinous the homily or seemingly irreverent the presider. I can say that because the renewal that comes from the Liturgy isn't primarily dependent on the priest but rather on us, on what the Council calls our "full, conscious, and active participation in the Liturgy,"[11] which this book is going to explore and encourage.

Again, an important way that the Council aimed to help us enter more fully, consciously, and actively into the liturgy was by its decision to translate the liturgical texts into the vernacular. The idea is that when we hear the prayers of the Liturgy in our own language, we'll better grasp the meaning of the prayers than if they were in a language we didn't understand.

Now, all of this is consistent with a major theme of the Council, namely, "the universal call to holiness."[12] Essentially, this means the responsibility of holiness falls not just on priests and religious but on everyone, including the laity. In the context of Liturgy, this call serves as a strong reminder to laypeople that they truly share in the priesthood of Christ by virtue of their Baptism. And because they're priests, because they share in the common priesthood of the faithful, laity most certainly have the right to unite themselves to the ministerial priest's offering at the altar at Mass. But that's not all. Laypeople also have the solemn obligation to bring with them, at the Eucharistic offering, the pains and sorrows of our broken human family that God may have mercy on us and on the whole world.[13]

Because the Mass includes not only the Liturgy of the Eucharist but also the Liturgy of the Word, Vatican II further encouraged everyone, including the laity, to more prayerfully read Sacred Scripture.[14] This was part of another theme of the Council, namely, a "getting back to the sources" ("*ressourcement*"), where of course, the most original source of all is the Word of God. Incidentally, by advocating a return to the sources, the Church seemed to be saying that her response to the challenge of the modern world would not simply be a return to a medieval theological synthesis. Four centuries earlier, the Council of Trent had already emphasized such a synthesis in its response to the challenge of the Protestant Reformation. But as the Second Vatican Council faced a different challenge, namely, the hypocrisy-inducing effects of the modern world, it adopted an approach *even more traditional* than that of the Council of Trent. For, whereas Trent relied heavily on medieval theology, Vatican II deliberately turned to the most traditional sources of all: Sacred Scripture and the early Fathers of the Church.[15] In a sense, then, you might say that, with Vatican II, the Church went even further back than Latin to Scripture's original Greek.

This book aims to promote the renewal called for by the Council *through the Sacred Liturgy*, by focusing on the two main parts of the Mass, namely, the Liturgy of the Word and the Liturgy of the Eucharist, as a way of responding to the modern world and avoiding the perilous pitfall of hypocrisy. But whereas the Council tended to be general in its approach, I want to get very specific as to how we will proceed along the trajectory of renewal laid out for us by the Council.

I'll begin by telling the story of one of the greatest graces of my life.

*M*ERCY FOR *M*ICHAEL: *T*HE *G*OSPEL OF *J*OHN. The Jubilee Year of 2000 was a time of extraordinary blessing for the whole Church, and I'd say, especially for me.

In September of that year, I began a 12-month novitiate in a religious congregation, a time set apart for intense prayer and conversion that was filled with what seemed like a lifetime of grace. Just two months into it, I got one of the greatest gifts in that year of gifts, and it came in an unexpected way.

Here's the background: I and the other men in my novitiate class weren't able to get out much. (After all, we were novices.) So, when the opportunity came to attend a local play, we jumped at it, even though none of us were very much into plays.

The play was produced and performed by Catholic actor, producer, and father of seven children, Leonardo Defilippis, and it was based on the Gospel of John. Actually, it wasn't just based on that Gospel, it *was* that Gospel. The whole thing. There was just one actor, Leonardo, and it lasted more than two hours — and to my great surprise, I totally loved it. I can't explain why, but seeing and hearing the whole Gospel in one sitting absolutely blew me away. Actually, I think I can explain why: The Gospel of John is the Word of God, and the Word of God is *powerful.* Moreover, the Gospel of John is a work of extraordinary beauty. In fact, based on the opinion of many saints, it's the most sublime book in all of Sacred Scripture, the Gospel that soars high above the others.[16]

Well, that's what I experienced that night.

So, after the production, I greeted Leonardo, who was still dressed as Jesus, and I bought one of the audio CDs of the production with what was left of my measly novitiate allowance. Now, that was probably the best purchase I've ever made in my whole life. Problem was, I had to wait about 10 more months before I could listen to it, because we novices weren't allowed to listen to CDs until after we made our first vows. Well, like a good novice, to torture myself, I put that CD right up on my desk where I could see it every day. I could hardly wait to listen to it to relive the experience of the play. In the meantime, I frequently read the Gospel of John, and while much of it confused me, I nevertheless fell deeply in love with its sacred mystery.

Finally, after I made my vows, I listened to the CD — *a lot.* Let me put it this way: If it were possible to wear out a CD, then that one would have been toast. After just a year, I basically had the whole thing memorized, and I still loved it. In fact, I never got tired of it. Even to this day, I still listen to it frequently, and I honestly believe that nothing has theologically formed me more in all of my 15 years of studies toward the priesthood than the Gospel of John, especially through that CD.

Now, before you run off and buy the CD, which beautifully weaves what I believe is one of the most beautiful pieces of music ever composed (the Russian chant of Rachmaninoff's *Vespers*) with a masterful dramatic presentation by someone who is not only a professional actor but who clearly loves the Lord and his Gospel — yes, before you run off and buy it — here's some good news in the time of mercy: *I'm going to give it to you*. Well, not the CD but the digital download. And, well, it's not me who's going to give it to you but Leonardo and his wife, Patti.

Before getting to the next section, let me briefly tell you how this came to be and how you can get the download.

About a week before I started working on this book, I gave a retreat to priests at Mt. Angel Benedictine Abbey in Oregon. A few days before I left, Leonardo, who lives near the Abbey, heard that I would be in town and contacted me, inviting me to meet. We did meet, and over the course of our conversation, I shared with him and his wife that I wanted to write a book based on the Gospel of John and how much his production meant to me and had inspired me. Leonardo then surprised me by saying that the place where I'd be giving the retreat (the Abbey) is where he'd rehearsed and opened the live production of *The Gospel According to John*. He also shared his own love for this Gospel but also his disappointment that not everyone appreciates it. I told him I shared the same disappointment and that one goal of my book would be to help people fall in love with this beautiful Gospel, as we had. I then felt inspired to make a very bold request. I said, "Leonardo, to help spread the Gospel of John, do you think you might be willing to give the download of your audio version away for free?" Without hesitation, he said, "Absolutely."

In the next section, I'll tell you more about how we'll be incorporating that audio of the Gospel of John into this retreat. But if you'd like to download it for free now, simply visit StLukeProductions.com/John and enter the code GLORY at checkout. When you do, please say a prayer of thanks for the generosity of Patti and Leonardo Defilippis. (You might also order a few copies of the CD for friends and family and peruse their other many fine productions.)

But now let's get back to this book and how it aims to bring us into the riches of the greatest Gospel, the greatest book of the Bible, the greatest story ever told.

*M*ERCY FOR A MONTH: GREATER GLORY. In 2012, I wrote a book called *33 Days to Morning Glory* to help people make a total consecration to Jesus through Mary. In 2016, I wrote another consecration book called *33 Days to Merciful Love,* a kind of sequel to the previous one, a consecration to Divine Mercy. Well, this book is the third in the series. And while you can read them in any order, I think it's best to read this one last. Why? Because this one is the culmination of the other two, the "*Greater Glory*" after *Morning Glory* and the fulfillment of *Merciful Love.*

Now, *Morning Glory* is about Mary and, at least implicitly, her Spouse, the Holy Spirit. But it doesn't end with Mary and the Holy Spirit. They bring us to a personal encounter with Jesus in his mercy, which is what *Merciful Love* is all about. But it doesn't end with Jesus, either. Jesus brings us home to God, our Father, which is what this book is about. It's the greater glory of the Mass that brings us through Christ, with Christ, and in Christ, in the unity of the Holy Spirit *to the Glory of God the Father.* It's the greater glory of God the Father fully revealed to us in the Gospel of John, the greatest of the Gospels.

Here's how it works.

1. Listen to the Gospel of John. Like *33 Days to Morning Glory* and *33 Days to Merciful Love,* this book is a 33-day preparation for consecration. In this case, though, it's the fullness of consecration that unites us to the perfect consecration of Jesus as he offers himself, in the Spirit, to the Father for the life of the world. And because this perfect consecration, as we'll learn in the Gospel of John, is to be *set apart* from the world, during these 33 days of preparation, I invite you to set yourself apart from digital distractions and devices as much as possible, except for this: Listen to the Gospel of John recording so graciously given to you by Leonardo and Patti. Listen to it over and over again during the course of your 33-day retreat. Put aside other things that you normally would listen to or watch and, instead, stick with the Gospel of John. It will reinforce the daily reading of this retreat and help free us from our worldliness by the power of the Word of God. (If you'd rather not listen to the whole Gospel, you can always read it. See Appendix Two for my favorite translation of the Gospel of John, the same translation that Leonardo uses in his audio production.)

2. Ponder with Your Heart. Like *33 Days to Morning Glory* and *33 Days to Merciful Love,* this book has daily readings. Like the other books, it's a 33-day do-it-yourself retreat in preparation for consecration that's based on *heart-pondering prayer.* In other words, this preparation doesn't focus on lots of vocal prayers each day of the retreat but, rather, on short spiritual readings that you can easily ponder in your heart throughout the day. So, you'll want to go over the daily reading each morning or the night before. That way, you can have the whole day to reflect on it. Of course, you should try not to miss a day of reading, but if you do, don't worry. You can always make it up the next day.

Now, you might be wondering when to schedule your 33-day retreat. Ideally, you should begin your preparation 33 days before an appropriate feast day. For *33 Days to Morning Glory* and *33 Days to Merciful Love,* the appropriate feast days were basically any Marian feast or other liturgical celebration associated with Divine Mercy. In this case, the options are much greater. Because this consecration is about a more full, conscious, and active participation in the Mass, I recommend that you make the consecration *at any Sunday Mass or Holy Day of Obligation.*

So, essentially, you can start the retreat at any time, and when you end, a Sunday Mass won't be far off, which is when you can make your consecration. Now, if you're aiming to consecrate on a *specific* Sunday, you'd simply take out your calendar and count back 33 days from that Sunday so your Day of Consecration would be the 34th day. In short: This retreat is 33 days *of preparation* followed by the Day of Consecration.

Simple enough.

Alright, so now let's look at the structure.

3. Know the Structure of the Weeks. Packing the Gospel of John into four weeks (28 days), with the last five days being a review, has been something of a challenge. But as I was preparing to write, a four-part structure suddenly dawned on me, one that lets us cover the whole Gospel in the *33 Days* format. That four-part structure is as follows: Opening Characters, The Seven Signs, The Upper Room, and Greater Glory.

Let's briefly look at how we'll apply this structure to the weeks of our retreat.

Week One, dedicated to the *Opening Characters*, covers the first four chapters of the Gospel (with one exception) and introduces several key people.

Week Two, dedicated to *The Seven Signs*, covers the seven miracles that Jesus works in the Gospel (chapters 2-11). But John[17] doesn't call them "miracles." Rather, he calls them "signs" to emphasize that each of them points to that truth to which Jesus came to bear witness, the truth we'll discover during our retreat.

Week Three is dedicated to *The Upper Room*, the place where Jesus speaks to the disciples and to the Father as he prepares to enter into the hour of his Passion (chapters 13-17).

Week Four, *Greater Glory*, focuses on the Passion and Resurrection of Jesus, where his glory and that of the Father is most fully revealed (chapters 12; 18-21). It's also during Week Four that we'll delve more deeply into the Liturgy of the Eucharist.

4. Follow Up with the Consecration to St. Joseph. One last thing: Because this book is essentially a consecration to the Father, after you've completed it, you may find it helpful to get to know the Father better by making a consecration to St. Joseph, who is a kind of image of God our Father.

Back in 2014, I wrote and published such a consecration, called *Nine Days to Joseph*, which I've included in Appendix One of this book. For years, I intended to expand that consecration into a more comprehensive presentation. Then came some terrible disappointments. Subsequently, with the support of my provincial superior, I freely chose to respond to those disappointments in the spirit of St. Joseph and put aside my earlier plans.

Now, that wasn't easy. But at this point, I'm beginning to see the blessing. Specifically, I wonder if perhaps the Lord just wanted me to keep the consecration to St. Joseph very simple and understated, like St. Joseph himself. Perhaps he wanted it to remain a brief consecration to our spiritual father so as not to distract from but to better complement the more important consecrations to Mary, to Divine Mercy, and to our Heavenly Father. Perhaps this is the way that St. Joseph himself prefers it.

But who knows for sure?

Certainly not me. And who knows if the Lord will eventually move me to write that longer consecration after all? Until then, if you do decide to consecrate yourself using *Nine Days to Joseph*, know this: It's *very* easy. You simply read the brief, daily prayers as a novena-style preparation nine days before a feast of St. Joseph, the main ones being March 19 (Solemnity of St. Joseph), May 1 (Memorial of St. Joseph the Worker), and the Second Sunday after Christmas (Feast of the Holy Family).[18] Also, since Wednesdays are traditionally dedicated to St. Joseph, you could make your consecration to him on any Wednesday of the year.

Alright, so amid the present time of turmoil, let's now find greater mercy and greater glory in the greatest of the Gospels. Let's get back to the original source, the Word of God, and let it set us free from our hypocrisy so we might become authentic witnesses of Christ and the beauty of the Church. Let's learn from the apostle who rested his head on the Heart of Jesus and there discovered the deepest mysteries of the Father's love.

Opening
Characters

This week covers the opening characters of the Gospel of John. They are as follows: A Prophet Like Moses, John the Baptist, the First Apostles, "The Jews," Nicodemus, the Woman at the Well, and perhaps surprisingly, the Woman Caught in Adultery.

DAY 1
A Prophet Like Moses
John 1:1-18

"Do not come near."

Thus God spoke to Moses from a bush that burned with a fire that did not consume it. But while Moses was not allowed to draw near, he still got to behold the glorious sight and had the privilege of hearing the voice of the Lord, the all-powerful Word of God.

And what did that Word reveal?

It revealed God's compassion and mercy, for God said, "I have seen the affliction of my people ... and have heard their cry ... I know their sufferings, and I have come down to deliver them" (Ex 3:7-8).

And the Word also revealed the name of God: "*I AM WHO AM*" (Ex 3:14).

That divine name, full of power and life, like the burning bush, is aflame with existence without needing any fuel from which to draw its power. For God himself IS. God himself is existence. God himself is power and life, the source of all life and all that is.

That merciful, all-powerful God then used Moses to deliver the people of Israel from their slavery in Egypt, leading them across the Red Sea to Mount Sinai in the desert. And on the third day at Sinai, God called Moses to the top of the mountain, which was shrouded in smoke because the glory of the Lord descended on top of it like a consuming fire. But that fire did not consume Moses, who received the Law as a spark to set God's people alight with a burning love for their God.

In response to the Word of the Law, God's people proclaimed, "All that the Lord has spoken we will do, and we will be obedient" (Ex 24:7).

But they were not obedient. For when Moses returned to the top of the mountain, the people made a god of their own, a golden calf, and worshiped it instead of the only God. At that, God's anger flared up. But Moses interceded, and the Lord relented of the punishment he had planned. Why? Because as the Lord said to Moses, he is a God "merciful and gracious, slow to anger, and abounding in mercy and faithfulness" (Ex 34:6).

And the one to whom God showed the greatest mercy of all was Moses himself. For Moses enjoyed an intimacy with God unlike anyone else on the face of the earth. After all, it was to Moses that God revealed his name, to Moses that God spoke as with "a friend," to Moses that God granted the familiarity of "face to face" dialogue (though without actually seeing God's face).[19]

Having already tasted the sweetness of the Lord and his friendship, Moses longed for more. He pined for more. And so, despite those earlier words of the Lord from the bush, "Do not come near," *Moses did draw near* as he expressed his desires in a heartfelt plea to the Lord: "I beg you, show me your glory" (Ex 33:18).

Sadly, God could not grant that prayer. To see the fullness of his glory would be to see his face, and to see God's face would have consumed poor Moses, as the Lord himself explained: "You cannot see my face; for man shall not see me and live" (Ex 33:20).

But God loved Moses, and in his great tenderness, he revealed to him as much glory as the man could bear, saying,

> Behold, there is a place by me where you shall stand upon the rock; and while my glory passes by I will put you in a cleft of the rock, and I will cover you with my hand until I have passed by; then I will take away my hand, and you shall see my back; but my face shall not be seen. (Ex 33:21-23)

The Lord's back. That was the most glory ever revealed to man — up to that point. It was the limit decreed by God, and yet our good and gracious God strove to give Moses even more. He did so by revealing the *promise* of a greater glory. And even though Moses himself would not see it in this life, he could at least become the messenger to point to it, and he is indeed that messenger precisely when he writes in Deuteronomy: "The Lord your God will raise up for you a prophet like me from among you" (18:15).

And how would that future prophet be like Moses? He would speak with God "face to face" (Ex 33:11). And how would that prophet experience a greater glory? He would not just speak with God face to face but would actually *see* God's face, as Pope Benedict XVI explains:

> The promise [from Moses] of a "prophet like me"
> … implicitly contains an even greater expectation:
> that the last prophet, the new Moses, will be granted
> what was refused to the first one — a real, immediate vision of the face of God, and thus the ability to
> speak entirely from seeing, not just from looking at
> God's back.[20]

Jesus is that Prophet, the one with "a real, immediate vision of the face of God." And more than a prophet, Jesus himself is the Word become Flesh, the Word who was with God, and the Word who is God. So, he doesn't just see God; he is God. He's the Only Begotten Son of God who's in the bosom of the Father, and he shares with us where he is from, what he has seen, and who God is.

The conclusion to the Prologue of John's Gospel summarizes it best: "*No one has ever seen God; the only-begotten Son, who is in the bosom of the Father, he has made him known*" (1:18).[21]

That last phrase describes Jesus' mission, his passion, and his purpose. It's to make the Father known and loved, to reveal the truth about God, to allow us to see what Moses could not see: the glorious face of the Father shining forth from the face of Christ, revealing not only the truth about God, but also the truth about ourselves, as we'll learn tomorrow.

Today's Prayer:
I beg you, Father, show me your glory. Show me your face. Let me behold your glory shining forth from the face of Christ.

DAY 2
John the Baptist 3|5
John 1:19-34; 3:22-30

To set his people free from their slavery in Egypt, God gave Moses power to work terrible wonders in the sight of Pharaoh.

The most terrible was the last.

To prepare his people for it, God gave them specific instructions: On the appointed evening, each household was to sacrifice an unblemished lamb, sprinkle its blood on the lintels and doorposts, and then, that night, they were to eat the roasted flesh of the lamb with unleavened bread. Finally, on the same night, God would send "a company of destroying angels" (Ps 78:49) to strike down the firstborn son of every house in Egypt, unless that house was marked by the blood of a lamb, unless the people of that house had eaten the flesh of the lamb (Ex 12:7-13).

And so it happened. The firstborn sons and even the firstborn animals from every Egyptian household, including that of Pharaoh, were slain that night.

After discovering his dead son and hearing the cries of the Egyptians, Pharaoh sent God's people away. But then he changed his mind and proceeded to pursue them with his "horses and chariots, horsemen, and army" (Ex 14:9). Finally, the Lord himself consumed Pharaoh's worldly power in the waves of the Red Sea and led his chosen people safely home to freedom.

Of course, we've heard all that before, especially every Easter. But we should bring it back to mind as we reflect on John the Baptist's words in the Gospel of John. Seeing Jesus walking toward him, he said, "Behold the Lamb of God who takes away the sin of the world."

Now, only the Gospel of John includes those words, and there's a lot from the other Gospels that John does not include. Why? Because John approaches the mystery of Christ from a deeper and more personal perspective.

Let's look at this aspect of the Gospel of John more closely through its treatment (or, rather, non-treatment) of the Baptism of Jesus.

The other three Gospels (Matthew, Mark, and Luke) describe Jesus' Baptism in this way: The clouds open, a dove descends, and the voice of the Father is heard, saying, "This is my beloved Son." The author of the Gospel of John also wants us to hear these words of the Father — although he never actually mentions them. Instead, he shares his own name.

John?

No. In his Gospel, John doesn't go by the name "John." Rather, he's the "Beloved Disciple." And by calling himself this, it's like he wants to tell us, "What the Father said to Jesus at his Baptism, 'You are my beloved,' *he also wants to say to you.*" In other words, John is telling all baptized believers that we, too, are God's beloved children, we too, are "beloved disciples" of the God who "so loved the world that he gave his only-begotten Son" (3:16).

Alright, so God loves us, and he also loves the world. But in the Gospel of John, "the world" is a reality ruled by the prince of this world, the devil. And whereas the other Gospels show Jesus, after his Baptism, being led to the desert to be tempted by the devil, which reveals the ways of the world (riches, honors, and pride), John doesn't report that at all. Rather, he unveils the sin of the world *throughout his Gospel.* In fact, right here, with the witness of John the Baptist, he gets directly to the task of unmasking the pride of the world. How? By revealing one of the most fundamental attitudes of Christ that prepares the way to Divine Love and discipleship in such love, namely, *humility.* So let's see how the Baptist and the Beloved Disciple help prepare the way for the revelation of God's love by showing us the path of humility in Christ.

First, John the Baptist himself is utterly humble. Regarding Christ, John says that he himself is not even worthy to do the slave's work of untying his master's sandals. Later, when some of John's disciples tell him that Jesus is also baptizing and "all are going to him," there's no jealousy in John, no ego, no rivalry or competition. Rather, he reveals the very heart of humility, which is to recognize that we have nothing on our own and can do nothing on our own, for everything comes from God: "No one can receive anything except what is given him from heaven." He further speaks of himself as "the friend of the bridegroom," as one who "rejoices greatly at the bridegroom's voice." Why does he speak like that? Because whereas others would envy the success of a potential rival, John sees a friend in Jesus and simply rejoices at his coming. Finally, speaking of Christ, he expresses what could be the very definition of Christian humility: "He must increase, but I must decrease." In other words, Jesus must increase and our bloated egos must decrease.

Second, the image of a lamb is also utterly humble. Think of it. A lamb is a young sheep that still suckles from its mother. It is a meek, docile, and gentle animal. So, *that* is what's going to take away the sin of the world? Absolutely. Again, at the heart of the sin of the world is pride. And just as the Passover lamb saved Israel's firstborn sons from death, so the humility of the Lamb of God saves the Children of God from the spiritual death that comes from the pride of the world.

In the Book of Revelation, also attributed to John, there's a curious scene where John is weeping and an elder says to him, "Weep not; behold, the Lion of the tribe of Judah ... has conquered" (5:5). A lion? Now that's more like it! That seems like the right image for a world-conquering God. But then you'd expect John to turn around and see a powerful and glorious lion, right? Instead, he says, "I saw a Lamb standing, as though it had been slain ..."

What? Talk about a powerless image: A dead lamb standing? That's certainly not the way of the world, but it's right in line with the humble way of Christ.

Again, think of it.

God in Christ first came to us in the form of a powerless little baby, born of a woman. As a child and adolescent, he grew up in a nowhere town with simple and humble parents. Finally, as a grown man, he needed someone as spectacular as John the Baptist to point him out. Why? Because on his own, nobody would have noticed Jesus. According to Isaiah's prophesy, his appearance wouldn't be particularly striking as, on the surface, nothing would set him apart or served to attract others to him (Is 53:3). (Although those who did draw close would discover astounding attractiveness, as we'll see tomorrow.)

So, Jesus, the grown man, really is like a lamb. He's a Lion, but he comes in the appearance of a Lamb.

The Prologue of John's Gospel speaks of a power Jesus gives us, the power to become "Children of God" (1:12). It's a power to say no to the world and yes to Christ, no to pride and yes to humility, no to the need for control and yes to letting God lead us, just as a Shepherd leads his flock of sheep — and of lambs.

Today's Prayer:

> *Look at an image of a lamb and reflect:* That *is the animal that most reveals who God is.* That *is the image of the Son, in whom the Father is well pleased.*

DAY 3
The First Disciples
John 1:35-51   3|6

John the Baptist must not have been a very attractive sight. He wore simple garments of camel hair, lived in a dusty desert wilderness, and was probably emaciated from his meager diet of locusts and wild honey.

So why did so many people go to him?

Because he was otherwordly. Because there's a hidden yet powerful attractiveness in that which is not of the world. Regarding John the Baptist, it's the promise of a light, life, and love that brings brightness, energy, and warmth to our often dismal human existence. Amid the "nothing new under the sun" of everything being "vanity" (Eccl 1:2, 9), it's the hope of something truly different, fresh, and new.

The promise of such a hope must have drawn the Beloved Disciple and Andrew to become followers of John the Baptist. They were men of sensitive hearts who searched for something more than what this world has to offer. Meeting the spirit-filled ascetic from the desert surely moved something in their spirits and helped form their hearts to recognize the Light of the World that would soon be dawning in their lives.

"Behold the Lamb of God."

Apart from the poignant connections with the history of Israel, the very image of a lamb, as we've seen, has an objective beauty. And so, the Baptist was essentially saying, "Behold the beauty of God's humility." For that's who Jesus is. He's the humility of God, the God who emptied himself and took the form of a slave and the image of a helpless lamb.

Attracted by the beauty of that Lamb, the Beloved Disciple and Andrew begin to follow Jesus. Turning, Jesus suddenly looks at them with a gaze of great tenderness and love, for while they don't yet know it, Jesus already knows everything that they will be to him. He then kindly asks them, "*What do you seek?*"

What *did* they seek? They probably didn't know what to say. Overwhelming beauty sometimes makes a person say senseless things. Think, for instance, of Peter at the Transfiguration when he basically blurted out, "Lord, it's good that we're here. Let me build some tents" (see Mt 17:4). Despite being dazzled by the light of Christ, John and Andrew give a beautiful response. They ask Jesus, "Where do you abide?"

Where *does* Jesus abide? The Prologue of John's Gospel already answered that question for us: He abides in "the bosom of the Father" (1:18). Jesus, who sees the Father, lives in the love of the Father as his dearly beloved Son and radiates the Father's love to all people. Again, whoever sees Jesus sees the Father also — that is, he sees the goodness of the Father who "so loved the world that he gave his only-begotten Son" (3:16).

So, Jesus responds to John and Andrew's beautiful question with a no less beautiful invitation: "Come and see." In other words, "Come and see the love of the Father. See where I abide, and abide with me in the Father's love."

And the disciples did just that. They stayed with Jesus that day, and while we don't know exactly what transpired, John reports a curious detail: the time. He says, "It was about the tenth hour" (or 4 in the afternoon). Now, why would he include a seemingly meaningless detail like that? Because to him it wasn't meaningless. When the Beloved Disciple was writing his Gospel as an old man in his 90s, he could still clearly remember the time he first encountered the love of Jesus. He could never forget it. That was the moment, that was the time, when everything changed. That was the moment when he found Love.

And then, what do John and Andrew do after meeting Jesus and encountering his love? They immediately go and tell others, because they had found what they sought — and what all of us seek.

First, they tell Simon, who became Peter, and then they find Philip and Nathanael. To each of these men, John and Andrew bear witness to what they themselves had experienced, even though they don't quite know what to make of it. In their enthusiasm, these first disciples call Jesus every name they can think of for a great man of Israel: "Rabbi," "Messiah," "King of Israel," and "Son of God." (The title "Son of God" in first-century Judaism did not mean the eternal Son, who is God.) Of course, Jesus is all of those things, but he's also so much more. And while the disciples don't yet know that Jesus is the Word become flesh, they do know that they've found something very special, something they now feel compelled to share with others.

This all brings us to a crucial concept that often comes up in John's Gospel. It has to do with the fact that the Beloved Disciple doesn't talk about *evangelization*, the spreading of the Gospel, like the other Gospel writers do. Rather, his word for evangelization is "witness." In other words, for John, to evangelize is to invite others with the same invitation Jesus offered to his first disciples. It's the invitation to "Come and see." It's the invitation to come and behold the beauty of God's glorious love shining forth from the face of Christ by bearing witness to that experience. For John, then, there's no evangelization without first encountering Christ. In fact, when Nathanael cynically responds to John and Andrew's testimony with the words, "Can anything good come out of Nazareth?" the disciples give the same response that Jesus himself first gave to them: "Come and see."

And why is this Jesus' invitation to us? Why come and *see*? Again, it's because he's the prophet like Moses who is greater than Moses, the one *who sees the Father*. Again, it's because Jesus' whole mission is to make the Father known. And just as John and Andrew, after beholding Christ's beauty, wanted to tell others about it, so also, because Jesus has seen the Father's glory, he, too, wants to tell everyone about it.

This desire to make the Father's glory known gets to the very heart of Jesus' Heart. It's at the center of why he came.

Again, Jesus loves the Father. He has seen the Father. But the world does not know this good and gracious Father. The world can't see him or understand him. The Father's love, humility, tenderness, and kindness are alien to a world that's still in bondage to sin. So, Jesus needs to train people to see, and he sometimes does so through the jarring action of over-turning the categories and status quo of the world, which we'll get to tomorrow.

Today's Prayer:
Hear the Lord ask you, "What do you seek?" Heed his invitation: "Come and see."

DAY 4
"The Jews"
John 2:13-22

Up until now, we've been following the basic progression of John's Gospel. First came the Prologue (Day 1), then John the Baptist (Day 2), and yesterday, the calling of the disciples (Day 3). That should now bring us to the Wedding Feast at Cana. However, we're going to have to skip the wedding — for now. The wedding at Cana is the first of Jesus' seven signs, which we'll be covering in Week Two.

Alright, so where do we go from here?

To Jerusalem, and for a less happy event. Here in Jerusalem, Jesus is going to cleanse the Temple and get into his first conflict with "the Jews." Before we get to all that, however, we should first take a brief look at the term "the Jews."[22]

In his Gospel, John usually uses the term "the Jews" in a negative way. Those words, however, do not refer to the Jewish race but, rather, to those religious leaders in Jerusalem who oppose Jesus and seek to kill him. Moreover, it should be obvious that John does not mean all Jewish people when he negatively writes of "the Jews." After all, John himself was a Jew, as were Jesus and Mary and many of the early Christians.[23]

Unfortunately, throughout much of the Church's history, this distinction was not always so obvious. In fact, John's use of the term "the Jews" to refer to those who sought Christ's death has sometimes been taken by Christians to justify persecution of the Jewish people, which has included mass expulsions, violence, and massacres.[24] Ironically, such Christians were precisely the kind of vicious, self-righteous people that John negatively refers to as "the Jews." (In that case, John himself might have considered such so-called Christians as "the Jews.")

Speaking of so-called Christians and given that so much worldliness has infiltrated the Church, the cleansing of the Temple provides a startling lesson. For Jesus, who is the meek Lamb and gentle shepherd full of tenderness and compassion for the weak and the broken, suddenly becomes the Lion in the face of worldliness in the Temple.

Let's read the actual text to grasp the ferocity of the Lion as he bears his claws:

> In the temple he found those who were selling oxen and sheep and pigeons, and the money-changers at their business. And making a whip of cords, he drove them all, with the sheep and the oxen, out of the temple; and he poured out the coins of the money-changers and overturned their tables. And he told those who sold the pigeons, "Take these things away; you shall not make my Father's house a house of trade." His disciples remembered that it was written, "Zeal for your house will consume me." (2:14-17)

Alright, now that's some zeal — maybe too much? In other words, might Jesus be overreacting here? I don't think so. To help us better appreciate exactly why the Lord would be so fired up, it may be helpful to reflect on the specific setting of the scene.

The buying and selling was taking place in what's called "the Court of the Gentiles." That's the one place into which God-fearing pagans could seek God at the Temple, the closest they could get to the divine presence in the Holy of Holies. And because that court was also for the Gentiles, who were seen as worldly and profane, "the Jews" had no problem prostituting it out as an emporium, a house of trade. Thus, among the hustle and bustle of what should have been a place of quiet and prayer, "the Jews" filled their moneybags while blocking the Gentiles from an experience of the one true God (see Mk 11:17).

And now, what about us? Are we also like "the Jews"? Do we sometimes look down with disdain on others who are not Catholic (or not Catholic enough)? Do we welcome materialism, gossip, and fear-mongering politics into those places of our hearts and minds that should be reserved for God? Do we allow the rush and clamor of daily life to crowd out opportunities to encounter Jesus through prayer and contemplation?

Such questions may, perhaps, upset us in the same way that Jesus upset "the Jews." After all, he overturned the tables of their worldly status quo — and then what? Then, they demanded a sign from him to justify his actions, to which Jesus responded: "Destroy this Temple, and in three days, I will raise it up." "The Jews" misunderstood him, thinking he was talking about the Temple building, but John clarifies that "he was speaking of the temple of his body."

Now, the ruler of this world, who is Satan, really did destroy the temple of Jesus' body on the Cross. But St. Paul tells us that we also are the Body of Christ and temples of the Holy Spirit (see 1 Cor 6:19; 12:27). In that case, we might ask, "Does the same diabolical, worldly spirit that destroyed the physical body of Jesus on the Cross seek to destroy our bodies as well?" In other words, does Satan want to destroy the temples that *we* are?

He does. Saint Peter himself tells us that "the devil prowls about the world like a roaring lion, looking for someone to devour" (1 Pet 5:8). Well, in the first century, that evil lion used Judas, the Romans, and "the Jews" to devour the body of the Lamb of God by means of the Cross. Now he wants to devour us, the Body of Christ, by other means. For instance, he wants to steal our souls through a worldly, materialistic, consumer culture that places having before being, things before people, and rights before responsibility. He wants to smother our spirits through a culture of death where the weak are aborted, the stranger is despised, and the environment is exploited. He wants to destroy our bodies through a convenient, throw-away, junk-food culture where we rarely exercise, fill ourselves with garbage, and become overweight, lazy, and terminally ill.

Again, Jesus is not just a Lamb but a Lion, and he won't let Satan devour us without a fight. And so, he cleanses the Temple of his Body, the Church. He bears his teeth, makes a whip of cords, and drives out the influence of the ruler of this world that we might be raised up, have life to the full, and become a more convincing light to the world.

And what is Jesus' whip? Here, during our retreat, it's the Gospel of John, written in the cleansing power of the Spirit — a power we'll learn more about tomorrow.

Today's Prayer:
> *Jesus, cleanse the temple of my body and soul. Destroy in it whatever is not of the Father and raise it up to new life in you.*

DAY 5
Nicodemus   ℨ\Ɣ
John 3:1-21

As we learned yesterday, when John uses the term "the Jews," he means the religious leaders in Jerusalem who oppose Jesus. But again, not all Jewish people were "the Jews."

Take Nicodemus, for instance. John describes him as "a ruler of the Jews," and rightfully so. After all, Nicodemus is a Pharisee and a member of the Jewish high council, the Sanhedrin — but he's certainly not one of "the Jews" in the negative sense of those who oppose Jesus. I say that because, later in the Gospel, he defends Jesus before others, and then, after the Crucifixion, he provides costly ointments for the Lord's burial, which reveals his compassion and love.

I think you could say, then, that Nicodemus was a good man. And yet, as is the case with all of us, he had his weaknesses. We see this, for instance, in the important detail about how he went to Jesus "by night." Why by night? Probably because, being a wealthy man of power, Nicodemus was afraid of what others might think if they caught him in a meeting with Jesus. Nevertheless, his goodness shines forth by the more important fact that, while others kept their distance, he actually did go out to see the Lord.

But then, we're right back to this man's weakness when he says to Jesus, "Rabbi, we know that you are a teacher come from God; for no one can do these signs that you do, unless God is with him."

Now, wait a minute, how is that weakness? Nicodemus sure seems to be saying everything in the right way. After all, he addresses Jesus with the respectful title "Rabbi," and he also affirms the truth that Jesus is "a teacher come from God." So, where's the weakness?

The weakness is in his *knowing*. Nicodemus has made a deduction about Jesus. He has seen the signs and deduces that only someone sent by God would have the power to do what Jesus does. Moreover, he has confidence in his judgments based on the categories of what he knows.

Now, there's no problem with having certitude based on categories — until we come to persons, especially the Person of the Incarnate Word. I say that because each and every person is a mystery that ought to be approached with respect and awe and not as a mere object to be categorized, classified, and have all figured out. Indeed, each person has an infinite depth, for we're all made in the image of God — but Jesus himself is the perfect image of the invisible God, the eternal Son of God. To know him in his mystery, we need new eyes, a new mind, and a whole new reality. We need to be transformed by faith and the power of the Spirit.

Unfortunately, Nicodemus still lacked all that. But Jesus loves this ruler of the Jews who had the courage to come to him, and he wants him to receive the gift of faith. So he challenges Nicodemus, telling him, "Truly, truly, I say to you, unless one is born anew, he cannot see the kingdom of God."

Now, the word Jesus uses, "anew" (*anōthen*), can also mean "from above." Not surprisingly, with his earthly way of thinking, Nicodemus assumes the former meaning and wonders if Jesus is saying that he must re-enter his mother's womb and be born again.

But obviously that's not what Jesus means.

So, what does he mean?

He means that to be set free from earthly thinking and the way of the world, we must be *born anew from above*. We need to be born of our Heavenly Father as his dearly beloved children through water and the power of the Holy Spirit:

"Truly, truly, I say to you, unless one is born of water and the Spirit, he cannot enter the kingdom of God." In other words, to come to know God, to see God, and enter into God, *we must be baptized.*

At this point, words spoken by the disciples later in the Gospel come to mind: "Ah, now you are speaking plainly, not in any figure!" (16:29) That is, we hear the word "Baptism" and think, *Oh, great! I know that. So that's what Jesus is talking about. (Why didn't he just say so?) Alright, let's move on.*

Now, that's certainly one way of approaching the ocean of mystery that is the Gospel of John, namely, by finding familiar islands and camping out on them.

But the Lord is inviting us to swim in the sea.

Let me put it this way: Baptism is so much more than we often realize. It was the moment of our deepest consecration, of when we were set apart from the world. Prior to Baptism, because of original sin, each of us belonged to the prince of this world, the devil. After Baptism, we are set free from Satan and belong to God as his dearly beloved children. And then we're supposed to live that way. We're to live "in the world but not of it," to live as lights in the midst of darkness. Too often, however, the darkness of the world smothers the light we received at Baptism. Or, at least it tries to force that light under the bushel basket of our greed, gluttony, anger, envy, pride, lust, laziness, and fear. But as sons and daughters of God, we're called to be a light in the darkness that shines for the world to see.

Alright, but how can we more faithfully respond to that call? How can we more effectively be that light?

Jesus explains to Nicodemus:

Do not marvel that I said to you, "You must be born anew." The wind blows where it wills, and you hear the sound of it, but you do not know where it comes from or where it goes; so it is with everyone who is born of the Spirit. (3:7-8)

There is the answer: The Christian life is the life of the Spirit. It's a life whose energy comes not from us but from the power of the Spirit, who blows where he wills. It's a life that does not follow the categories of this world and the ways of the flesh but, rather, the ways of the Kingdom of God. It's a life animated by the Spirit of Love, who's at odds with this world of sin, but at that same time, loves the created world.

Jesus tells Nicodemus that "God so loved the world that he gave his only-begotten Son, that whoever believes in him should not perish but might have eternal life." He then goes on, "For God sent his Son into the world, not to condemn the world, but that the world might be saved through him."

And how is the world saved through Jesus Christ?

In one sense, it's saved through us, through the baptized, who truly are his Body. It's saved when we, the children of light, come out of the darkness to do what is right. It's saved when we do the works of love through the power of the Holy Spirit, that it may be clearly seen by the world that our deeds, like those of Jesus, have come from the God who is Love.

Tomorrow, we'll learn more about this life in the Spirit.

Today's Prayer:
> *Come, Holy Spirit, help me to keep my baptismal promises by rejecting Satan and all his works of darkness and all his empty promises, that I may walk in newness of life and be the Light of Christ to the world.*

DAY 6
Woman at the Well 3|9
John 4:1-42

Yesterday, we learned that our Baptism makes us born anew into the life of the Spirit — and that the Spirit blows where he wills.

In today's scene from John's Gospel, Jesus is led by the Spirit to Jacob's well in Samaria, where he teaches us more about the life in the Spirit.

Now, think for a moment of the central image of this scene: A well. What an image! A well is deep. This Gospel is deep, and there's a very deep meaning here.

Let's get into it. Let's dive down into this well.

So, what's down a well? Water. Refreshing water. Refreshing, especially if you're Jesus, who has just sat down after a long journey on dusty paths in the hot sun. From a place of great weariness and thirst, he now says to us what he said to the woman at the well: "Give me a drink."

Think of it. Jesus wants us to give him a drink. But with what water? Does he want the water in this particular well, here in Samaria?

Recall that on Day 4, when he cleansed the Temple, Jesus said, "Destroy this temple and in three days I will raise it up." "The Jews" thought he was speaking of the Temple building, but he actually meant the temple of his body.

Here, when Jesus asks for a drink, we may think he wants us to draw from this well, here in Samaria. But once again, he's referring to his body — more specifically, his Heart. And the water he wants us to draw from his Heart is the living water of the Holy Spirit, the Spirit of Love.

Now, up to this point, as we've been looking at the darkness of the world and how the Gospel of John challenges us to step out of it and into the light, we may at times have felt overwhelmed. I know I have. As I said in the Introduction, part of why I'm writing this book is to try to own what I myself profess to believe. But, I tell you, between the times of writing, as I still get annoyed and short with the kind and caring people around me, I'm often thinking, *I can't live up to this call to love. I'm a hypocrite.*

But now comes this story of the woman at the well.

Here, Jesus wants us to give him a drink. If you're like me, though, you probably feel you've got nothing: no bucket, no water, no love. Yet, again, Jesus himself says to us, "If you knew the gift of God and who is saying to you, 'give me a drink,' you would have asked him, and he would have given you living water."

The gift of God is the living water that is the Holy Spirit, the Spirit of Love. That's what we're missing.

Alright, so do we just have to ask for it?

Well, let's look at the Gospel. The woman wants the living water that Jesus seems to offer her, and so she says to him, "Sir, give me this water."

No problem, right?

Actually, it's not that simple. Before this woman can draw from the well of the Heart of Jesus, the Heart of Jesus first needs to draw from her well, a hidden well of profound sadness and shame. With Jesus, then, let's descend to that place as we get to know this woman of Samaria.

First, as a woman, she likely has experienced second-class status in the land of ancient Israel, at least by way of social, political, and religious institutions.

Second, as a Samaritan, she no doubt has deeply felt her minority status in a region dominated by Jews who deride and despise the Samaritans not only for being a mongrel race of Jew and Gentile but for practicing a mongrel religion that mixes the Law of Moses with pagan idolatry.

Third, as someone who has had five husbands and is living with a man who is not her husband, this woman knows shame. In fact, she's likely the talk of her small town, which probably explains why she's come to draw water in the heat of mid-day, when nobody else is around.

It's interesting that, of all the people from whom Jesus could ask for a drink, the Father would lead him to this one, to this sad and shameful woman. (What does that say about the Heart of the Father?) It's further interesting that before Jesus will give this woman a drink, he first presses on the sorest part of her heart. Let's see what that will tell us about his Heart.

Jesus begins by telling the woman, "Go, call your husband." Not surprisingly, the woman answers briefly without elaborating: "I have no husband." The Lord presses further, "You are right in saying 'I have no husband;' for you have had five husbands, and he whom you now have is not your husband. What you've said is true."

Surprisingly, the woman's response is not one of anger. For instance, she doesn't berate Jesus for calling her out, nor does she retreat to the shadows of even deeper shame. Rather, she responds by saying, "Sir, I perceive that you are a prophet."

Now, some quick background here. For the books of their Bible, the Samaritans accepted the Law of Moses but not the Prophets and the Writings. Therefore, for Samaritans, there was only one prophet — the prophet announced by Moses, the prophet who would be like Moses and who would speak to God "face to face as one speaks to a friend" (Ex 33:11).

So here, suddenly, this woman declares that Jesus is that most important prophet, long awaited by the Samaritans? Why?

I suggest it's because even as Jesus touched the Samaritan woman at the most painful place of her shame and guilt, he did so with the tenderness of the closest and most compassionate friend. The look on his face and in his eyes must have reflected the face of the Father in Heaven, who is "merciful and gracious, slow to anger and abounding in mercy and faithfulness" (Ex 34:6). Seeing that face must have melted this woman's heart and filled her with insight as she realized that he was indeed the prophet like Moses. Her words to the people of her town put it best: "Come and see a man who told me all that I ever did." That's what Jesus' look did for her. She could see that *he saw it all*, and yet he still loved her.

There, in the place of her most profound brokenness, this woman could receive the living water of Merciful Love from the tender Heart of Jesus and, thereby, give him a drink.

And so, also, with us.

When we enter into dialogue with God as with a friend, when we speak with Jesus from the deep well of our brokenness, pain, sinfulness, self-doubt, and personal darkness, he looks at us, loves us, and gives us the balm of his mercy, the living water of his Merciful Love. In other words, as he pulls us out of the dark pit, the well of this world, he does so with love, and he surrounds us with love. He doesn't shame us or guilt us. He sits down with us, at the well, and he asks us for a drink.

Again, the drink we give him is our brokenness, our worldliness, our sin.

The drink he gives us is his love and mercy, his tenderness and friendship.

That is the life of the Spirit.

Tomorrow, we'll learn more about this Spirit of Love, this tenderness of mercy, and the gentle judgment of Jesus that is really no judgment at all.

Today's Prayer:

Jesus, I invite you to drink from the well of my broken-ness and sin. Pour into my heart the living water of your mercy.

DAY 7
The Woman Caught in Adultery
John 8:2-11

Thus far, with the exception of the Wedding Feast at Cana, which we'll cover tomorrow, we've been able to progress through the characters and events of the Gospel of John in the order of their appearance. So, yesterday, with the Woman at the Well, we were in chapter 4. Nicodemus came in chapter 3. The cleansing of the Temple was in 2, and the Baptist and the Prophet like Moses were in 1.

So now, why are we getting to a story that doesn't show up until chapter 8?

Because it could go almost anywhere — literally.

The verses that tell the tale of the woman caught in adultery have a complex history. Scripture scholars unanimously agree that they were not originally part of John's Gospel. Rather, they were inserted later by editors, and early manuscripts show that the editors couldn't agree as to where to put them. For instance, they appeared in various places within John's Gospel, and one ancient manuscript even had them in the Gospel of Luke.[25]

Well, does this mean that the story is not the Word of God? Not at all. There's no doubt that it is. It's just that the

Holy Spirit seems to have had to fight to get it to be recognized as such. Why? Because many copyists, the people who wrote out the Gospels before the printing press, took it upon themselves to remove it. And why on earth would they do that?

Because they thought it had too much mercy.

One Scripture commentary explains:

> St. Augustine said that the reason doubts were raised about the passage was that it showed Jesus to be so merciful that some rigorists thought it would lead to a relaxation of moral rules — and therefore many copyists suppressed it from their manuscripts.[26]

Thank God for those rigid copyists. Were it not for them, this beautiful story might have ended up in another Gospel. Praise the Holy Spirit, who knew just how precious this story is, and reserved a place for it in the most beautiful Gospel, the Gospel of John.

Now, I hope you don't mind that I'm bringing this story of mercy in early. (Again, the history seems to allow for that.) But after a week filled with meditation on the sin of the world, it doesn't hurt to end with a word of mercy.

So, in this story, the religious leaders in Jerusalem bring a woman caught in the act of adultery and place her right in the middle of what was likely a growing crowd. She's not only humiliated because now everyone knows her sin, but she's also absolutely terrified of being stoned.

And what about the man she was with? Where is he?

Now that would be a good question if this were about justice. But the religious leaders aren't looking for that. They just want blood, Jesus' blood. And if they have to sacrifice this poor woman to get it, so be it. To them, she's nothing. A nobody. They couldn't care less.[27]

But Jesus cares, as we'll see.

As for the religious leaders, they know that if Jesus instructs them to stone this woman, as the Law of Moses calls for, then he's breaking the Roman Law, and the Romans will kill *him* (see 18:31). On the other hand, if he disregards the Law of Moses, then he'll be discredited before his followers as a weak compromiser.

Jesus is completely unperturbed by their trap. As they bluster, the very one who composed the Law of Moses bends down and writes on the ground. After a moment, he stands up and says, "Let he who is without sin cast the first stone." With that, he bends back down and continues to write on the ground.

Of course, we know the rest of the story. The Lord's enemies all depart, beginning with the elders, until it's just Jesus and the woman alone.

But then notice something. It's a small detail but astonishingly beautiful. When Jesus addresses the woman, he doesn't bother to stand up. Rather, he simply *looks up*. In other words, Jesus humbles himself. He places himself below this poor woman. He speaks to her from a lower place out of respect and compassion. Think of that gesture. He speaks to her from below, not from above, not from a position of judgment or condemnation. In fact, he specifically asks her: "Has anyone condemned you?"

She replies, "No one, sir."

He continues, "Neither do I condemn you; go and sin no more."

Let's hear those words now for ourselves, those scandalous words that led copyists to try to suppress them. Let's hear those words and realize who God is. As John tells us in his first Letter, "God is love" (4:8). Yes, he is Love and Mercy itself.

Then is there no judgment, no condemnation?

Yes, there is, but the judgment is simply God's love. It's his love that's a light in the darkness. Now, those who love the darkness and choose to remain in it condemn themselves by hating the Light. But there is no hatred in God. Again, "God so loved the world that he gave his only-begotten Son, that whoever believes in him should not perish but have eternal life" (3:16). Jesus did not come to condemn the world but to save it by being a light in the darkness, by revealing the ways of God to a sinful world, as we've seen.

Again, the whole purpose of Jesus' coming was to reveal the glorious face of the Father of us all, a face of love and mercy (Day 1). Jesus revealed through John the Baptist's call to "Behold, the Lamb of God" the humility that overcomes the pride of the world (Day 2). He revealed to the first disciples that he abides in the bosom of the Father, that we might find the love that we seek (Day 3). He revealed the zeal he has for his Father's house, that we might awaken to the wiles of the devil (Day 4). He revealed to Nicodemus the life in the Spirit that gives us power to overcome the world's darkness (Day 5). He revealed to the woman at the well that he gives us the drink of his Merciful Love when we give him the drink of our sins (Day 6). And finally, he revealed to the woman caught in adultery that there is no condemnation in him, but only Love and Mercy itself (Day 7).

With this summary, we're ready to begin Week Two and the seven signs that point us to the Father, seven signs that will lead us to even greater glory.

Today's Prayer:
   Go and sin no more.

WEEK TWO
The Seven Signs

This week covers the seven signs Jesus worked in the Gospel of John that point to the Father, whom he came to reveal. Those signs are as follows: Wedding at Cana, Healing the Official's Son, Healing on the Sabbath, Feeding the Multitude, Walking on the Water, Healing the Man Born Blind, and the Raising of Lazarus.

DAY 8
Wedding at Cana   3/11
John 2:1-12

"On the third day, there was a marriage feast at Cana."

Why does the text say "*on the third day*"?

To the ears of those steeped in the Law of Moses, that phrase immediately would bring them back to Mount Sinai.

Since that's where the story is pointing, let's return to that mountain.

When the Israelites first arrived at Sinai, God spoke to Moses and told him to get the people ready for *the third day*:

> And the Lord said to Moses, "Go to the people and consecrate them today and tomorrow and let them wash their garments, and be ready by the third day; for on the third day the Lord will come down upon Mount Sinai in the sight of all the people." (Ex 19:10-11)

God tells Moses to get the people ready, to get them prepared for the manifestation of his glory on Sinai, when he'll give the gift of the Law and ratify the covenant. But how, specifically, does Moses get them ready?

He consecrates them.

Recall from the Introduction that consecration means to be "set apart" for God. God wanted Moses to set the people apart because the Law they were preparing to receive and the covenant they were preparing to make would, in fact, set them apart as God's Chosen People. On the third day, they would belong to God, and God would belong to them in a sacred covenant of love. They would become different from all the other nations on the face of the earth, as a people peculiarly God's own. They would be bound to the Law so as to live in holiness and become a light to all peoples. And while others remained in bondage to their idols made of human hands, Israel would love and serve the one God, living and true.

And through Moses, God gave Israel a summary of their consecration, which they called "the Great Commandment" or the "Shema Israel" ("Hear Israel"), a name that comes from its opening words:

> Hear, O Israel: The Lord is our God, the Lord alone; and you shall love the Lord your God with all your heart, and with all your soul, and with all your strength. And these words which I command you this day shall be upon your heart; and you shall teach them diligently to your children, and shall talk of them when you sit in your house, and when you walk by the way, and when you lie down, and when you rise. (6:4-7)

As we've seen earlier, to this Law, this Covenant, this love, Israel responded: "All that the Lord has spoken we will do, and we will be obedient" (Ex 24:7). Following this, Moses ratified the covenant through the blood of a slaughtered animal, which he sprinkled on the people.

Now think of this. Everything we've covered so far during this retreat has been in preparation for this *new third day*. For instance, we've been getting ready by renewing the consecration of our Baptism by turning away from the sin of the world and recommitting ourselves to being set apart for God. For we, too, are a chosen people, set apart in love, and called to be a light to the nations.

And what has all our preparation been for? It's been to get us ready for the revelation of this day at the Wedding Feast at Cana. Recall that at Sinai, Israel got ready for the third day, the giving of the Law of Moses, amid signs and wonders. Now, here at Cana, on another third day, we see the Lord's glory in a miracle that *points* to the New Law in Christ. I say it "points" because it's not just a miracle but a sign, a sign that points to a New Law that's not yet fully revealed here. And why do I say it's not fully revealed here? Because Jesus himself tells Mary at the wedding, "My hour has not yet come." That future hour will be the full manifestation of God's glory, the greater glory of his love on the Cross, the glory of his sacrificial suffering and death that manifests the New Law of Love that should always be in our hearts and on our lips.

Now, in response to the gift of the New Law, just as Israel responded to the Old Law with the words "All that the Lord has spoken we will do," so Mary *points* us to the similar response that we're called to give to the New Law when it comes. That is, just as she says to the servants, "Do whatever he tells you," so when the Lord's hour comes and he gives us the New Law of love, Mary will tell us, "Do what he tells you: Love one another as he has loved you."

And as Israel ratified the covenant by the blood of a beast of burden, so the New Covenant will be ratified by the Blood of the Lamb of God, to which the miracle of changing water into wine points. For when Christ ratifies the New Covenant with us, he will change not water into wine but wine into Blood, the Blood of the Eucharist.

And just as Israel made a covenant with God on Mount Sinai such that he would be their God and they would be his people, so the sign at Cana points to a greater covenant, a covenant of marriage between the Bridegroom, who is Christ, and his bride, which is the Church — that is, us.

So, this first sign at the Wedding at Cana points to our wedding with God as his new Chosen People through a New Covenant ratified in the Blood of the Lamb, which gives us a New Law of Love.

Finally, just as Israel cherished a summary of both the Law and the Covenant in their "Shema," which they were to keep in their hearts and on their lips, so the summary of the New Law and New Covenant in Christ is the sign both of his gift of love in the Eucharist and of his gift of love for us on the

Cross. And just as Israel overcame hypocrisy when they kept the Great Commandment, the Shema, in their hearts and on their lips, so we should keep the Word of God that we are pondering during this retreat in our hearts and on our lips. Why? Again, it's so we may overcome our modern hypocrisy, so we may bring the love of Christ from head to heart to life, and so we may become an authentic light of love to the nations as a people wedded to the Lord in the marriage feast of the Lamb that we celebrate at every Eucharist.

Today's Prayer:

> *The Lord is our God, the Lord alone; and I will love the Lord my God with all my heart, and with all my soul, and with all my strength. I will keep this commitment in my heart and on my lips, and I will reveal it to others through both my words and by my deeds of love.*

DAY 9
Healing the Official's Son 3\\12
John 4:43-54

Yesterday, we covered the first of the seven signs in John's Gospel, a glorious miracle that points to an even greater event: the New Covenant of Love. And now, we turn to the second sign, which points us to the Eternal Fountain of that Love, who is God our Father.

On the first day of this retreat, we learned that Jesus is the Prophet like Moses, who sees God face to face, and that his mission is to make God the Father known. But as he makes his way to Galilee, the region where he is from, Jesus seems a bit frustrated. I say that because he's just left Samaria, where the woman at the well had witnessed to her whole town, and her whole town came to profess that Jesus is "the Savior of the World" (4:42). But now, the Prophet like Moses testifies that "a prophet has no honor in his own country."

So, as Jesus arrives in Galilee, his spirit is weary. Yes, the people crowd around him when he arrives, but that's just because they've all heard about how he overturned the tables in Jerusalem and perhaps about how he changed the water into wine — but they don't give him a drink, as the Samaritan woman had done. They don't give him the faith that is deep like a well. Instead, they have a superficial interest in a wonder-worker, and Jesus' spirit is heavy because he didn't come to be a spectacle. Rather, he came to reveal the Father, but they still do not understand.

Then, Jesus arrives again in Cana, where he changed the water into wine. Perhaps his spirit becomes even heavier here. After all, the servants at the wedding, who never forgot how they had filled jars with water and drew out wine, have likely spread the word of the miracle throughout all of Cana. And now, in this moment, here comes someone who wants another miracle, a royal official from the court of Herod. Jesus immediately puts him off: "Unless you see signs and wonders, you will not believe." (By "believe," Jesus doesn't mean the deep faith for which he longs, but the superficial faith of one who has simply seen wonders.)

But the man is not put off. With the anguish of a loving father for his gravely ill son, he simply pleads, "Sir, come down before my child dies."

Touched by this man's love and recognizing the work of the Holy Spirit in him, Jesus responds, "*Go; your son will live.*"

Now, what was Jesus thinking at that moment?

Certainly a variety of opinions are possible. After all, according to St. Augustine, even if an interpretation of Scripture does not square precisely with what the author intended, if it builds up love, it achieves the Author's goal.[28] So here's my interpretation, for what it's worth (love, I hope).

When Jesus, who is already weary, first saw the official coming to him, he may have thought to himself, *Here comes another one.* In other words, *Here comes another one who just wants me to work a sign without recognizing the Father to whom my signs point.* But what Jesus may not have realized at the time was that it was the Father himself who was preparing a special gift to console his incarnate Son.[29]

Let's look at the passage in that light.

The official is a father, and he has anguish because of the suffering of his beloved son, who is sick. This father, I believe, was sent by God the Father, through the Spirit, because our Heavenly Father felt anguish at seeing the suffering of his beloved Son, Jesus. (After all, right here at the very beginning of his public ministry, Jesus' Heart is already growing weary.) It seems, then, that the Father wanted to give a gift of consolation and encouragement to his Son. For when Jesus said to the anguished official, "Your son will live," I believe that's when it hit him. I believe Jesus suddenly realized that he was also speaking to *his* Father. I believe that as he said those words of consolation to the official, at the same time, he knew that the Spirit of Love was also consoling his Father in Heaven. That, I suggest, is what floored Jesus in that moment and is also what brought *him* consolation. In other words, by way of illustration, we might imagine Jesus turning to his Father and saying:

> Ah, Father. You, too, are weary at seeing me weary. You, too, will be in anguish when I am in anguish on the Cross. But loving Father, gracious Abba, do not be in anguish, for *your Son will live.* You know that your Son will live, for you yourself will raise him up. And you are raising me up even now from my anguish by reminding me that, although I feel alone among these people, I am not alone, for you are with me, sharing in my anguish.

If it seems unlikely that the Father would work to console his Son in this way, we could very well ask: But doesn't the Father do the same for us? Indeed, he does. Every day. After all, God is the Father *Almighty*, the one who guides us with his loving providence, a beautiful providence that the Son tenderly describes for us in another Gospel:

> Look at the birds of the air: they neither sow nor reap nor gather into barns, and yet your heavenly Father feeds them. Are you not of more value than they? And which of you by being anxious can add

one cubit to his span of life? And why are you anxious about clothing? Consider the lilies of the field, how they grow; they neither toil nor spin; yet I tell you, even Solomon in all his glory was not clothed like one of these. But if God so clothes the grass of the field, which today is alive and tomorrow is thrown into the oven, will he not much more clothe you, O you of little faith? Therefore do not be anxious, saying, "What shall we eat?" or "What shall we drink?" or "What shall we wear?" For the Gentiles seek all these things; and your heavenly Father knows that you need them all. (Mt 6:25-32)

Now, we see something of a confirmation of this sign of the Father's providential love at work in the later action of the official. I say that because, after the official believes Jesus' word, he starts home and meets some of his servants on the way. They tell the father that his son is alive and well. The father then asks them the hour[30] when his son began to mend. The servants tell him, and the father realizes that that was the very hour when Jesus had said, "Your son will live." The Gospel tells us that after the official recognized this connection, "he himself believed, and all his household." Now, the official had already believed when he heard Jesus say, "Your son will live," but his faith deepened, and so it more powerfully consoled the Heart of the Son, which is exactly what the Father wanted. We, too, will console the Son and the Father when we better recognize the many signs of love that the Father's tender providence works for us every day — and so come to believe in that love even more deeply.

Tomorrow, we'll meet those who do not recognize the Father's works of love.

Today's Prayer:

Father, give me the eyes to see each day the wonders of your love and the generosity to praise and thank you with all my heart and soul, and with all my mind and strength.

DAY 10
Healing on the Sabbath 3|13
John 5

"Do you want to be healed?"

Of course the guy wants to be healed. He's been paralyzed for 38 years! Also, he's made his way to this pool in Jerusalem, known for its healing properties, and has been lying here for a long time. So, clearly, his answer to Jesus is going to be "Yes! I want to be healed!" Right?

Not exactly. Here's his surprising response: "Sir, I have no man to put me into the pool when the water is troubled, and while I am going another steps down before me." So, instead of exclaiming, "I want to be healed!" he responds by making an excuse? And doesn't he realize how implausible it sounds that, for 38 years (or however long he's been there), he's always gotten beaten in the race to the pool?

There's a saying that "even the blind squirrel finds a nut." So, how does this guy not find one? I suspect he actually could have gotten to the pool first if he wanted to. I just don't think he wanted to. And why not? Maybe because he's got a good spot in the sun by the water, a nice comfy mat, and a community of friends who are just as hard up as he is. Maybe he's grown to love self-pity. Maybe he's allowed his handicap to define his whole identity. Well, whatever his mindset, Jesus decides to heal him and tells the man, "Rise, take up your mat, and walk."

The man obeys, and he's healed. But he also seems a bit bitter about it. I say that because he doesn't thank Jesus or even ask him his name. Also, he has to be told by Jesus, "Sin no more, that nothing worse befall you." Finally, he reports Jesus to "the Jews," who were irate when they saw this man carrying his mat on the Sabbath.

So why would Jesus heal someone who doesn't even seem to want to be healed? I believe it's because the Lord wanted to send a message. Let's see what it is.

As we know by now, the Gospel of John doesn't call Jesus' miracles "miracles." Rather, they're "signs," and they're signs because they point to something. So, what is this sign pointing to? Yes, it points to the truth that our merciful Father heals the sick. But there's something more: It's that Jesus has authority, like his Father, to give life *on the Sabbath*. That's really what this healing is all about.

Let's look at it more closely.

The Sabbath was meant as a day of rest in commemoration of God's rest after he created the world (see Gen 2:2).[31] But Jewish tradition teaches that God doesn't *completely* rest on the Sabbath. Rather, there are two things he still does on that day: He gives life, and he judges. He gives life because babies continue to be born on the Sabbath. He judges because people still die on the Sabbath and go on to "meet their maker," who judges them.[32]

Now, couldn't Jesus have just picked another day to heal? Of course he could have, but he purposely chose to heal on the Sabbath in order to provoke "the Jews." Better yet, he chose to do so because he wanted to heal "the Jews" by revealing to them his Father. It's like he wanted to say to them, "Look, I know you're upset that I healed on the Sabbath, but I actually have the authority to do so — to give life on the Sabbath. I also have authority to judge you on the Sabbath. Why? Because God is my Father, and he can be your Father, too, if only you'll listen and believe."

Of course, "the Jews" don't buy it. They don't really listen, and they certainly don't believe. In fact, at this point, they seek all the more to kill Jesus. (Ironically, they feel it's all right to seek to kill someone on the Sabbath but not to give life.) Now, if they won't listen, then Jesus at least wants us to listen and believe more deeply in the goodness of the Father, who has given authority to the Son to give life and to judge.

So, Point One: *The Father gives life to the Son*. "For as the Father has life in himself, so he has granted the Son also to have life in himself." This may be one of the most important lines in the entire Gospel of John. Why? Because it reveals the heart of the identity of both the Father and the Son. Let's start with the identity of the Son.

The Son knows and understands that he receives *everything* he has and is from the Father. He has *nothing* on his own. Everything that he is, the life that he has, is the result of the Father's goodness, love, humility, and generosity. For as the Father eternally begets the Son, if he were to hold anything back, the Son would not be equal to the Father. But the Father gives himself so fully and so completely to the Son that the Son *is in no way less than the Father.* They are totally equal because the Father gives without holding anything back. What humility! What generosity!

Traditionally, the Father is called the Source in the Deity, the *Principium Deitatis.*[33] In the case of the Son, the Father is the source of the Son, even though the Son has no origin in time. This is why Jesus could say, "The Father is greater than I" (14:28). They are equal, but the Father is the one who eternally begets (not creates) the Son in an act of total, self-giving love. The Son knows all this. That is why he delights in the Father, is just as generous with the Father, and returns the Father's love without holding anything back.

Now, in the incarnate Son, we see this generosity. For instance, we see it in Jesus' zeal to do the Father's will and *to give life*: "For as the Father raises the dead and gives them life, so also the Son gives life to whom he will." By the will of the Father, Jesus wants to give to us the same life that he himself has from the Father, which brings us to point two.

Point Two: *The Father gives all judgment to the Son.* Jesus says, "The Father judges no one, but has given all judgment to the Son." What a gift! That the Father gives all judgment to the Son is an act of unfathomable mercy. I say that because, again, the Father "so loved the world that he gave his only-begotten Son, that whoever believes in him should not perish but have eternal life" (3:16). And he sent his Son "not to condemn the world, but that the world might be saved through him" (3:17). As the *Catechism of the Catholic Church* puts it, "The Son did not come to judge, but to save and to give the life he has in himself."[34] Now, whoever believes in the Son has eternal life, but if we choose not to believe, then we judge (condemn) ourselves by choosing not to receive the gift of life that the Father wants us to have through the Son. Jesus himself says later in the Gospel, "If anyone hears my sayings and does not keep them, I do not judge him; for I did not come to judge the world but to save the world" (12:47). He goes on to say the word that he spoke is what judges a person. What word? This one: Whoever believes in Jesus has eternal life, and whoever does not believe has it not.

But such belief includes a commitment to following the light of love. And here is the judgment: Some prefer darkness rather than light because their deeds are evil (see 3:19). Take, for instance, "the Jews," who seek to kill Jesus. What is their preferred darkness? Jesus sheds light on that: He says their darkness is that *they accept human praise rather than the praise of God* (see 5:44; 12:43). In other words, they seek adulation, fame, power, and worldly glory rather than the only glory that really matters, that of the one true God. And so, they do not believe, do not come to the light, and like the paralytic, do not really want to be healed. Jesus cares not for human praise and glory but only for the glory of God his Father, which he continues to reveal through the sign we'll cover tomorrow.

Today's Prayer:

> *Jesus, free me from the desire for human praise and worldly glory that I may more fully believe in you and pass from judgment to life.*

DAY 11
Feeding the Multitude
John 6:1-15, 22-71

Yesterday, in the sign of the healing on the Sabbath, we learned that Jesus has authority to give life and to judge. With today's sign, the feeding of the multitude, we learn more specifically how he gives that life and how he judges.

Here's the scene: A large crowd of about 5,000 people has followed Jesus because they witnessed the miracles that he worked on the sick. Seeing such a crowd, and knowing they need to eat, Jesus miraculously feeds them all with just five barley loaves and two fish. In response, the people want to take him by force and make him their king, but the Lord avoids them and withdraws to the hills by himself.

Clearly, the large crowd had misread the sign. Actually, they didn't read the sign at all. They simply followed their stomachs, and their stomachs told them, "Make Jesus your king so he can keep feeding you." Later, Jesus himself assessed the situation, saying, "Truly, truly, I say to you, you seek me, not because you saw signs, but because you ate your fill of the loaves."

Well, what is the sign that the people missed?

I think what we learned yesterday gives us the best clue.

Yesterday, we learned that the Father gave authority to the Son *to give life* and *to judge*. Let's start with his authority to give life.

The sign of the miracle of feeding the multitude is that Jesus gives life, for bread is life. After all, without bread, without food, we'd starve to death. But the sign of the bread that gives life points to *a greater bread* that gives *eternal life*. Later in the chapter, after the people follow Jesus to the other side of the Sea of Galilee, Jesus tells them about this greater bread. He says, "I am the bread of life; he who comes to me shall not hunger." He then goes on to explain the wonders of this bread:

> I am the bread of life. Your fathers ate the manna in the wilderness, and they died. This is the bread which comes down from heaven, that a man may eat of it and not die. I am the living bread which came down from heaven; if anyone eats of this bread, he will live for ever; and the bread which I shall give for the life of the world is my flesh. ... Truly, truly, I say to you, unless you eat the flesh of the Son of man and drink his blood, you have no life in you; he who eats my flesh and drinks my blood has eternal life, and I will raise him up at the last day. (6:48-51, 53-54)

Jesus goes on to connect what he'd said about the Father giving life to the Son (which we read about yesterday) with the bread of life that he talks about here. So, yesterday we read: "For as the Father has life in himself, so he has granted the Son also to have life in himself" (5:26). In other words, everything that the Son is comes as a gift from the Father. But that gift of life that the Son has from the Father is a gift that *the Son wants to give to us.* Why? Because the Son always does what he sees the Father doing: "Truly, truly, I say to you, the Son can do nothing of his own accord, but only what he sees the Father doing; for whatever he does, that the Son does likewise" (5:19). And what does the Father do? He gives himself to the Son without holding anything back, that the Son may have the same life as the Father. And what does the Son do? He gives himself to us, especially in the Eucharist, without holding anything back, that we may have the same life as the Son. What life? The eternal life of the Son: "As the living Father sent me, and I live because of the Father, so he who eats me will live because of me."

So, Jesus gives himself to us completely just as the Father has given himself to the Son. And as the Son has eternal life because of the Father, so we can have eternal life because of the Son. But we must receive the gift. And to receive the gift means to come to Jesus, believe in him, and eat his flesh, which is the Bread of Life.

And here again is the judgment. It is not so much Jesus who does the judging as the word that he has spoken. And that word is this: If we eat the flesh of Christ, then we will have eternal life; if we don't eat his flesh, then we won't. Ultimately, then, the question of judgment is the same question that permeates the Gospel: What do you seek? What are you hungering for? What are you thirsting for? *That* is the question, and the judgment all depends on how we answer it.

It's like this. The one who satisfies the deepest desires of our hearts is here. Why? Because of love. Because the deepest desire of our hearts is love, and God is Love, and Jesus Christ is God, and Jesus Christ gives himself to us completely in love.

But do we seek him? Do we thirst for him? Do we hunger for him?

He certainly thirsts for us. As he said to the woman at the well, "Give me a drink" (4:7). As he says on the Cross, "I thirst" (19:28). But then he asks us: What do *you* seek? For what do *you* thirst? For what do *you* hunger?

If we seek him, he is there to be found: Behold the Lamb of God, who invites us to come and see where he abides. If we thirst for him, he is there to be drunk: "If anyone thirsts, let him come to me and drink!" (7:37). If we hunger for him, he is there to be eaten: "I am the bread of life; he who comes to me shall not hunger."

But do we really seek him? Do we really thirst for him? Do we really hunger for him? That is where the judgment comes to us most personally. That is where we have our choice. And yet, it's not entirely our choice. For Jesus has said, "No one can come to me unless the Father who sent me draws him."

So, is the Father drawing us to his Son?

Absolutely.

How?

The Father draws us through the restlessness of our hearts. As St. Augustine famously wrote, "You made us for yourself, O God, and our hearts are restless until they rest in you."[35] The Father draws us through the loneliness that we sometimes feel. He draws us through the hunger we all have for love, the thirst for communion. But the question is where do we seek the satisfaction of our thirst?

The Father has given us manna in the desert, as Jesus told us, "My Father gives you the true bread from heaven." But is this bread the desire of our hearts? Is the Eucharist the source and summit of our lives? Is it that for which we long above all else?

Here, then, is the sign of the feeding of the multitude. It points us to the bread that can truly satisfy our hunger, the Bread of Life that gives us eternal life. The judgment is whether or not we thirst for he who thirsts for us, of whether we hunger for him who hungers for us, of whether we want eternal life or whether we're simply happy to settle for this earthly life that doesn't truly satisfy and that comes to an end.

Today's Prayer:

> *Father, draw me to thirst and hunger for your Son, that I may have the eternal life and love that you have prepared for me from before the foundation of the world.*

DAY 12
Walking on the Water
John 6:16-21

Yesterday, we learned that Jesus is the Bread of Life and that he who eats his flesh and drinks his blood "has eternal life." Now, there's a very important point in those words. The tense that Jesus uses is not future, "*will have* eternal life," but rather, present, "*has* eternal life." In other words, the eternal life that the Father wants for us begins *now*.

The fifth sign in John's Gospel, the walking on the water, points to how eternal life already begins here and now.

Let's start by picturing the scene: After the multitude has eaten of the loaves and has tried to force Jesus to be their king, Jesus escapes to the hills to pray. Meanwhile, the disciples jump into a boat and make their way across the Sea of Galilee. On their way, a strong wind blows and stirs up the sea, and then Jesus suddenly comes toward them, walking on the water. The disciples are frightened, but Jesus says to them, "I AM; do not be afraid." The disciples are glad to take him into the boat, and then they immediately arrive at the shore to which they are going.

Alright, so what's this sign all about? What is Jesus trying to say to the disciples and to us? What's the meaning of this miracle?

Well, let's start with the first thing Jesus said to the disciples: "I AM." Now, some translations render that as "It is I." However, the original Greek for that phrase is "*ego eimi*," which is used dozens of times in John's Gospel, and is sometimes translated as "I AM." One place where that translation particularly fits is John 18:3-6, which is when Jesus was arrested in the garden. Let's picture that scene.

A whole cohort of Roman soldiers (several hundred) and the temple guard go out to arrest Jesus. When they arrive in the garden, Jesus asks them, "Whom do you seek?" They respond, "Jesus of Nazareth." Jesus then replies, "I AM." With those words, "they drew back and fell to the ground." Think of that: Hundreds of Roman soldiers, part of the most powerful military on earth, fall down to the ground simply at the sound of the divine name, spoken by Jesus.

That, I suggest, is how we ought to read Jesus' words to the disciples in the boat. When he says to them "I am," he means "I AM," the divine name that is full of power and might (see Ex 3:14).

And why is this important? It's important because, again, as the Prophet like Moses, Jesus is one who sees the Father and who wants to make the Father known. In this miracle, this sign, Jesus is pointing to one of the most important aspects of the Father's identity, the one that we mention Sunday after Sunday when we profess the Creed: "I believe in God, the Father *Almighty*." That is to say, our Father, the Father of Jesus, is all powerful, the one whom the winds and seas obey. Knowing this fact and bringing it deeply into our hearts brings us to experience eternal life *now*.

Let me explain.

Often in life, we'll feel such things as stress, anxiety, worry, fear, nervousness, and agitation. That's all natural. Everyone experiences these emotions. However, as Christians, we should deal with such emotions differently from how people of the world handle them. Let me tell a quick story about this.

Shortly after recreational marijuana was legalized in my home state, a dispensary opened up close to my house. One Sunday morning, I happened to drive by it, and I couldn't believe the size of the line. Literally hundreds of people had lined up to get their supply of the drug. Why? Well, I imagine most of them were struggling with stress, worry, and anxiety, and they were looking for the passing relief that popping some gummies or lighting up a joint might bring.

Now, Karl Marx, the founder of Marxism, infamously once said that "religion is the opiate of the people." If he means that religion deadens our senses and destroys our motivation, then of course, he's wrong. But in the case of Christianity, he may be onto something. How so? Because Christianity does indeed bring relief to the stresses and anxieties of this world. Recall the words of Jesus that the Father cares for the birds of the air and the flowers of the field and, even more so, how he cares for us. Believing in the promise of such words brings the relief that Christianity proclaims, a relief called peace, a peace that the world cannot give — thank God. I say that because the peace of Christ is much richer, deeper, and longer lasting than the numbing relief that comes from such things as pot or alcohol. In fact, Christ's peace is of a completely different order, and he wants to give it to us, the beginning of Heaven, not later but *now*.

Of course, we all have our ways of dealing with stress. If it's not drugs or alcohol, it may be food, television, video games, movies, music, or even pornography. The way of the Christian, however, is to find relief from the anxieties of life primarily by turning in faith to our Almighty Father. He has the power to calm the storms of our lives. He has the might to immediately bring us safely to shore even as we're being tossed about in the middle of the sea. He's the one who hovers above the water, above the chaos, above the stormy winds, and who can calm them all by uttering one Word. In fact, that's exactly how he does calm them, as we learn in this Gospel: He sends his Word who proceeds to tell us "I AM; do not be afraid."

"Do not be afraid." These are Jesus' words to us, which he heard from the Father. Remember, before Jesus came walking on the water, he'd gone to the hills by himself — but he wasn't really by himself. As usual, he was communing with the Father. The Father then told him to go out to the disciples, because the Father is always sending the Son, who loves to do the Father's will, which is a will of love for us his children.

Like the Son, we do the Father's will when we believe the Son, but this means more than just believing what he says. It means believing *in* the Son. It means giving ourselves to him, including all our worries, anxieties, problems, difficulties, and concerns. It means entrusting everything to the Father through him.

In the Christian life, sometimes familiar words become a bit worn out. For instance, take the word "mercy." It's used so much nowadays that one might miss the beauty of its meaning. So, I prefer another word that highlights an aspect of mercy that helps us better appreciate its wonderful reality. That word is "tenderness," and it's like this: When the Lord shows mercy to us, when he bends down to help us, he does so with tenderness, which has the connotation of *extreme kindness and gentleness*. Now, who doesn't love to be treated with kindness and gentleness? Mercy, then, as *tenderness*, is unmistakably beautiful.

The word "faith" is also one of those familiar words that sometimes feels a bit worn out. Another word highlights an aspect of faith while getting to the heart of it. That word is "trust." Trust highlights the Lord's *goodness* because you can't trust someone unless you believe that person to be good. Interestingly enough, the word "trust" is one that the Lord himself seems to highlight for us in the high anxiety environment of the modern world. He does so through the Divine Mercy message and devotion, which has been endorsed by several popes. That devotion includes the Image of Divine Mercy with the prayer "Jesus, I trust in you" at the bottom. This sacred Image reminds us of Jesus walking on the water. This mighty image reveals the power of God the Father. This consoling image invites us to find relief by praying, "Jesus, I trust in you." That prayer, that faith, helps bring the peace of eternal life, the peace of Heaven, into our lives *now*.

Today's Prayer:
> *Jesus, I trust in you.*
> *Jesus, I trust in you.*
> *Jesus, I trust in you.*

DAY 13
Healing the Man Born Blind   3/16
John 9 (see also 7 and 8)

To appreciate the sign of the healing of the man born blind, let's start with what has led up to this moment.

After Jesus fed the multitudes, walked on water, and spoke to the crowds about giving them his flesh to eat, there was something of a crisis. Many who had followed Jesus up to that point left him. (The idea of "eating his flesh" was just too much for them.) Thankfully, Jesus' twelve apostles stuck with him, even though they, too, did not understand. Then, they all remained in Galilee, where the Lord was from, because "the Jews" in Jerusalem were still seeking to kill Jesus.

But now, perhaps realizing that their family's reputation is taking a major hit, the Lord's "brethren" push him to get back into the game. (Yes, in their unbelief, they do see it as a game: the worldly game of power, prestige, and influence.) They see the most popular feast of the year, the Feast of Booths in Jerusalem, as a perfect opportunity for Jesus to win back the disciples who left him. They even tell Jesus "Leave here and go … that your disciples may see the works you are doing" (7:3). Giving voice to their doubts, they also add, "If you do these things, show yourself to the world" (7:4). In other words, *if* you really are the Messiah, then prove it by working more wonders for us.

And why not? Surely, Jesus could just storm into Jerusalem and, with one hearty shout of "I AM," destroy all his enemies and become king not only of Jerusalem but of the whole world. But that's not why he came.

So why did he come?

He came that we might see. Again, as the Prophet like Moses, who is greater than Moses, Jesus sees God the Father, face to face. He came to reveal the Father, whom we can't see, in his own humanity, which we can. As he expresses it later, "He who has seen me has seen the Father" (14:9). The Christian life is about seeing Jesus and also the Father, through him.

Last week, we often came across the theme of seeing. Recall that John the Baptist invited everyone to see Jesus: "*Behold* the Lamb of God" (1:29). Also, Jesus invited the first disciples to "come and *see*" (1:39), and he told them they would "*see* greater things" (1:50). To Nicodemus, Jesus said, "Unless one is born anew, he cannot *see* the kingdom of God" (3:3). The woman at the well testified to Jesus by telling those in her town, "Come and *see* a man who told me all that I ever did" (4:29). She testified to what she herself had *seen* and experienced of Christ.

But how do we see?

That question brings us to the healing.

Picture the context: Jesus had gone up to Jerusalem not openly, as his relatives wanted, but in secret. His presence there, however, didn't remain a secret for long, because Jesus began to witness to the Father. This led to "the Jews" picking up stones to throw at him, and so he left the temple to hide himself from them.

As Jesus was leaving, he saw a man, blind from his birth. Now, right there, that last phrase already says so much. This man was blind right from the beginning. He was blind from the time of his birth, which describes us all. We were all born into this world unable to see the love of the Father through Jesus. Then, shortly after our birth, most of us were baptized, and as we grew up, we heard about Jesus. But have we ever seen him? Baptized Christians often go through their whole lives without ever really seeing the Lord.

I think this all too common blindness is linked to the widespread problem of Christian hypocrisy. That is, we often speak of someone we've heard about rather than of someone we know and have seen. But as we learned earlier, in the Gospel of John, to evangelize means *to witness*. It means to witness to what we have seen. It's to make the same Easter proclamation as the apostles: "I have seen the Lord!" (20:18)

Now, am I saying we all need to experience an apparition or some kind of mystical phenomenon? Not exactly. But let me tell you what I do mean through an experience I once had in prayer.

The fall after my college graduation, I joined a religious congregation in the Northeast. As soon as I arrived, the superior told me I was to start a retreat. He then gave me a sheet with Psalm 139 printed on it and instructed me to go and pray with it. I did as I was told, and soon after I read the opening words, "O Lord, you search me and you know me," a striking image came to my mind. It was that of a father, lovingly gazing at his newborn child with delight. Now, the eyes of the baby were going all over the place (as the eyes of infants often do), without seeing those of the father. Nevertheless, the father kept looking at his child even more lovingly, hoping and waiting for his baby's eyes to meet his own.

As I reflected on that scene, I suddenly realized I was that newborn baby and God was the father. I further realized that all my life, up to that point, my eyes mostly had been going in every other direction except toward the Lord. I knew he wanted me to see him, that he wanted me to recognize his love and understand that I am his dearly beloved child. He wanted me to see him seeing me. He wanted me to behold him beholding me. He wanted me to recognize how precious I am in his sight, not because of what I do but because of who I am: his beloved son.

The Prologue of the Gospel of John says that Jesus gives us the "power to become children of God" (1:12). Of course, that power is realized in us through Baptism. After all, when we're baptized, we truly become God's beloved sons and daughters in the Divine Son. But the Christian life goes far beyond simply being baptized. It's also about recognizing what the Sacrament of Baptism has given us. It's about seeing God's love for us in Christ, in his gaze. It's about living under the gaze of that love, of knowing that we are God's beloved children, as St. John tells us:

> See what love the Father has given us, that we should be called children of God; and so we are. ... Beloved, we are God's children now; it does not yet appear what we shall be, but we know that when he

appears we shall be like him, for we shall see him as he is. (1 Jn 3:1-2)

But do we see the love that the Father has for us? Do we really know what it means to be children of God? It means this: *The Father loves us with the same love with which he loves his eternal Son.* Did you hear that? The love could not be greater! From the time of our Baptism, the Father always says about us what he said about his Son: "This is my beloved." With the author of the Gospel of John, each of us truly is a "beloved disciple." And that love *does not change.* As the parable of the Prodigal Son from the Gospel of Luke teaches, the gift of being children of God does not change. So, even if we reject the Father, run away from him, and live with the pigs, the Father is always calling to us. He's always ready to run out to meet us and embrace us as soon as we turn back to him. Why? Because just as a child of a parent always remains that parent's child, so a child of God always remains a child of God, no matter what.

But again, here's the problem: We don't recognize it. We doubt God's love. We don't see that God loves us not for what we do but because of who we are: God's children, his dearly beloved. Jesus came to heal us of this blindness so we might receive the Father's love and become even more like him in glory — a glory that will be revealed next week.

Until then, we have one more sign to conclude this week.

Today's Prayer:

Father, I beg you, let me see your love for me.

DAY 14
Raising of Lazarus
John 11 (see also 10; 12:1-8)

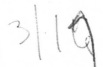

The story of the raising of Lazarus gives us an extremely touching and beautiful glimpse into the humanity of Jesus — and so also, into the tenderness of the Father. It reveals the depths of the Lord's love in his friendships, which went beyond the circle of his apostles.

The house of Martha, Mary, and Lazarus in Bethany was something of an oasis of peace and joy for Jesus. He deeply loved the family there, and their home became the place that the Father specially prepared for his Son to strengthen and console him six days before his death. On that occasion of the Lord's visit, the ever-attentive Mary noticed the heaviness on her dear friend's Heart. And so, in an unforgettable gesture of generosity and love, she took a pound of costly aromatic ointment and used it to anoint the feet of Jesus, which she then tenderly wiped with her hair. Despite the protests of Judas, Jesus gratefully accepted Mary's gift of love as the smell of the ointment filled the whole house.

Now, there are many beautiful spiritual interpretations about what the ointment represents and the symbolism of this or that in the scene. But the heart of it, I believe, is very simple: Jesus rejoiced in the love of a family, a family that became the centerpiece of the most wondrous of his signs. Actually, the most wondrous of all his signs is his Resurrection, but here's the greatness of this seventh sign: It unites the death of God's friends with that of the death and Resurrection of Christ.

We'll get to that soon enough. First, however, so as to give some background to this seventh sign, I'd like to share a unique interpretation about one of the characters in the story, an interpretation that may shed even more light on the mystery of love at the house in Bethany. It comes from Jean Vanier, the founder of L'Arche, a community for people with disabilities:

> In this gospel, Lazarus is present but he never speaks and is never described. In Luke's gospel, when Jesus visits this family in Bethany, the home is described as the "home of Martha," not the home of Lazarus. In the home, we find Martha and Mary, but Lazarus is not present. Lazarus seems to be a "nobody," except to his sisters and Jesus, who love him deeply. He seems to be at the centre of the family, living with his two unmarried sisters. As I read all this I cannot help but come to the conclusion, which of course

comes from my experience in L'Arche with people with disabilities, that Lazarus has a handicap and probably a serious one. The [Greek] word *asthenés* ["sick," "without strength," "feeble," "insignificant"] can imply this. Were the two sisters unmarried in order to look after him? The words of his sister [to Jesus], "the one you love is sick," seems to me significant. To me, these words imply "the one that you visit and bathe, the one you love with tenderness and affection, is in danger of death." This is of course only a supposition and is in no way central to what John seeks to reveal here about the love of Jesus for each one in his family.[36]

Vanier is right in saying that his interpretation is not central to the story. And of course, while I myself believe it, we cannot know for sure if it is correct. However, we do know this: Jesus did have a particular love for the weak, the broken, and the sick. We know that his heart went out to the poor. But the greatest poverty of all may very well be in those who face death, and so death in this story evoked a particularly strong response from the Heart of Jesus.

Of course, all of us will die. And most of us have probably suffered the death of a loved one. If we have, it's hard to describe the anguish. But imagine if there were no hope of ever seeing the loved one again. Imagine if death were the miserable end. Imagine if our own deaths meant that we would be no more. What a terrible evil! Jesus, in the sign of raising Lazarus from the dead, confronts that evil head-on. And what is his reaction?

Let's read what the Gospel itself has to say:

Then Mary, when she came where Jesus was and saw him, fell at his feet, saying to him, "Lord, if you had been here, my brother would not have died." When Jesus saw her weeping, and the Jews who came with her also weeping, he was deeply moved in spirit and troubled; and he said, "Where have you laid him?"

They said to him, "Lord, come and see."
　Jesus wept.
　So the Jews said, "See how he loved him!"

Jesus wept. The Father, in Jesus, wept. God the Father, who so loved the world that he gave his only Son that it might not perish, wept through the humanity of his Son when the one he loved had died. Thus, the Father is not a God who rejoices over evil and suffering. Thus, in tragedies and pain, when people ask, "Where is God?" he's right there, weeping with them.

But if the Father is God almighty, why doesn't he do something about it?

Well, let's not get ahead of ourselves. There's more to the story.

The Gospel of John shows not only that God in Christ weeps with those who weep and grieves with those who grieve, but in the face of death he also becomes "troubled." Apparently, the original Greek word for "troubled" implies that Jesus is actually *fiercely angry*. Angry at what? It seems that Jesus (and the Father, through him) is angry at death and the prince of this world who causes so much suffering for God's children. In fact, he's so angry, he's going to do something drastic about it.

And what does he do?

Jesus, the Good Shepherd, lays down his life for his beloved sheep. By so doing, he doesn't immediately take away suffering but transforms it into love: "No greater love has a man than if he gives up his life for his friends" (15:13). Jesus gives his life for his friends, and Lazarus is one of his best friends. And while he doesn't take away Lazarus' illness or prevent him from dying, Jesus tenderly loves him in his illness and raises him up. And the sign of raising up Lazarus leads to the sign of our also being raised up with Christ.

How so? Because by raising Lazarus from the dead, Jesus knew he had signed his own death warrant. As it turned out, for "the Jews," the raising of Lazarus was the last straw. It was too much. They feared that everyone would now come to believe in Jesus, and so, after this sign, "they took counsel about how to put him to death." You might say, then, that Jesus' earlier anger at death was provoked not just by the prospect of Lazarus' demise but also by his own. But Jesus would not shy away from it. With the courage of a hero, he would take death upon himself and destroy death that we might all have life in him. Tomorrow, we will enter into the mystery and drama of that heroism and love as we ascend the steps to the Upper Room.

Today's Prayer:
    See how he loves us.

The Upper Room

This week covers the sublime words Jesus speaks to his disciples and to the Father in the Upper Room before he enters into his Passion. We begin with an introduction, and then, each day after that will cover chapters 13-17. Finally, we'll end with a conclusion.

DAY 15
Ascending the Steps
There are no specific Scripture passages for today.

The Upper Room, also called the Cenacle, is a place of mind-blowing glory. Not only is it where Jesus instituted the priesthood and the Eucharist, it's also where we can listen in on his "farewell" words both to the apostles and to his Father.

I shared in the Introduction that, for many years, I've often listened to an audio version of the Gospel of John. What I didn't share is that most of the time I listened to chapters 13-17, the "Farewell Discourse" of the Upper Room. The words of those chapters, expressed just before Jesus descended into the depths of his Passion, touch the soul like few things in this world — just ask the Missionaries.

The community I work with, the Marian Missionaries of Divine Mercy, have a tradition that, every Holy Thursday, after the Mass of the Lord's Supper, we go to our chapel and listen to the entire Farewell Discourse of John's Gospel.[37] Many of the Missionaries have described that spiritual exercise as one of the highlights of their whole year. They say it facilitates an encounter with God, through his Word, unlike any they've ever experienced.

But why is it so powerful?

Of course, it's powerful because the Word of God is God's own self-revelation. But what makes the chapters of the Farewell Discourse so extraordinary is that they stand at the very pinnacle of that revelation.

Let me explain.

God reveals himself to us through Sacred Scripture, and according to the *Catechism*, the "*Gospels* are the heart of all the Scriptures."[38] But among the four Gospels, John particularly stands out. Not only does it follow a unique story line, but it surpasses the other Gospels in terms of the weight of glory it reveals. This is why a tradition of the Church marks the Gospel of John with the symbol of an eagle and describes it as the Gospel that "soars" and "takes a loftier flight."[39]

And where are the highest heights to which this Gospel ascends? I suggest they're in the Farewell Discourse, because it's in those chapters that the most important mystery of Christian faith and life is most fully revealed: The Mystery of the Most Holy Trinity.[40] But John doesn't reveal this mystery using the often intimidating language of theology. Rather, he uses the easily accessible language of love, and that love, the Divine Love of the Trinity, comes forth in the chapters of the Farewell Discourse with a depth and beauty unlike anywhere else.

Looking back on the rest of our retreat, you might say that what we've covered thus far has been something of an appetizer. In other words, the earlier chapters of the Gospel of John have given us tasty bits and pieces of the love of the Trinity. But now, as we take our seat in the Upper Room, we get to drink and dine at the feast of Divine Love itself.

But isn't the Mass that feast? Yes, it is, and that's the point. Let me put it this way: It's not a coincidence that the Upper Room, the place where Jesus gives us the Eucharist, the banquet of his Body and Blood, is also where we eat and drink of the most sumptuous banquet of the Word of God.

But if the Farewell Discourse of the Gospel of John provides such a wonderful meal, then why doesn't John include an institution narrative of the Eucharist? In other words, why don't we read in his Gospel the words of Consecration: "This is my body ... this is my blood"? The other Gospels have them, and even St. Paul includes them in one of his letters.[41] So why does John leave out what many would say is the most important part of the Mass?

I believe it's because John's Gospel, which was written years after the other Gospels and presupposes them, is meant to give us something even more profound. And that greater profundity is this: John doesn't describe the surface details of how the Eucharist is given, but rather, he unveils the inner mystery of what it means. And what does it mean? It means love. It means the fullness of Divine Love. It means the fullness of divine, self-giving Love that is Father, Son, and Holy Spirit.

In the Introduction, I wrote that one of the goals of this book is to help people come to a more full, conscious, and active participation in the Mass. Well, a key to accomplishing this is the Farewell Discourse. I say that because these chapters, with their strong emphasis on the Trinity, get us to rethink what we usually consider to be the "highest point" of the Mass. And what's that? Well, I think for most of us, if we had to pick the highest or most important moment of the Mass, we'd probably choose the one that's highlighted in the Gospels of Matthew, Mark, and Luke, namely, *the Consecration*. Of course, that's the glorious moment when the priest at the altar speaks the words of Jesus, "This is my body ... this is my blood," and bread and wine are truly transformed into the Body and Blood, Soul and Divinity of Christ.

Now, as important and exalted as the moment of Consecration is, my reading of the Gospel of John leads me to yet another summit, what I believe is the highest and most important Liturgical moment of all, the moment I'd describe as the Consecration's culmination: the Concluding Doxology.[42]

And what is that? It's the glorious Trinitarian prayer of the priest at the altar, who, taking the Body and Blood, Soul and Divinity of Jesus into his hands, offers it to the Father with these words:

> Through him and with him and in him, O God almighty Father, in the unity of the Holy Spirit, all glory and honor is yours, forever and ever.

As the priest speaks these words to the Father, the rubrics of the Mass (the instructions for the priest at the altar), direct him differently than during the Consecration. At the Consecration, the rubrics instruct the priest to hold the bread and wine "slightly raised" above the altar and then, after the words of Consecration, to "show" the Body and Blood of Jesus. At the

Concluding Doxology, however, the instruction is to take the chalice and the paten with the host and *to raise them* as they're offered to the Father. That's one reason I call the Concluding Doxology the "high point" of the Mass. It's when Jesus in his Body and Blood is indeed raised highest, but it's more than that. It's also when we, too, are swept up through Christ, with Christ, and in Christ, in the unity of the Holy Spirit, to the one who dwells in highest Heaven: the Father.

And then, what follows the Concluding Doxology? What do we pray immediately after we're swept up to the highest Heaven? The priest at the altar clues us in as he says: "At the Savior's command and formed by divine teaching, we dare to say ..." And what is it that we dare to say? That's right. We pray, "Our Father." As we'll learn this week, our Heavenly Father is the culmination, the final end of our worship and praise, and his will is not only that we praise him but that we become sharers in the life of the Trinity itself. Here's how the *Catechism* puts it, turning to the testimony of the author of the Gospel of John:

> But St. John goes even further when he affirms that "God is Love": God's very being is love. By sending his only Son and the Spirit of Love in the fullness of time, God has revealed his innermost secret: God himself is an eternal exchange of love, Father, Son, and Holy Spirit, and he has destined us to share in that exchange.[43]

God has destined us to share in the eternal exchange of his love! And as the *Catechism* also points out, that destiny culminates in the Father:

> [God's] will was that men should have access to the Father, through Christ, the Word made flesh, in the Holy Spirit, and thus become sharers in the divine nature.[44]

So, with all that, we've arrived at the Upper Room. For the rest of this week, we'll find here our "access to the Father," discover more fully God's "innermost secret," and be filled with awe at the glorious gift of becoming "sharers in the divine nature," a nature that is love.

Today's Prayer:

> *Come, Holy Spirit, enlighten my mind and heart that I may behold God's glorious love given to me here in the Upper Room.*

DAY 16
Love to the End
John 13

3|19

The Farewell Discourse begins with these words:

> Now before the feast of the Passover, when Jesus knew that his hour had come to depart out of this world to the Father, having loved his own who were in the world, he loved them to the end.

To the end. Jesus loved them to the end. He loved us to the end. But what is that end? Again, as we saw yesterday, it's the Father. Jesus loves us home to the Father, to the house of God, our Father. That is the goal of Jesus, and it's our goal, too: the Father.

But who is the Father?

The Father is Love. He's the one who has life in himself and who eternally gives life to his Son in a total gift of self-giving love. Jesus Christ, the incarnate Son, fully knows what the Father does for him. And so, Jesus delights in the Father, loves the Father, and always does the Father's will. And what is the Father's will? It's that we be given the life and love that the Son himself has received, that we may also call God our Father. But for us to receive it, to truly be God's children, Jesus must first consecrate us and cleanse us.

Recall that on Day 8, the Wedding at Cana, we read about how Moses prepared the people for "the third day" on Mount Sinai. And how did he do it? He consecrated them and had them wash their garments.

Recall that on Day 1, we read that when God spoke to Moses from the burning bush, he told Moses to take off his shoes. Well, here in the Upper Room, where God manifests himself in the burning Heart of Jesus, not only must the disciples take off their shoes, but the dirt on their feet must come off, too. For, here, in this place, they're on the holiest of holy ground.

And so, to prepare his disciples for the gifts he'll give in this Upper Room, Jesus begins by washing their feet, which he says makes them "clean all over." But why does washing a man's feet make him clean all over? It's because this foot washing has a twofold power. It not only washes dirt off of feet, but it also takes the dark grime of worldliness away from minds and hearts. More specifically, Jesus' humble gesture cleansed the disciples of the notion that greatness comes from being first, esteemed, and high up on a pedestal. It replaced that notion with the concrete fact of the great and eternal God revealing his glory through lowly service.

That, at least, was the plan. The reality, however, was much different. As Jesus was washing the disciples' feet, they didn't understand what he was doing. After all, they still did not recognize that the one who washed them is the eternal Son of the Father. They did not know that it was God himself who washed their feet.

But we do. We know it was God. We believe it was God, and if we let that reality sink down into our hearts as we contemplate the foot washing, it can make us clean all over. So, think of it: The one who washes the feet is he who, "though he was in the form of God, did not deem equality with God something to be grasped at but emptied himself, taking the form of a slave, being born in the likeness of men" (Phil 2:7). Think of it: The eternal Son not only took on the form of a slave, but here, he's actually doing the work of a slave.

To help us appreciate all this, John carefully describes the gestures that lead up to the foot washing. Specifically, he points out that Jesus "rose from supper, laid aside his garments, and girded himself with a towel." These gestures speak of the self-emptying of the Incarnation. For, when Jesus "rose from supper," he's reminding us of how he rose from the beatitude of the Trinity. When he "laid aside his garments," he's reminding us of how he laid aside his divine glory. When he "girded himself with a towel," he's reminding us of how he girded himself with our fragile human nature.

So, the washing of the disciples' feet really does have the power to make us "clean all over." And it's not just the humility of the action but the identity of the one who performs it: It's God. It's God revealing the humility of God. It's God the Son revealing the humility of God the Father. It's God the Father revealing the humility of God the Son. It's God the Holy Spirit revealing the humility of God the Father and God the Son through words that he himself has inspired John to write. Thus, the power of the humble God, humbly washing the feet of his creatures, cleanses us of the central sin of the world — pride — if we let it. If we let the meaning of Christ's actions in the Upper Room wash over us, it will cleanse us of our vanity and pride as it also fills us with the very humility of God and his self-emptying love.

But the cleansing is not finished with the washing of the feet. There's one more piece of "dirt" that must go: Judas. Judas remains unclean because he rejects the love of Christ that's offered to him at the first Holy Communion. For, when Jesus gives him the morsel of his Body, instead of uniting himself with the Lord in love, Judas breaks from him in disgust. Why disgust? Because Judas respects power, worldly power, and he'd expected Jesus to be a messiah of might, who would deliver the Jews from the Romans by force. But now, all those dreams are dashed by the sight of his "king," down on his knees, washing the dirt off of other men's feet. That was too much for Judas. And so, in that moment, he rejected Love and accepted Satan, who immediately "entered into him." Then, filled with the Prince of Darkness, Judas departed, "and it was night."

After Judas' departure, the Upper Room became fully consecrated, set apart. The remaining disciples were washed and prepared. God's glory could finally come down as the gift of the New Law of Love.

Now, before we get to that New Law, let's not miss how the glory comes down. Did you see it? This time it doesn't descend, as it did on Mount Sinai, as flames of fire and ominous smoke. Rather, it simply comes through the rejection of a friend that goes unnoticed in a room full of people. Actually, Jesus notices it, and while the rejection breaks his Heart, it also allows him to announce the arrival of his long-awaited hour of glory. And so, at the very moment of Judas' departure, Jesus declares to the disciples, "Now is the Son of man glorified, and in him God is glorified."

But why is rejection God's glorification?

Because God is Love, and his love is revealed through the self-giving of the Incarnate Son, especially through his suffering and death. Now, here in the Upper Room, Judas' rejection of Jesus has started the first turning of the wheels of the Lord's Passion. And so, the betrayal of Jesus by Judas really is the beginning, the first streaks of light from the dawn that fully reveals God's love on the Cross. It's fitting, then, that the Lord would choose this moment, this background of glory shining through Judas' inglorious betrayal to unveil the New Law of Love:

> A new commandment I give to you, that you love one another; even as I have loved you, that you also love one another. By this all men will know that you are my disciples, if you have love for one another. (13:34)

So, we are to love one another as God has loved us. And how did he love us? The eternal Son did not grasp at his equality with God. Rather, he emptied himself, took the form of a slave, and then served the slaves to set them free. Furthermore, the Incarnate Son allowed himself to be betrayed and then beaten, scourged, crowned, and crucified. He loved us to the bitter end that we ourselves might have a glorious end, the glorious end of being able to call God "our Father."

Today's Prayer:
Lord, please cleanse me of my selfish pride through the power of your humble love, and then help me to love others as you have loved me.

DAY 17
The Father's House
John 14

Chapter 14 of the Gospel of John begins as follows:

> Let not your hearts be troubled; believe in God, believe also in me. In my Father's house are many rooms; if it were not so, would I have told you that I go to prepare a place for you?

Yesterday, we learned that our end is the Father. Today, Jesus tells us more about that end. Specifically, he describes our end as home, as "my Father's house." This phrase brings us back to the Prologue of John's Gospel, where we read about "the only-begotten Son, who is in the bosom of the Father" (1:18). And what is the "bosom of the Father"? It's the Father's house, where the eternal Son dwells.

Another word for "bosom" is chest. And what's inside a person's chest? His heart. So, if the Father's house is his bosom, then inside that house is his Heart. Again, as St. John tells us, dwelling inside that house is the Son, the Son who lives and rests at the Heart of the Father. This is who the Son is. He lives at the very Heart of the Father, surrounded by the Father's love. This also is the place Jesus prepares for us through his suffering and death. It's the place of the Father's love. It's our true and lasting home.

But Jesus tells us that in his Father's house are many rooms. So, what does that mean? I suggest it means that the Father's love for each one of us is not some general concept but, rather, very personal and particular. It's as personal and particular as Jesus' love for us on the Cross, as we read in the *Catechism*:

Jesus knew and loved us each and all during his life, his agony, and his Passion and gave himself up for each one of us: "The Son of God ... loved me and gave himself for me" (Gal 2:20). He has loved us all with a human heart.[45]

Yes, Jesus loved us all with a human heart, by the will of the Father, to show us the Father's particular love for us. This is why the Father's house is not some large open space where everyone gathers simply to experience some far out, cosmic, general love. No, we each have our own room in the Father's house where we find the Father's particular love for us, a love of great intimacy. Because it is so intimate, Jesus tells us to go to our rooms, shut the door, and pray to the Father in secret (see Mt 6:6).

So, our room in the Father's house is very personal and intimate. It's a place where we're invited to open our hearts to the Father as to no one else. It's a place where the Father calls each of us by a new name that's only known to him and his beloved (Rev 2:17). It's a place where, as we learn in Psalm 139, the Father knows whether we sit or if we stand, where all our thoughts lie open to him, where before even a word is on our lips, he already knows it (but wants to hear it anyway, because he loves us). It's a place where he gazes on us with great tenderness as he lovingly numbers every hair on our heads. That is the particular and personal love of our Father for each one of us.

But there's more, and that more comes from *the only words* that the Father repeats in the very few times his voice is heard in Sacred Scripture. What are those words? They're the words the Father spoke at the moment of Jesus' baptism: "This is my beloved Son." They're also the words the Father speaks to us at the moment of our baptisms: "*You are my Beloved.*"

"You are my Beloved." These are the words that Jesus wants us to hear from the Father. These are the words that the Father wants to speak to us. These are the words that set us free, give us life, and fill us with peace and joy. These are the words that always bring us back to our true home: the Father's house, the Father's love, the Father's bosom.

In his book *The Return of the Prodigal Son*, Fr. Henri Nouwen offers a moving reflection on the importance of finding our true homes in the word of love spoken to us by the Father: "You are my beloved." Nouwen writes that "this is the voice that speaks to all the children of God and sets them free to live in the midst of a dark world while remaining in the light." And then he shares from his own experience:

> I have heard that voice ["You are my beloved"]. It has spoken to me in the past and continues to speak to me now. It is the never-interrupted voice of love speaking from eternity and giving life and love whenever it is heard. When I hear that voice, I know that I am home with God and have nothing to fear. As the Beloved of my heavenly Father, "I can walk in the valley of darkness: no evil will I fear." As the Beloved, I can "cure the sick, raise the dead, cleanse the lepers, cast out devils." Having "received without charge," I can "give without charge." As the Beloved, I can confront, console, admonish, and encourage without fear of rejection or need for affirmation. As the Beloved, I can suffer persecution without desire for revenge and receive praise without using it as proof of my goodness. As the Beloved, I can be tortured and killed without ever having to doubt that the love that is given to me is stronger than death. As the Beloved, I am free to live and give life, free also to die while giving life.[46]

I believe Nouwen is right. The love of the Father for us as his dearly beloved children is the secret that sets us free from fear and of the need to be affirmed by others, praised by others, rewarded by others. For the Father's love is enough. In fact, it's more than enough. It's everything. It's our home. Problem is, we don't listen to the voice of the Father. We even run away from home, as Nouwen also describes:

Yet over and over again I have left home. I have fled the [Father] and run off to faraway places searching for love! This is the great tragedy of my life and of the lives of so many I meet on my journey. Somehow I have become deaf to the voice that calls me the Beloved, have left the only place where I can hear that voice, and have gone off desperately hoping that I would find somewhere else what I could no longer find at home.[47]

Let's not leave home. Let's listen to the Father's voice. Let's stay in his house, abiding in the love of the Heart of Jesus in the love of the Heart of the Father. (More on that tomorrow.)

Today's Prayer:

Father, purify my heart of the noise and ways of the world, that I may always hear your word of love for me: "You are my Beloved."

DAY 18
Abide in My Love   3|21
John 15

Chapter 15 of the Gospel of John begins as follows:

I am the true vine, and my Father is the vinedresser. Every branch of mine that bears no fruit, he takes away, and every branch that does bear fruit he prunes, that it may bear more fruit. You are already made clean by the word which I have spoken to you. Abide in me, and I in you. As the branch cannot bear fruit by itself, unless it abides in the vine, neither can you unless you abide in me. I am the vine, you are the branches. He who abides in me, and I in him, he it is that bears much fruit, for apart from me you can do nothing.

The fruit of love is impossible without Christ. Apart from him, we're selfish, noisy gongs that simply draw attention to ourselves. The fruit of love is impossible without the Cross, those daily prunings that can make us more open to love if we let them. The fruit of love is impossible without the Word of God, which cleanses us of the world and its narcissistic ways. The fruit of love is impossible without the Holy Spirit, who is the "sap" in the vine that gives energy and power for the works of love. The fruit of love is impossible without our abiding in Jesus, for apart from him we can do nothing.

As Chapter 15 of the Gospel of John continues, one theme from the opening verses resonates throughout the rest of the chapter, a theme that also appears several times in John's later reflections in the First Letter of St. John. It's the theme of "abide."

Saint Thomas Aquinas writes that what Jesus wants to convey through this theme comes down to three things: "(1) To abide in Jesus is to abide in his love; (2) to abide in his love is to keep his commandments; (3) to keep his commandments is to love."[48]

Well, then, it looks like it's all about love, which makes sense because, again, as John himself teaches, "God is love" (1 Jn 4:8).

Now, this emphasis on love so impacted St. John that in his Gospel, he simply refers to himself as "the Beloved Disciple." It's also something that, apparently, he talked about all the time. I say that because a tradition in the Church, attributed to St. Augustine, tells us that John's disciples got a bit tired of hearing him always repeat, "Love one another." So, one day, they asked him whether Jesus had anything else to say that was important. The Beloved Disciple simply responded: "Love one another."[49]

But wasn't there anything else?

For John, that's it. That's what it's all about. And to learn to love each other, we first need to experience God's love for ourselves: "We love, because he first loved us" (1 Jn 4:19). God himself shows us what it means to love, and without him, we would not know what it means — at least not Divine Love, which is the love to which we're called.

So, what is Divine Love?

Throughout this retreat, John has been teaching us about Divine Love, and he will show us even more when we arrive at the Passion. For the Passion reveals the greatest love: "Greater love has no man than this, that a man lay down his life for his friends." And as John later writes, "By this we know love, that he laid down his life for us; and we ought to lay down our lives for the brethren" (1 Jn 3:16). So, let's review how Jesus has revealed love to us in what we've already covered.

Through the Word becoming flesh, we literally see the love of God shining forth from the face of Christ, and we also see that the Father so loved us that he sent his Only Begotten Son that we might have eternal life. Through John the Baptist, we see the love of God in the humility of the Lamb of God, who takes away the sin of the world. Through the first disciples, we get a glimpse of the attractiveness of love in Jesus, as he invites them to "come and see" where he abides. Through "the Jews," we see the love of God in the way that Jesus is at pains to win them over to love by speaking with them at length, provoking them, and performing many signs. Through Nicodemus, we see the love of God in the way Jesus challenges him to a deeper faith that he might see the Kingdom of God's love. Through the woman at the well, we see the love of God in the great tenderness with which Jesus meets her in her brokenness and brings her to faith and salvation. Through the woman caught in adultery, we see the love of God in the way Jesus restores her dignity by speaking to her "from below" and by not condemning her. Through the Wedding at Cana, we see the love of God in the gift of our tender mother, Mary, and in our glorious Bridegroom, who takes us as his spouse. Through the healing of the official's Son, we glimpse the compassion of the Father, whose loving providence consoles his Son and does the same for us. Through the healing of the paralytic, we see the love of God, who strives to heal us even when we don't want to be healed. Through the feeding of the multitude, we see the love of God, who cares for our physical needs and spiritual life not only by giving us bread but also his own flesh. Through the walking on the water, we see the love of God that calms the storms of our lives, that we might have the peace the world cannot give. Through the healing of the man born blind, we see the love of God incarnate, standing before us in Jesus Christ. Through the raising of Lazarus, we see the tender love of God for us, his dearly beloved friends, for whom he will give up his life. Through the events of the Upper Room, we see the love of God for us as the Lord opens his Heart, revealing the deepest secrets of the love to be found in the Father's house. But Jesus doesn't just tell us. He also shows us through his loving humility as he washes the disciples' feet, making us clean all over.

Now, *that* is the Word that should abide in us. That is the Word that reveals the amazing love God has for us. But then, having seen God's love for us, we should also love one another just as he has loved us. Following the example of Jesus, we should look at others with tenderness, feed them with our bread, console them when they grieve, serve them in humility, and do any other work of love that the Holy Spirit will inspire.

If we do all that, we will bear the fruit of love. We will abide in the love of Christ and of the Father, and we will have eternal life now and in the future, particularly through the joy that comes from friendship with Christ. As the Lord himself puts it: "These things I have spoken to you, that my joy may be in you, and that your joy may be full." Tomorrow, we'll look more closely at the divine power that gives us the joy that comes through love.

Today's Prayer:
Jesus, help me to know and experience the depths of your love for me, that I may love others as you have loved me.

DAY 19

The Spirit of Truth

John 16

Yesterday, we learned that "it's all about love" — not worldly love, but Divine Love. It's the love that Jesus shows us, the love we've been discovering throughout the Gospel of John. But just because we've read the Gospel, just because we have Jesus' example of love, that doesn't mean we will love. It doesn't mean we'll abide in love. In order to love and to abide in love, we need help. We need power. We need the divine power that is the Holy Spirit, the Spirit of Love, the Spirit of Truth.

In the following, Jesus tells us about this Spirit:

> I have much more to tell you, but you cannot bear it now. But when he comes, the Spirit of truth, he will guide you to all truth. ... He will glorify me, because he will take from what is mine and declare it to you. Everything that the Father has is mine; for this reason I told you that he will take from what is mine and declare it to you. (16:12-14)

The apostles in the Upper Room could not bear the full truth. They could not understand the truth of who Jesus is. And what is that truth? What is the fullness of truth, the "all truth," that the Holy Spirit will guide them into?

A clue to the answer comes from the only line above that Jesus repeats: "*He will take from what is mine and declare it to you.*" What is it about Jesus that the Spirit of Truth takes and declares to us? It's Christ's Sonship. Jesus is the Son, and that is what belongs to him. Let me put it this way: There is only one thing in the Trinity that Jesus has that the Father and the Holy Spirit do not have — Sonship. The Father is not the Son. The Holy Spirit is not the Son. Only Jesus is the Son.

But what about us? Are we also the Son?

Well, let's listen to what the Spirit of Truth declares: Jesus is the eternal Son of God, *and we also are God's sons and daughters in the Son.* That is the truth. That is the truth that sets us free. It's the truth not only that Jesus Christ is God, the Son of God, who is eternally begotten of the Father but also the truth that we are sons and daughters in the Son. It's the truth that we become "divinized" by the Son. In other words, in a sense, *we become God.*

What? It's true. The Fathers of the Church had a saying, "God became man that man might become God."[50] And remember those quotes from the *Catechism* we read earlier? It's worth reading them again:

> God's very being is love. By sending his only Son and the Spirit of Love in the fullness of time, God has revealed his innermost secret: God himself is an eternal exchange of love, Father, Son, and Holy Spirit, and he has destined us to share in that exchange.[51]

And again:

> [God's] will was that men should have access to the Father, through Christ, the Word made flesh, in the Holy Spirit, and thus become sharers in the divine nature.[52]

We are "destined" by the will of the Father to share in the eternal exchange of love of the Trinity — Father, Son, and Holy Spirit. We are called to become "sharers in the divine nature" (2 Pet 1:4). In a sense, we are called to become divine. But how can that be?

Well, the exchange of love of the Trinity is only three Persons: Father, Son, and Holy Spirit. So if we "become God," then this must mean we somehow "become" one of those divine Persons. Alright, but which one? Do we become the Father? No. The Holy Spirit? No. Do we become the Son? Yes!

Again, the Holy Spirit declares to us this truth: Jesus is the eternal Son of God, *and you also are God's sons and daughters in the Son.* In other words, we have been transformed into the Son as sons and daughters in the Son. And when did that happen? At our Baptism. When we were baptized, through the power of the Holy Spirit, we were "born again from above" and transformed into the Body of Christ. We were not transformed into the head of the Body, Jesus Christ, but we were truly made members of the Body of Christ. We are Christ because we are his Body, and so we truly are God's sons and daughters.

So, the Spirit of Truth not only declares to us the truth of who Jesus is and who we are in Christ, he's also the power that makes us into Christ. Again, he did so at our Baptism — and that's not all he did at our Baptism. He also filled us with himself, as St. Paul teaches:

> For you did not receive the spirit of slavery to fall back into fear, but you have received the spirit of sonship. When we cry, "Abba! Father!" it is the Spirit himself bearing witness with our spirit that we are children of God (Rom 8:15).

> And because you are sons, God has sent the Spirit of his Son into our hearts, crying "Abba! Father!" (Gal 4:6)

This is the glorious truth that was too much for the apostles to bear. It's the truth that Jesus Christ is God and that he has made us sharers in his own divine nature, through the power of the Holy Spirit.[53] But we need to listen to the Holy Spirit, because we forget who we are. We forget that God is our Father. We forget that that is enough. We forget that the Father loves us with the same love with which he loves his eternal Son. We forget that the Father's love for us could not be more.

The spirit of the world, who is Satan, tries to get us to forget all this. He does so by redirecting us from the fullness of love that we find in the Father to people or places or things instead. For instance, he moves us to make idols of our spouse or girlfriend or boyfriend as if a creature could fully satisfy the longing for love that moves the heart of a child of God. He gets us to think that we must earn love and become "somebody" to be loved. But we already are somebody. We're the children of God! We're totally and completely loved by the Father. But again, we easily forget this truth and strive to find our identity in what we do instead of who we are in Christ.

So what should we do?

Throughout the Farewell Discourse, Jesus reassures us with some of the most consoling words in Sacred Scripture: "Truly, truly I say to you, if you ask anything of the Father, he will give it to you in my name" (see also v. 24; 14:13, 14; 15:16). For what, then, should we ask? After all, we're already God's children and have all the love of the Father. So, what else do we need?

We need a deeper outpouring of the Spirit. We need the Holy Spirit, the Spirit of Love, the Spirit of Truth, to open our eyes to the gift we've already been given. We need the Holy Spirit to enlighten our minds to understand the Truth of who Jesus Christ is and who we are: God's dearly beloved children. We need the spirit of sonship to well up and overflow in our souls to the point where we cry out, "Abba, Father!" We need the Holy Spirit to set our hearts on fire with love that we might love others with the same love that we ourselves have received.

Today's Prayer:

> *Come, Holy Spirit, Spirit of Truth, declare to me the Truth of who Jesus is, who I am, and move me to cry out with love, "Abba, Father!"*

DAY 20
Consecrated in the Truth
John 17:16-23

Yesterday, we concluded with those beautiful words of Jesus, "Whatever you ask the Father in my name he will give to you" (16:23). And, again, the great gift of God for which we asked is the Holy Spirit — but there's more. We can find that "more" if we ask, what is *Jesus'* prayer? What does *he* want? What is his deepest, most heartfelt petition before the Father?

It's for unity. It's for communion. It's that all of humanity be brought into the communion of love who is Father, Son, and Holy Spirit. It's that all may be one. But how does that happen? One key passage in the famous prayer of Jesus from Chapter 17 tells us. Speaking of we who are still in the world but not of it (we hope), Jesus says to the Father:

> They are not of the world, even as I am not of the world. Sanctify them in the truth; your word is truth. As you sent me into the world, so I have sent them into the world. And for their sake I consecrate myself, that they also may be consecrated in truth. (17:16-19)

Again, the "they" is us. It is all Christians, all those who believe in Jesus and who are called to be in the world but not of it. Now that last part gets to the heart of the Christian life: the call to be in the world but not of it. That is our mission in Jesus Christ. Again, Jesus says to the Father, "As you sent me into the world, so I have sent them into the world." He didn't send us into the world to be worldly Christians but, rather, to save the world through an otherworldly love.

Yesterday, we saw that we need extra help to be love in the world, and this help comes through the power of the Holy Spirit. But Jesus knew we also need something else, some extra help from him. And so, just before entering into his Passion, he speaks to the Father of this extra help, this extra help we need in order to love: "For their sake I consecrate myself, that they also may be consecrated in truth."

So, the help he gives us is his own consecration.

Okay, but what, again, does it mean to be consecrated?

It means to be set apart.

Alright, then, from what does Jesus set himself apart when he says, "I consecrate myself"?

He's setting himself apart from the world and its ways.

Now, throughout the Gospel, Jesus has been teaching us about being set apart from the world and overcoming worldly ways. For instance, earlier this week, we read about how he did so through the foot washing, which overcomes the pride of the world. But that was not the greatest way Jesus teaches us.

The greatest way, the fullness of his consecration, is his agony on the Cross. There, as we'll see next week, he completely sets himself apart from the world, consecrating himself so we also may be consecrated in the truth.

And what is that truth? Of course, Jesus is the Truth. But he's also the Way to the Source of all truth: the Father. Jesus is the Truth because he is the Son, and the very word "Son" implies a "Father." Jesus came to reveal the truth that he is the Son and God is the Father.

As we saw yesterday, we're also part of that truth, because we are in the Son. We're sons and daughters in the Divine Son and, with Christ, we witness to the truth that God is Father. But through his consecration on the Cross, Jesus also reveals the truth of what sonship means. It means total self-gift to the Father. It means obedience to the Father's will, even to the point of death on a Cross. It means loving the Father without holding anything back. This should be our love for the Father just as it was Jesus' love for the Father. For Jesus said, "I do as the Father has commanded me, so that the world may know that I love the Father" (14:31).

Now, does the world see in us that we love the Father? Or does the world see that we love the father of lies? According to St. John, "He who says 'I know [the Father]' but disobeys his commandments is a liar, and the truth is not in him" (1 Jn 2:4). And also, "If any one says, 'I love God,' and hates his brother, he is a liar; for he who does not love his brother whom he has seen, cannot love God whom he has not seen" (1 Jn 4:20). If we hate our brother, if we refuse to forgive, if we hold on to bitterness and resentment, then we are not in the truth, and our father is not God but Satan, the father of lies and of hypocrisy.

And it gets worse. Saint John is all about love, but sometimes it's tough love:

> Do not love the world or the things in the world. If any one loves the world, love for the Father is not in him. For all that is in the world, the lust of the flesh and the lust of the eyes and the pride of life, is not of

the Father but is of the world. And the world passes away, and the lust of it; but he who does the will of God abides forever. (1 Jn 2:15-17)

The world and its ways of riches, vanity, fame, pride, power, adulation, and status are from Satan, and they pass away. But God our Father wants us to have eternal life, to break free from the lure of this world. Speaking for the Father, Jesus says, "He who loves his life loses it, and he who hates his life in this world will keep it for eternal life" (12:25).

Ah, but that's all geared to people who make vows of poverty, chastity, and obedience. It's for priests and religious. They're the ones who need to be separated from the ways of the world, right? Right. At least, we're supposed to be. But the Second Vatican Council, through its "universal call to holiness," reminds us that holiness, the life of consecration, of being set apart for God, is not just for priests and religious but for *everyone*.[54] Indeed, I would go so far as to say that the Christian life *is* the consecrated life, in the sense of being set apart from the world, in the sense of being in the world but not of it. Why? Because the Christian life begins with Baptism, which is our fundamental consecration. At our Baptism, the prince of this world, who is Satan, loses the rights he had to us as a result of original sin. At our Baptism, the God who created us in love reclaims us as his own. At our Baptism, God becomes our Father, and we become his children — and then he wants us to act like it. Why? Because that's how the world will be saved.

Before returning to the Father, Jesus commissioned us to go out into the world to be the light of the world. He sent us out to reveal the Father, telling us, "Greater works than these will [you] do, because I go to the Father" (14:12). What works? The works of love. How? Through the power of the Holy Spirit that he sends into us. But we need to ask for the Spirit, receive him, and live his life so as to reveal the face of the Father to the world. And what is this life of the Spirit? Saint Paul tells us by first contrasting it with "the works of the flesh" (what John calls "the world"):

Now the works of the flesh are plain: immortality, impurity, licentiousness, idolatry, sorcery, enmity, strife, jealousy, anger, selfishness, dissension, party spirit, envy, drunkenness, carousing, and the like. (Gal 5:19-21)

Paul goes on to describe the life in the Spirit according to its fruits:

But the fruit of the Spirit is love, joy, peace, patience, kindness, goodness, faithfulness, gentleness, self-control ... . And those who belong to Christ Jesus have crucified the flesh with its passions and desires. (Gal 5:22-24)

Jesus surely allowed his flesh to be crucified, and he overcame the world by his Cross. That was how he consecrated himself. We also must be consecrated in this truth, the truth of crucified love, by uniting ourselves to Christ on the Cross as we strive to love our neighbor as Christ has loved us, that the world may be saved, and that all may be one.

Today's Prayer:
Father, with Christ your Son, I pray that all may be one, and I ask that you use me as an instrument of unity by setting me apart even more from the world and its ways.

DAY 21
A Most Beautiful Truth   3\24
John 17:24-26

Yesterday we covered the idea of being consecrated in the Truth. Now, admittedly, that's a challenging reality. Believe me. I know.

As you may recall from the Introduction, part of why I'm writing this book is to better own precisely the kind of priest and Christian I want to be. I also invited you to join me on this journey. Well, my guess is that, at least by now, you're probably thinking what I'm thinking: *This is hard. This is challenging! I'm not so sure I'm up for this.*

Well, that's a good place to be. In fact, I believe it's exactly the place God wants us to be when we really dig into his Word. It's the place where we have to confront our weakness. It's the place where we better realize we haven't yet "arrived" (far from it). It's the place where we strongly feel the tension between "the person I am" and "the person I'm called to be." Still, being in this place shouldn't cause us to quit. Rather, it should move us to call out, in the name of Jesus Christ, to God our Father, and ask him to pour into our weakness the Spirit of Love, the Spirit of Truth. It's meant to push us higher toward the summit of love.

Here at the end of this week, we've arrived at that summit. We've come to a most beautiful truth, a truth that's found in what I believe is the greatest passage in all of Scripture. It's the passage that, if we ponder it deeply in our hearts, can set our souls on fire with love. It's the passage that comes at the very end of the Farewell Discourse, and like at Cana, the Lord has saved the best for last:

> Father, I desire that they also, whom thou hast given me, may be with me where I am, to behold my glory which thou hast given me in thy love for me before the foundation of the world. O righteous Father, the world has not known thee, but I have known thee, and these know that thou hast sent me. I have made known to them thy name, and I will make it known, that the love with which thou hast loved me may be in them and I in them. (17:24-26)

Now, why is this passage so great? In another book, I give a general argument as to why this is the greatest passage in all of Scripture, an argument I reproduce in this endnote.[55] Here I'll just share the main conclusions: The Gospels are the heart of Scripture; the Gospel of John is the greatest Gospel; the Farewell Discourse is the most sublime section of John's Gospel; Jesus' prayer to the Father in Chapter 17 is the most

important part of the Farewell Discourse; and the last verses of
Chapter 17 (which we've just read) are the most glorious of all,
the greatest passage in all of the Bible. Of course, you're free
to disagree. However, as we look more closely at the verses
themselves, I think you'll come to be convinced of their rich-
ness and beauty. Why? Because it's all there. The very heart of
Jesus' Heart.

Let me explain.

In the above passage, Jesus is speaking to the Father
immediately before he enters into his Passion. So, these really
are his last words prior to descending into the darkness. Before
he goes, however, he expresses the deepest desire of his Heart
to the Father.

And what is it that Jesus desires on the eve of his Passion?

He himself tells us: "Father, I desire that they also …
may be with me where *I am*." In other words, he wants us to
be "with him" in his divinity, where he is in the divine name,
"I AM." His deep desire is to do for us what the Father did
for him. So, just as the Father gives himself completely to
the Son without holding anything back such that the Son
is equal to the Father, Jesus also wants to give himself to us
without holding anything back so we may be as as equal to
the Father as is possible for a creature made in God's own
image. In other words, Jesus' desire is that we be divinized
in himself through the power of the Holy Spirit to the glory
of God the Father.

Now, that in itself is totally amazing — but it doesn't end
there. Jesus also wants us to see what nobody else gets to see.

Let me put it this way. There's a beautiful intimacy
between spouses that the children never see (and should never
see) and from which the children come. Well, for us, Jesus
wants to remove the veil that stands between us and the intimacy between the Father, Son, and Holy Spirit. He wants us
to see the love that was before any of us came to be. He wants
us to "behold the glory" that the Father gave to him, in his
love for him, before the foundation of the world.

Now *that* is mind-blowingly amazing.

But Jesus doesn't just want us to behold that glory; he also wants us to be in it, to share it, to participate in it.

At the very last part of the very last line of "the greatest passage," Jesus describes more fully what this intimacy will look like. Speaking to the Father, he expresses his desire that "the love with which thou hast loved me may be in them and I in them." In other words, as that marvelous passage from the *Catechism* we read earlier described it, God himself desires that we participate in the "eternal exchange of love" that is between the Father and the Son.

Alright, but where is the Holy Spirit?

He's in that word "love." For the Holy Spirit is "Love." And so, it's all here: Father, Son, and the Love between them, who is the Holy Spirit. You might say, then, that Jesus wants us to have it all, the fullness of God himself, the Trinity! He wants to do for us what the Father does for him. He wants to give to us without holding anything back. He wants us to have as much glory as he has insofar as a creature can receive it. Here, in the "greatest passage," he says it with words. In his suffering and death, he actually does it with deeds.

Great. But isn't all that a bit much?

It surely was for Lucifer, the highest of the angels. He couldn't accept God's plan of love for humanity. Now known as Satan, this fallen angel burns with envy at how God brings human beings, who are lower than the angels by nature, even higher than the angels by grace. He's enraged that we puny creatures have been invited into God's own inner life, into his "innermost secret," as the *Catechism* puts it.[56]

Unfortunately, while Satan clearly understands what God has done for us in Christ, we often do not. We rarely realize the most beautiful truth of God's mercy for us, namely, that he intends to "divinize us," that he wants to bring us to share in his own divine nature as fully as possible. Well, let's now come to realize it. Let's try to understand by considering this: There's one thing that kicks off the greater glory that Jesus wants to give us, one thing that leads to our receiving the very same love that the Father has for the Son.

And what is that?

Jesus himself reveals it in the "greatest passage." He does so when he says, "I have made known to them *thy name* and I will make it known that the love with which thou hast loved me may be in them and I in them."

So, everything hinges on knowing "thy name." All the love God wants to give us flows from that. That's why there's the word "that." Jesus says, "I have made known to them thy name *that...*" In other words, our Lord is saying, "I made known to them thy name *so that* the love with which you love me may be in them." But what name is he talking about here? What's the name upon which everything hinges? Is it the divine name "I AM"? No. It's something better, something greater. It's the name "*Father.*" Everything gets back to that. We have everything, all the love of the Trinity, when we have God as our Father. For if we can call God "Father," then we truly are his dearly beloved children. That is everything, because our Father's love is everything.

Of course, we already know that Jesus has made known the Father's name. After all, that's what we've been learning throughout the Gospel of John. But Jesus also says, "I *will* make it known." And when does he make the Father's name known in the future? We'll find that out this coming week.

Today's Prayer:

Jesus, thank you. Thank you for not holding anything back and for giving me everything, for giving me your Father as my Father.

Greater Glory

This week covers the suffering, death, and Resurrection of our Lord. The days are as follows: Rejection of the Truth, "I Thirst," Mary Magdalene, The Upper Room (Again), Going Fishing, "Do You Love Me?" and "Follow Me."

DAY 22
Rejection of the Truth 3/25
John 18 (see also 12:12-19)

"Are you the King of the Jews?" Jesus answers Pilate's question by saying that his kingship is "not of this world" and "not from the world." And then, as if out of the blue, he describes his kingship in terms of "the truth":

> For this I was born, and for this I have come into the world, to bear witness to the truth. Everyone who is of the truth hears my voice.

In response to this, Pilate dismissively asks, "What is truth?" Cynicism aside, that's a great question. The meditations of the last three days have attempted an answer. Before we get to that, however, one brief word about truth in general.

The classic, medieval definition of truth is the correspondence of the intellect with reality.[57] For example, if you know that the United States of America was established in 1776, then you have found that particular truth. The Scriptural definition, however, the one that the Gospel of John follows, is different. For John, the truth is what God reveals about divine reality and God's plans.[58]

Alright, so what's John's specific answer to the question, "What is truth?"

John tells us that Jesus himself is the Truth (see 14:6). He's the Truth because he's God the Son, who reveals God the Father and also the Love between the Father and the Son, who is God the Holy Spirit. He further reveals the loving plan of God for us, that we are called to be children of God who share in the very life of God the Trinity — if only we will believe the Truth that's revealed in Jesus Christ.

115

As we saw yesterday, all that is a most beautiful truth!

Alright, so why would anyone reject it?

Because of worldliness. Again, Jesus told Pilate that his kingdom is not of this world. It's not surprising, then, that those who are of this world have a hard time recognizing the Truth — even when, like Pilate, it's right there in front of them. Jesus basically said the same thing to Nicodemus: "Unless one is born from above, he cannot see the kingdom of God" (3:3). Also, he told "the Jews," who were blind to the Truth, why they could not see it: "You are from below, I am from above; you are of this world, I am not of this world" (8:23).

So, being of the world and "from below" is the great obstacle to recognizing, receiving, and accepting the Truth.

Now, to help us better understand the rejection of the Truth during the Passion, let's turn to some earlier examples of how worldliness blinds people to receiving Jesus.

Recall that after Jesus fed the multitudes with bread, they wanted to carry him away by force and make him their king (see 6:15). Clearly, they saw Jesus as an earthly king instead of a heavenly one. Such worldly thinking explains why they couldn't receive the truth when Jesus later told them, "I am the bread which came down from heaven" (6:41). In fact, shortly after he spoke those words, they flat out rejected him.

In the twelfth chapter of John's Gospel, we read of Jesus' triumphal entry into Jerusalem. There the people greeted the Lord with joyous cries of "Hosanna," because they saw him as a worldly king who would deliver them from foreign oppression. Now, one bit of data had sparked their zeal: Jesus had just raised Lazarus from the dead. With such power, might he also do the reverse and send the Roman legions to the dead?

Jesus made sure not to encourage such worldly ambitions. For instance, he came riding into Jerusalem not on a war horse or in a chariot but on "a young donkey." Hardly an image of worldly power. Actually, it's an image from Zechariah, who prophesied about a "humble" king who would stop war and bring peace to the earth (Zech 9:9-10). Jesus is such a king because his power comes not from the world but from the Father and his love, which brings true peace to the world through mercy and forgiveness. The crowds in Jerusalem, however, stuck as they were in their worldly perspective, could not receive such a king from Heaven. And so, the cries of "Hosanna" would soon change to "Crucify him!"

As we've seen earlier, Judas was not so different from the people in Jerusalem. In fact, his cries of Hosanna may have been loudest of all. I say that because he had personally witnessed the Lord's powerful signs. Unfortunately, however, he misinterpreted those signs, seeing in them the establishment of a worldly kingdom instead of a heavenly one. Again, this explains why it was too much for Judas to see Jesus washing the disciples' feet in the Upper Room. A meek, humble king, who did the work of slaves, just didn't fit with Judas' worldly ambitions.

And so, now, as the hour of Jesus' Passion begins, Judas reappears, this time with a band of soldiers and Temple guards carrying lanterns, torches, and weapons. Together, they all represent the world and its power, and they're the total opposite of the first disciples. For when Jesus asks these men in the garden the very same question he had asked the first disciples ("Whom do you seek?"), they don't ask where he abides, and they're certainly not invited to "come and see." Why? Because they can't see. They're too blinded by their worldliness. And so they answer Jesus' question as men who are "from below," as men who go no further than the merely earthly name of the Lord: "Jesus of Nazareth." As we read earlier, Jesus responds with the Divine Name, "I AM," a pronouncement that knocks them to the ground. While Jesus is still the all-powerful God incarnate, he'll now sheath the sword of his might and hand himself over to the powers of worldly darkness so as to overcome that darkness through the mystery of merciful love.

And what about Peter? What's his reaction to Jesus' arrest? Does the head of the disciples prepare to lay down his life in love? No. Instead, he draws his sword and attempts to take another man's life (only managing to cut off an ear). To his credit, Peter at least does follow Jesus to the house of

Annas, the high priest. However, the Gospel of Matthew adds the foreboding detail that he follows Jesus "from a distance" (26:58).

In the courtyard of Annas' house, Peter's inner distance from Jesus widens as he warms himself by a fire in the company of the very people who had gone to arrest his friend. Perhaps this scene shows that Peter's love for Jesus is growing cold. After all, he's now finding his light and warmth from the world instead of from the Light of the World. Actually, we have proof that his love has grown cold, because he goes on to deliberately and explicitly reject the Truth when he's asked if he is one of Jesus' disciples. In fact, he rejects the Truth three times. Why? Well, let's look at this more closely because, whereas we may not be ready to reject the Truth as dramatically as "the Jews" and Pilate did after Jesus' arrest, we may easily find ourselves in the position of Peter.

Why does Peter reject Jesus? Another Gospel gives us a clue. In Matthew, just after Jesus gives Peter the name "Rock," the Rock crumbles. He crumbles because he can't accept Jesus' announcement that the Son of Man will be arrested and killed. In fact, he rebukes Jesus for even saying it. In response, the Lord turns on Peter and exclaims, "Get behind me, Satan! You are a hindrance to me; for you are not on the side of God, but of men" (16:23).

A similar scenario happens in John's Gospel at the foot washing in the Upper Room. Like Judas, Peter didn't want Jesus to do the slave's work of washing his feet. Why not? Because, again, he was thinking from the perspective of men and not of God. In fact, right up to Jesus' Passion, Peter still shows himself to be a very worldly man. For instance, we already know his response to Jesus' arrest — violent anger. And then, again, it gets worse by the fire. As Peter warmed himself, we can imagine worldly thoughts filling his mind: *Jesus is weak. He's not defending himself. This is not the one I left everything to follow. He's not who I thought he was. He's a nobody.* Then, suddenly, a woman asks him, "Are you one of his disciples?" Instead of answering boldly with Christ, "I AM." He emphatically states, "I AM NOT." Peter denies Jesus and, in a sense, *he* becomes nothing, a nobody. He's surrendered his identity as a follower of Christ. And so, without the Holy Spirit's help, he will have no part with I AM and will remain "I AM NOT."

So, as Jesus enters into his Passion, the head of the disciples turns out to be a hypocrite, a worldly man, a disciple in name only. Despite three years of following Jesus, listening to him, and seeing his signs, he hasn't realized that the Lord's kingship is one of truth and love and not from this world. But once Jesus Christ the King is lifted up on the throne of his Cross, he will conquer the way of the world. Once he is lifted up in glory, he will overcome earthly glory. Once he is lifted up high as Love, all people will be drawn to look up from this selfish, prideful, power-hungry world and see the truth that God is Love. We, too, have to look up to see it and believe it so as not to end up like Judas and Peter: hypocrites. We have to go to the Cross. We'll do just that tomorrow.

Today's Prayer:
> *Lord Jesus, help me to be a true disciple by accepting the truth that the way of love is the way of the Cross.*

DAY 23
"I Thirst"
John 19:17-37

At the end of last week, we contemplated "a most beautiful truth," expressed in what I called the greatest passage in all of Sacred Scripture. One reason it's so great is that, on the eve of the Passion, it reveals the deepest desire in the Heart of Jesus expressed in his most heartfelt prayer to his Father.

Now, again, what was that desire?

Jesus himself tells us: "Father, I desire that they also ... may be with me where I AM, to behold my glory that thou hast given me in thy love for me before the foundation of the world" (17:24). What a beautiful longing! Jesus is saying that he wants us to be with him in the greatness of his divinity and to behold the glory that the Father gave to him from even before creation. But there's more. And we find that more at the one other place in John's Gospel where Jesus expresses the deepest desire of his Heart.

That other place is on the Cross. There, Jesus expresses his deepest desire when he cries out, "I thirst." At that moment, I believe Jesus wasn't so much thirsting for water. Rather, I suggest, with those words, he's revealing the very same desire he had expressed to the Father in the Upper Room. It's the same desire we already read in the greatest passage, but with this difference: It's now being expressed in the context of the Cross, which deepens the meaning of the greatest passage.

Let me explain.

From the Cross, in crying out "I thirst," Jesus is repeating his final words in the Upper Room, but with the following difference. Instead of saying, "Father, I desire that they also may be with me where I AM," I believe he's saying, "Father, I desire that they also may be with me where *I THIRST*." In short, the divine name "I AM" becomes on the Cross, "I THIRST." And rightly so. I say that because the great I AM fully manifests his true greatness to the world, above all, in his total self-emptying on the Cross. The God who doesn't need us (because he's God) shows his greatness in the vulnerability that he lovingly accepted in becoming incarnate, a vulnerability that's best expressed by the words, "I THIRST."[59] There is Jesus' greatest glory, a glory that is also part of the prayer of the Upper Room. How so? Let's see.

Again, in the Upper Room, Jesus' deep longing is that we behold his glory, the glory that the Father gave to him from before the foundation of the world. Well, as we've just seen, the glory that the Son had before the foundation of the world is fully manifested on the Cross. For us to behold it, therefore, we need to go to the Cross. We need to be with Jesus where he thirsts. For, there on the Cross, the invisible love between the Father and the Son is made visible. And so, if we want to see the glorious love of the Trinity, we simply need to look at Jesus as he's dying on the Cross. But as we've just seen, he's not only dying. He's thirsting. He's thirsting that we see his love. He's thirsting that we be with him where he thirsts, because that's where we'll see his glory.

Now, if we look to the wider context of Jesus' words, "I thirst," it confirms that his longing is that we be there with him at the Cross. It also opens up a clearer vision of the glory that is present there. So, let's turn to that wider context now:

> After this Jesus, knowing that all was now finished, said (to fulfill the Scripture), "I thirst." A bowl of vinegar stood there; so they put a sponge full of the vinegar on hyssop and held it to his mouth. When Jesus had received the vinegar, he said, "It is finished"; and he bowed his head and gave up his spirit. (19:30)

Now, what Scripture is Jesus fulfilling here? It's Psalm 69:22, which says, "They gave me gall for food, and for my thirst they gave me vinegar to drink." Okay. So, is that it? That's the clearer vision? Well, let me put it this way: John often cites a line or two from the Old Testament and then expects the reader to go to that passage and find something more. So, what's the more John wants us to find in Psalm 69? It's in the preceding verse, which says this:

> Insults have broken my heart, so that I am in despair. And I looked for one that would grieve together with me, and there was none: and I sought one that would console me, and I found none. (69:21)

Right there. That says it all. Jesus on the Cross, as he cries out, "I thirst," is looking for consolers. In other words, he wants us to give him a drink.

Now, wait a minute. Jesus wants us to give him a drink? Where have we heard that before? Of course, we heard it during Jesus' conversation with the woman at the well. So, let's go back to that, because John seems to be leading us to something.

Jesus said to the woman at the well, "Give me a drink." However, as we read, he really wanted to give *her* a drink —

which is just like Jesus. We quench his thirst by letting him quench ours. We feed him by letting him feed us. We console him by letting him console us.

Alright, so what's the drink that Jesus wants to give to the woman at the well, the drink that quenches his thirst? That's right. It's the "living water" that is the Holy Spirit, the Spirit of Love. And what is the drink he wants to give to us from the Cross that quenches our thirst? It's the same living water — but it's also something more.

We've already read that, on Calvary, Jesus "bowed his head and gave up his spirit." This prophetic gesture points to the coming of a very special gift of the Holy Spirit from the Cross, a gift we discover a few verses later:

> But when they came to Jesus and saw that he was already dead, they did not break his legs. But one of the soldiers pierced his side with a spear, and at once there came out blood and water. (19:34)

The blood and water from Jesus' pierced side is the drink he wants to give us that quenches his own thirst. Again, his desire here on the Cross is that we be with him where he thirsts, behold his glory (the glory of his love), and receive the love that comes from his pierced side. Specifically, it's the blood and water that are a fountain of mercy for us, the blood and water that are a sign of the Eucharist and Baptism, the blood and water that are a sign of love and the Spirit of Love. That is Jesus' thirst: that we would quench our thirst by drinking from the fountain of his pierced side. (This then gives us the Spirit of Love, enabling us to love Jesus with his own Divine Love.[60]) And to show us exactly how he wants us to do this, he says something very significant just before "I thirst":

> When Jesus saw his mother, and the disciple whom he loved standing near, he said to his mother, "Woman, behold your son!" Then he said to the disciple, "Behold your mother!" And from that hour the disciple took her to his own home. (19:26-27)

So, just as there was a "woman" at the well, here there's a "woman" at the Cross: Jesus' mother. And now, as a parting gift of love, from the Cross, Jesus gives us his mother as our own spiritual mother. Indeed, as disciples whom he loves, Jesus invites us to "behold" our mother. The one, then, who has gone to the Cross that we may have access to the Father, from the same Cross, has given us a Mother, that we may have better access to the Son. And just as Mary's love consoled her Son as he was dying on the Cross, so she will console us, too. How? By helping us to have the courage to come to the foot of the Cross, stand there with her, and quench our thirst from the blood and water that gush forth from the pierced Heart of Jesus as a fountain of mercy for us. She also helps us unite ourselves to the perfect consecration of her Son as he offers himself in the Spirit to the Father for the life of the world, as we'll see later this week. Before then, however (tomorrow, in fact), we'll get to know one of the other faithful people here at the foot of the Cross.

Today's Prayer:

O Blood and Water that gushed forth from the Heart of Jesus as a fountain of mercy for us, I thirst for you.

DAY 24
Mary Magdalene 3|27
John 20:1-18

"Standing by the foot of the cross of Jesus," John tells us, among other faithful women, "was Mary Magdalene" (19:25). And who was that? In the Gospel of Mark, we learn that she's the one out of whom Jesus cast seven demons (10:9). Some also believe that she's the one who washed the feet of Jesus in the house of Simon the Pharisee in the Gospel of Luke, the one about whom Jesus said, "She loved much" (7:47). Whether Mary Magdalene is that woman, we do not know. But here's what we do know: She loved Jesus much, very much.

How do we know this? Because, again, Mary was there at the Cross. While all of the apostles (except John) fled from

Jesus' crucifixion out of fear, Mary Magdalene went to the Cross without any fear. For "there is no fear in love, but perfect love casts out fear" (1 Jn 4:18). We also see Mary's love for Jesus in the fact that she went to his tomb early on Sunday morning, while it was still dark. And she wasn't just quietly visiting there. Rather, she was weeping, beside herself with grief at the loss of the one whom she loved. Reflecting on her tears, we can certainly take what John had said of Jesus as he wept for Lazarus and apply it to her: "*See how she loved him.*"

Now, as Mary was there at the tomb, weeping in the darkness, she suddenly realized that the stone that had blocked the entrance had been taken away. So, immediately, she ran (another sign of her love) and went to tell Peter and John. With her eyes still puffy from crying, and probably with desperation in her voice, she pleaded with the men, "They have taken the Lord out of the tomb, and we do not know where they have laid him."

Hearing this, Peter and John ran to the tomb, went inside, and saw that the body of Jesus was no longer there. Then, filled with exuberant joy, they ran throughout Jerusalem proclaiming the good news that Jesus had been raised from the dead. Well, no. That's not what they did. Instead, they simply went home. Why? Because, as John writes, "as yet they did not know the Scripture that [Jesus] must rise from the dead."[61]

Meanwhile, Mary Magdalene stayed at the tomb weeping (and so her love seems to be even greater than that of John). As she wept, she suddenly noticed two angels in the tomb where Jesus' body had been. The angels then said to her, "Woman, why are you weeping?"

Now, let's reflect on that for a moment.

The angels, who by nature far surpass human beings in beauty and greatness, well know what God has done for us in Christ. They know the Lord has raised humanity by grace even higher than the angels, bringing us into the very nature of God. And so, these angels are probably marveling at the Divine Mercy shown to humanity in that tomb. It's no wonder, then, that they ask Mary, "Why are you weeping?" It's as if they wanted to say, "Don't you have any idea what God has done for you? Poor little creature, you should be rejoicing! You now stand at the summit of creation with the resurrected Lord!" But they don't say that, because Jesus suddenly appears, and he, too, says to Mary, "Woman why are you weeping?" But he also adds, "Whom do you seek?"

Mary is so distraught, she doesn't recognize Jesus, and she's thought nothing of the fact that she's just seen two angels. All she seems to want is to be left alone with what's left of her Lord. And now the beasts who took his life have even taken away his body? The apostles have done nothing. They don't seem to care, which increases Mary's anguish. She just wants Jesus' body back so she can grieve in peace. She asks the Lord, whom she still does not recognize, whether he's removed the body. If so, she'll take it away.

Whom, then, does Mary seek? She doesn't seek a "someone" but a body, a corpse, because the one she loves is dead. While she certainly has no faith, she nevertheless has very deep love.

But the Lord's love for Mary is much deeper. Imagine how precious she is to him, this loyal woman whose love not only brought her to the Cross but now brings her to the tomb. And where are the men? Where are the apostles? There's only this poor woman? The sight of such a devout disciple moves Jesus to tenderly call her by name, "*Mary*." Hearing her name, this woman who's so filled with love, responds to love. Being a meek, little lamb, she knows the voice of her shepherd, the Good Shepherd, the one who gave his life for his sheep. Hearing her name, she also recognizes Jesus as the one who says, according to Isaiah, "Fear not, for I have redeemed you; I have called you by name, you are mine" (Is 43:1). It seems this is what Jesus is saying to Mary in calling her by name. He's subtly announcing the triumph of his Resurrection that overcomes sadness and fear and makes her (and us) truly belong to him.

Now, Mary's response to Jesus is also filled with meaning. Of all the things she could say to him, she addresses him as "Rabboni!" which means "Teacher." For he is the true Teacher, the one who gives the gift of truth (1:17), the one who is the Truth (14:6), and the one who will now give the fullness of truth.

After telling Mary not to hold on to him — she was probably weeping and hugging him — he tells her why. It's because he's not the end. Rather, his Father is the end: "Do not hold me, for I have not yet ascended to the Father."[62] And then he proceeds to bear witness to the truth, the truth for which he was born and came into the world, the fullness of the truth:

> Go to my brothers and say to them, I am ascending to my Father and your Father, to my God and your God. (20:17)

Right here is the Gospel, the good news, the truth that Jesus came to announce. Right here is the moment that Jesus referred to in the Upper Room when he said to the Father, "I have made known to them thy name, and I *will* make it known." Right here is when he makes "thy name" known. Right here is his Easter proclamation: *The Father*.

Fittingly, then, having accomplished the work the Father gave him to do, having now given those who receive him the power to become children of God, Jesus says to Mary, "Go to *my brothers*." This is the first time in the Gospel of John that Jesus refers to the disciples as his brothers. That's because, before, they weren't. But now, after Jesus' suffering, death, and Resurrection, *they are*. The blood of the Risen Christ has made them such, and now they have the same Father, we have the same Father — God.

Still, Jesus makes a distinction. He says "my Father and your Father." That is, we are all sons and daughters *in the Son*. We only call God our Father through the gift of being in the eternal Son. But why does Jesus call the Father "my God"? Isn't Jesus also God? Yes, of course. But the Father is his "God" in the sense that Jesus knows that *everything* he has, including his divinity, is a gift from the Father. He knows the goodness and humility of the Father who, as he loves, gives everything without holding anything back such that the Son is equal to the Father. And the Son has now done what the Father does for him: He has loved us without holding anything back, thus giving us his Father as our Father as we live in him as sons and daughters in the Son.

Hearing Jesus' words, then, the woman who loved much, very much, did as she was told. She went to the apostles as the "apostle to the apostles" and declared to them, "I have seen the Lord!" She then announced the good news that God is our Father and we are now brothers and sisters in loving communion with Christ. Alleluia.

Today's Prayer:
> *Lord Jesus, thank you for making the Father's name known to me so that the love with which he has loved you is now in me and I in you.*

DAY 25
The Upper Room, Again 3/28
John 20:19-29

Despite Mary Magdalene's proclamation "I have seen the Lord!" the apostles did not believe — or at least it seems that way. I say that because, had they believed, they would have been outside, boldly proclaiming the Resurrection. Instead, they were inside, behind locked doors, filled with fear.

Why were they afraid? Because they thought "the Jews" would come and do to them what they'd already done to Jesus. But the apostles weren't just afraid. They were also probably ashamed. With the exception of John, they'd been a bunch of disloyal cowards. And then, Mary Magdalene's words this morning served as salt in the wounds. The apostles all knew she'd been faithful, that she'd gone to the Cross. They all knew that she'd been weeping all morning at the tomb, while they hadn't shed a tear — except maybe for themselves and their hopeless future as fugitives from "the Jews." So, that woman was a better friend to Jesus than they'd ever been, and her love for the Lord put them all to shame. And now, just this morning, she was saying that Jesus had appeared to her? Her grief must have driven her mad. But even if it were true, Jesus surely wouldn't come *to them*. And even if he did, it certainly wouldn't be for a nice hug! Rather, he'd probably punish them, shame them, or rebuke them for their cowardice and disloyalty, and he'd be totally justified in doing so.

Now, while we can't totally be sure what the disciples were thinking, we do know this: The atmosphere in that Upper Room was very different than it had been before. The last time, the room had been bathed in the warm light of the Lord's love as he humbly washed his disciples feet. But now it was all darkness: the cold darkness of fear, shame, and confusion.

If anyone needed the hope of Easter, these men did.

And Jesus gave it. Despite the locked doors, the Lord suddenly appeared and stood in their midst. Although he fully knew their disloyalty, cowardice, and lack of faith, he didn't even mention it. Instead, he spoke a word that caused exactly what it meant: "Peace." "Peace be with you." Those words, coming from the lips of the Risen Savior, cause peace. They act with the same power as the words that Jesus had spoken in the garden: "I AM." However, instead of causing a whole cohort of Roman soldiers to fall to the ground, they cause fear, shame, and sin to disappear just as the dawn dispels the darkness of the night. That is what Jesus gave to the disciples, and not just that. He also proceeded to show them his pierced hands and side.

Now, as for Thomas, who wasn't there because he had isolated himself, Jesus made it up to him the very next week. He did so by letting the doubting disciple put his hand into the largest wound, the wound of his Heart, the wounded Heart that heals hearts. Thomas had been so shaken by the Lord's arrest, suffering, and death that his own heart needed particular attention, which Jesus lovingly gave. But again, that came a week later. Here and now, for these disciples, it's time to rejoice because they're finally seeing the Lord.

Still, after the fervor of the initial rejoicing subsides, Jesus says to the disciples again, "Peace be with you." In case there are any lingering doubts, he repeats himself. In case they're wondering if they've really been forgiven, Jesus says "Peace be with you," so they can hear it again. And they probably did need to hear it again. For while the Lord's suffering, death, and resurrection has overcome the world, the spirit of the world can still live in us. It can live in our thoughts and emotions, accusing us, shaming us, and driving us to despair. It can affect the way we see Jesus (and so also the Father) as if he no longer loves us and has condemned us. But as we've learned, there is no judgment in Jesus. Rather, the encounter with the light of his love exposes our lack of it, but that love is also mercy, a mercy that forgives every time we turn away from the darkness and toward the light, a light that's always there. It really is always there. And if the darkness of the world keeps pulling us back, the light is always shining forth from the Heart of Jesus as the blood and water that pursues us and makes us clean.

To emphasize this truth of his mercy, Jesus said to the apostles, "As the Father has sent me, even so I send you." And then "he breathed on them" and said, "Receive the Holy Spirit. If you forgive the sins of any, they are forgiven; if you retain the sins of any, they are retained." So that is what the Father sent the Son to do? He sent him to forgive sins, to show mercy? Well, then, what does that say about the Father? What do we discover in the fact that as soon as the proclamation is made that God is our Father and we are his children, he then wants us to know that he forgives us, will forgive us, and continues to forgive us as soon as we come back to him?

Here, then, Jesus reveals our Father as the Father of Mercy whom we encounter in the parable of the Prodigal Son. But instead of just waiting for his lost children to come back, here in the Upper Room, we learn that the Father actually sends his sons to go out and find us and forgive us. How else are we to understand Jesus' words, "As the Father has sent me, so I send you"? He's not telling the apostles and their successors to just wait in a confessional. Rather, he's sending them. He's asking them to be good shepherds who go out in search of the lost sheep. And when they find the sheep, they're not to yell at them and beat them. Rather, they're to say to them, "Peace be with you." Then, they're to gently place the sheep on their shoulders and carry them home. Home? Yes, back home to the Father's house, back to the Father's love. They're to bring them back to their rooms, where the Father can call them by the name that no one else knows, a name that's followed by the words, "*You are my beloved.*"

This is the work of the Holy Spirit, the Spirit of Love, the Spirit of the Father's love for his children. But the Holy Spirit doesn't want to just do this work through the apostles and through bishops and priests. It's a work he wants to do through *everyone.* Jesus says not just to the apostles but to each of us, "As the Father has sent me, so I send you." Now, you probably don't have the power to forgive sins, but we all have the power to love, which overcomes sin. That is what it means to be a child of the Father — it means to go out, to be sent, and to make the love of the Father known. But we should link Jesus' words, "As the Father has sent me, so I send you," with other words he spoke in the Upper Room: "Love one another as I have loved you" (15:12). Those two go together. In other words, Jesus wants to say to us, "As the Father has sent me to reveal love, to give love, and to be love to this broken, hurting world, so I also send you to reveal the love I have revealed to you, to give the love I have given to you, to be the love I always am for you."

Now, before we can be love to others, we first need to experience it ourselves. Alright, but how?

In the chapel of the Marian Missionaries of Divine Mercy, the community of men and women with whom I work, we have a giant image that depicts the scene of this day's meditation. That image, called the Image of Divine Mercy, gets to the heart of our whole spirituality and, dare I say, of all Christian spirituality. For, every day, each one of us is there in the Upper Room that becomes dark and cold with our shame, sadness, confusion, and sin. Jesus then wants to enter that room and bring the light and warmth of his merciful love. He wants to tell us, "Peace be with you." He wants to breathe on us and say, "Receive the Holy Spirit," that we might rejoice. He wants to then send us out to others with the same love, mercy, and joy that we ourselves have received. So, behold the Image of Divine Mercy. Be not unbelieving but believe. Pray, "Jesus, I trust in you." Allow the peace and mercy in. And then, as the Father has sent the Son, know that the Son also sends us to be living Images of Divine Mercy to others as we reveal the merciful face of the Father and bring the peace and joy of the Gospel to a Church and a world that so badly need it.

Today's Prayer:

Jesus, I trust in you. Please breathe on me the Holy Spirit. Let me rejoice in your mercy, and then send me out as a living image of Divine Mercy.

DAY 26
Going Fishing 3/29
John 21:1-14

Jesus is Risen! The apostles have seen the Lord! They've received the Holy Spirit, the Spirit of love and mercy, and now they've been sent out to bring that same love and mercy to the world.

Great. So why did they just go fishing?

The last chapter of John's Gospel begins with a touching but somewhat confusing scene. Here's a summary: Peter says to the other apostles, "I am going fishing," and they go with him. After fishing all night, they catch nothing. As day breaks, Jesus calls out to them from the shore (although they don't know that it's Jesus). He says, "Children, have you any fish?" They answer him, "No." Jesus then tells them where to cast the net to catch some. The disciples obey and bring in a huge number of fish. John recognizes that it's the Lord, tells Peter, and Peter is so excited that he jumps into the water and swims to the shore. Meanwhile, the other disciples follow in the boat. Once on shore, they see that Jesus has made a fire and cooked breakfast, which he then gives to them. The end.

That's basically the story.

So what does it mean?

Of course, there are many ways of reading it. Here's my take: Jesus' greatest prayer to the Father is being fulfilled, a prayer for unity and communion. Let's see how.

Peter announces that he's going fishing. But should he have been going fishing? Should he have been going back to his old job, back out into the world? Well, maybe so. After all, the apostles do need to eat. What's interesting to me, though, is that they all go out *together*. And in fact, when Peter made the announcement, the text says the disciples "were together." By going out with Peter, they remain together.

So, they're out on a boat all night long together, and they don't catch anything. There's no excitement from the fish, no TV, no smartphone, not even any light so as to gaze upon the shore. They're just stuck in a boat together. But do they feel stuck?

These are men who have just received the Holy Spirit, the Father's love and forgiveness. They've just seen the Lord! They're now resting in all that. They can be in a boat all night long, catch nothing, and be at peace. They can be together for hours, doing nothing, and be fine with just being together. Why? Perhaps because what they've heard and seen is sinking in: God is their Father, and they are now brothers. Yes, they're brothers. They're a family. Loneliness is over.

When Jesus appears on the shore, I don't see the disciples as disappointed that they didn't catch any fish. They're fine. They're together. They have each other. The Father loves them. Jesus is Risen. It's all good.

Jesus seems to confirm such a sentiment by calling the disciples "children." For, now, they are the Father's children, which is the deepest source of their peace. So, while they're out in the boat, they're also in the Father's house, in the Father's love. But Jesus' words from the shore, "Children, have you any fish?" gently reminds them that the communion they enjoy is not just for themselves. It's meant to bear fruit, and it does bear fruit in the large catch of fish.

Now there are many spiritual interpretations regarding the symbolism of the fish. But let's keep it simple: What are the disciples going to do with all that fish? It's more than they can eat. Well, before answering that, let's first see what Jesus has done with the one fish that he has, here on the shore.

The Lord has already made a charcoal fire. He's cooked his one fish. He's warming some bread. Then, he says to the disciples: "Bring some of the fish that you have just caught." With that, Jesus makes them a little potluck meal. He gives them the bread and the cooked fish, and they all enjoy breakfast together.

And that's it? That's it.

With this event, perhaps Jesus is reminding us that the radical love he reveals on the Cross, in day to day life, often manifests itself in the simple things. It's manifested in things like going fishing or out on a walk with others. It's manifested in the effort to be truly present to one's family and friends. It's manifested in creating spaces for community, where people can be drawn out of the loneliness of the world and into the love of Christ that's incarnated when Christians gather together — which brings us to the fish.

What will the disciples do with all that fish? If the great commandment is Jesus saying, "Love one another as I have loved you," then how did he just show his love for his disciples? He prepared a meal for them. So, are the disciples now called to do the same? Well, unless they salt all that fish, it's not going to last for long. Thankfully, it's only morning, so there's plenty of time to organize a big evening meal, a celebration perhaps. After all, Jesus has risen. Surely others need to be told, but in what context? The Gospel isn't just something to tell people about. It's something to show. It's something to celebrate. It's the communion of a family. So, wouldn't the appropriate place to share the Gospel be at a big, celebratory meal?

If this seems a bit far-fetched, let me ask you this, "Where was the very first place that Jesus took his disciples?" As far as we know, it was to a marriage celebration, a wedding feast, a party so lively that the wine ran out. And might Jesus and the disciples have had something to do with that? Well, whatever the case, thanks to Mary, Jesus took care of it. He turned water into wine — a *lot* of wine.

And now, isn't the Risen Savior the Bridegroom (see 3:29)? Hasn't he returned from the dead to claim his bride and celebrate the Father's love? So, isn't the mark of authentic Christianity joy and celebration? Alleluia! Yes, it is, because Christians are brothers and sisters in Christ who have a loving Father in Heaven who, if we know him, if we stay in the house of his love, fills us with overflowing joy — the joy of the Gospel.

Yesterday, I shared that the Marian Missionaries with whom I work have a big Divine Mercy Image in their chapel. I didn't share that they also have one in their restaurant. Well, it's not a commercial restaurant that's open for business but the place where the Missionaries gather and invite others to join them for meals. Anyway, since opening the restaurant, we've discovered that sharing meals with others is a most effective way for experiencing the joy of the Gospel. In fact, we've found that during such meals, people encounter the Image of Divine Mercy as a living image, present in all those gathered in community. And so, we've focused on bringing back the lost art of hospitality, an art that goes back to the beginning.

In the early Church, the way the Christians won over the their neighbors and converted the Roman Empire was through love. Indeed, the pagans would say of the Christians, "See how they love one another."[63] Of course, they were also impressed by the martyrs, who joyfully gave their lives for Christ. But they also must have been impressed by the day-to-day living of Christian men and women who radiated peace and joy as they lovingly cared for each other. But how can believers reveal their love without inviting people into that love, through hospitality?

The New Evangelization, the way to spread the Gospel today, is not primarily about preaching with words. Rather, it's about revealing the Trinity through Christian community, through a brotherhood and sisterhood in Christ that says we all have one Father: God. Such living community can feed so many hungry hearts starving in this lonely modern world. It's how we can all go fishing and bring in a big catch for Christ.

Today's Prayer:

Jesus, give me the courage to get out of my comfort zone and work at building moments of community that let the light of your love shine out to others.

DAY 27
"Do You Love Me?" 3/30
John 21:15-17

Why did Peter decide to go fishing? Was it just to have something to eat? Perhaps something was eating at him.

People who like to go fishing often say that part of the attraction is that when you're out on the water, you forget all your problems. That may help explain why Peter went fishing.

Now, what problems could Peter have had? After all, hadn't he rejoiced with everyone else when the Lord appeared? Hadn't he also experienced the gift of forgiveness when the Lord said, "Peace be with you"? Indeed, he had. So what's the problem?

The problem is that Peter hadn't forgiven himself. He clearly remembered how he'd denied the Lord in Annas' courtyard. He knew he'd been a terrible friend. And so, despite the Easter joy, Peter suffered a hidden sorrow, a sorrow that, I suggest, came out on the night of fishing. In other words, while it was dark and no one else could see, I believe Peter silently shed some tears in secret.

But I don't think they really were a secret. The other disciples, having spent three years with Peter, had seen the sorrow in his eyes and in his demeanor. The always perceptive John had noticed it when the Lord appeared to them in the Upper Room, because Peter wasn't at the front as usual. Rather, he stood at distance. Sure, he rejoiced with everyone else, but he still felt the weight of his threefold denial. In that case, Peter's heart may have been like that of a formerly unfaithful husband who, even after repentance and forgiveness, still feels burdened by the goodness and beauty of the beloved he betrayed.

So, the other disciples noticed it, and when Peter said he was going fishing, they wanted to be with their brother. They didn't want to leave him alone. The new reality of the Father's love and the family of God was growing in their hearts. So they all went along with Peter, letting him know by their presence that they loved him and that God had forgiven him.

But again, Peter hadn't forgiven himself. Of course, Jesus knew this, which may explain why he suddenly appeared on the shore. It may also explain why, after Peter jumped out of the boat and swam to the shore, instead of running up and embracing the Lord, more than likely he stopped. In other words, the sudden memory of his betrayal likely became a wall that kept him at a distance. Of course, he loved Jesus, but there was a space, a separation that the Lord wanted to heal. The healing, however, would not only be for Peter but for all of us who carry hidden wounds, which the Lord also wants to heal.

So what does Jesus do? As we know from yesterday, he makes Peter and the disciples some breakfast. But there's another detail from that breakfast we didn't cover yesterday, a detail that would have been very important to Peter. Before we get to it, however, we should briefly go back to an earlier scene in John's Gospel, the scene with the woman at the well.

Recall that during Jesus' dialogue with the woman at the well, the Lord was not afraid to push on the deepest wound of her heart. Again, that wound was her dark well of shame that came from a history of broken relationships involving no less than five husbands. Jesus touched that wound by telling the woman to go call her husband. And when she said she had no husband, Jesus pushed harder on the wound: "You are right in saying 'I have no husband' for you have had five husbands and he whom you now have is not your husband. What you said is true" (4:18). But Jesus spoke to her with such tenderness and a look of so much love that the woman was healed. Her shame disappeared. And with newfound dignity, she became a fearless apostle to her whole town.

Now, back to Peter and the important detail at breakfast. It's the charcoal fire that Jesus had built on the beach. And why is that important? Well, at what other place did we hear about a charcoal fire in John's Gospel? It was in the courtyard of Annas. That was the place where Peter stood, warming himself. That was the place where he denied Jesus three times. That was the place where he went from I AM to I AM NOT. That was the place where he'd lost his identity and broken his friendship with Christ. Now here, at another charcoal fire, Jesus is going to restore Peter's dignity and their friendship. Of course, on Jesus' side, all has already been forgiven. But Peter is still a mess inside, and his wounded heart needs surgery.

So, after breakfast, Jesus makes the first incision. He does so by addressing Peter as "Simon, son of John." Now, Jesus hadn't called Peter that name in three years. Hearing that old name, then, spoken by his Lord, must pierce Peter's poor heart. For Peter knows it means that the Lord, who takes words seriously, has taken Peter's words seriously. What words? "*I am not.*" Are you his disciple? "*I am not.*" Are you Peter? "*I am not.* Not anymore. I have denied my Lord." So, Jesus calls him Simon, because by denying Jesus, he's no longer Peter.

And then, it gets worse — only because Jesus wants to make it better. Healing only comes when we get to the wound, open it up, and let love and mercy in.

So, Jesus says to Simon, "Do you love me more than these?"

Again, with those words, heartache. Peter knows what Jesus is referring to. In the Upper Room, at the Last Supper, after Jesus had washed Peter's feet, Peter had boldly proclaimed in front of all the others, "I will lay down my life for you" (13:37). Jesus is now asking him, "Do you love me more than these?" In other words, "Simon, you once indicated that you loved me more than everyone else. But then you turned right around and were the only one who denied me. But Simon, I'm giving you another chance to tell me that you love me."

Humbled, Peter replies, "Yes, Lord, you know that I love you."

Jesus then responds, "Well, then, don't let that ever happen again." No. That's not what he says. Instead, he restores Peter's dignity by entrusting him with greater responsibility, showing Peter that he trusts him, despite everything. And *that* is astounding mercy. For, while we may forgive people after a betrayal but, with good reason, no longer fully trust them, Jesus shows Peter not only that he forgives him but that he also fully trusts him. In fact, he trusts him with what is dearest to him in all the world: his precious flock. Specifically, he says to Peter, "Feed my lambs."

But then Jesus repeats the question, "Simon, son of John, do you love me?" Peter responds, "Yes, Lord, you know that I love you." Jesus then says to him, "Feed my lambs." A third time, Jesus says to him, "Simon, son of John, do you love me?" With this, Peter is grieved. Three times. Peter had denied Jesus three times, and three times Jesus has asked him if he loves him. Surely, all this is not meant to torture poor Peter but, rather, to rehabilitate him, to restore him to himself. It's exactly what Peter needs. He needs the opportunity to reaffirm his love and hear himself say it. He needs to know that the Lord trusts him. He also needs the humility that comes from his fall, so he can then worthily lead the Lord's flock.

Now, Jesus knows exactly what we need for our healing. And while it's not always easy and rarely pain-free, he does it with tenderness. For instance, he showed that tenderness to the woman at the well. He also showed it to Thomas, who got to touch the Lord's Heart in the Upper Room. Here, he shows it to Peter not only by letting him retrieve what he'd thrown away but also by entrusting him with great responsibility. The Lord will show it to us, too, that we also may be healed and restored in the Father's love and rest in the Father's House.

So, what in us needs to be healed? What hidden walls have we placed between ourselves and Jesus? Are they feelings of self-loathing, unworthiness, or hatred toward those who have hurt us? Whatever they are, Jesus is saying to us, "Do you want to be healed? Then, don't go fishing. Give me a drink instead." In other words, give me your pain. Give me your wounds. Give me your hurt. Give me your anger, your resentment, your bitterness. Let me hear it. Let me heal it. And then, come follow me.

Today's Prayer:
  Jesus, heal me.

DAY 28
"Follow Me" 3/31
John 21:18-19

Yesterday, we read about how Jesus healed Peter's heart. What we didn't cover were Jesus' words to Peter afterward: "Follow me." Those are the last words that Jesus speaks in John's Gospel. Actually, because John wrote his Gospel after the others had been written, you might say they really are Jesus' last words. So, let's hear them now at the end of Week Four as he speaks them to us: "Follow me."

Alright, but follow him where? At this point of the retreat, it should come as no surprise that he wants us to follow him to the Father. After all, that's where Jesus is always going. That's where he always wants to bring us. And if we do follow him, that's where we'll always remain, forever — eternally with him in Heaven.

But one thing John likes to make clear in his Gospel is that Heaven is not just for later. Rather, it begins now. So, we can follow Jesus to the Father and be in the Father's house right now, right here in our daily lives. How? By hearing the Father gently speak to our hearts, "You are my beloved." By following Jesus' commandment to love one another. By coming together to "worship the Father in spirit and truth" (4:23).

And where is that? Where's the most privileged place for coming together to worship the Father in Spirit and Truth? Of course, it's at Mass. It's where we get to enjoy in a veiled way the love that for all eternity we'll experience in an unveiled way. It's where we're taken up into the very Heart of the Father through Christ, with Christ, and in Christ, in the unity of the

Holy Spirit. It's where we fully live our consecration, our being set apart from the world.

Now, because this retreat is meant to prepare us for Mass as a total consecration to the Father through Jesus, let's look at all this more closely, starting with the beginning — and I do mean the beginning.

The Prologue of John's Gospel opens like this:

> In the beginning was the Word and the Word was with God, and the Word was God. He was in the beginning with God; all things were made through him, and without him was not anything made that was made. In him was life, and the life was the light of men. (1:1-4)

In the original Greek, the word "Word" in the first sentence is "*Logos.*" Now, *logos* had a rich meaning in the ancient world, especially among philosophers. They saw the *logos* as the order, harmony, and rationality of the world. But for believers, there's even more. *Logos* not only evokes our awe and wonder at all that God has made. It's not only the beauty, majesty, and splendor of creation. What's most awe-inspiring of all, as John tells us later in his Prologue, is that the *Logos* has become flesh. In other words, all the order, harmony, and beauty of the world (and more) has become incarnate in Jesus Christ. Now, of course, that's great. It's absolutely great. But according to John, isn't "the world" a bad thing?

It is. When John writes about the world, he's usually referring to the power of sin in the world. He means all the ugliness of pride, vanity, and selfishness that make up the worst of fallen humanity. But the world as the cosmos, as creation, is remarkably beautiful and good. Again, it's beautiful and good with the same beauty and goodness that is in Christ Jesus, the *Logos* become flesh. After all, everything was made through him and with him. So, when we look at Christianity as a life of consecration, of being set apart from the world, the world we're talking about being separated from is the world of sin, not the world as cosmos and creation. In fact, regarding the world as creation, our consecration is really about engaging it with even greater closeness and intimacy. Before we get to that, however, let's first delve more deeply into the sin of the world by reflecting on what it does to us.

The "sin of the world" leads us to approach the beauty of creation in a disordered way. For instance, it tempts us to exploit natural resources, take them for granted, and waste them. It entices us to see people as objects instead of as persons. It causes us either to lose the sense of wonder for creation or to turn creation into an idol, an end in itself. In short, the sin of the world makes us forget or reject the Father Almighty, Creator of Heaven and earth.

Now, when we forget or reject the Almighty Father and Creator, we begin to see ourselves as God, which is the heart of the sin of the world. It's the sin of seeing ourselves as the center of the universe with everything and everyone revolving around us. But we are not God. The Father is God, and while he wants to make us sharers in his own divine nature, we only receive that gift by doing his will and not our own. Unfortunately, our first parents took the latter path. According to the *Catechism*, their sin was that they wanted to be "like God" but "without God, before God, and not in accordance with God."[64] Alright, then. So, how do we become "like God" and even, so to speak, "become God," in the way that God wants?

As we've seen, we "become God" by being and living as sons and daughters in the Son. We "become God" by being consecrated in that truth, the truth of divine sonship, which sets us apart from the world of sin. But Jesus wants to set us apart from the world (the world of sin) because he loves the world (the world of creation) and wants us to join him in bringing it back to the Father.

So how do we bring the world of creation back to the Father? We do it by letting Jesus reveal the Father to us through creation. It's like this: Jesus tells us that "he who sees me, sees the Father" (14:8). Well, when we recognize the *Logos* in creation, when we see the beauty, life, and goodness of the created world, we're seeing the image of the Son through whom and in whom all of it was made. And with the eyes of faith, we may even begin to perceive in creation the longing of the Son that all may be one, that all may be brought back to the Father. For, as St. Paul tells us, "the creation waits with eager longing for the revealing of the sons of God" (Rom 8:19). We are those sons, God's children, who with Christ are called to bring fallen creation back to the Father through the Son. That is our consecration to the Father through Jesus. It requires that we step back with Christ from the world of sin to see the beauty and goodness of the world of creation, and then, instead of keeping it all to ourselves, we give it back to the Father through Jesus, the *Logos* who has become flesh.[65]

Of course, the beauty and goodness of creation includes us. Men and women are part of it, and so Jesus' desire to bring everything back to the Father includes all people. And we help fulfill his desire at Mass. There, we can bring ourselves, with all our sufferings and joys, hopes and fears, and also our loved ones (and maybe not-so-loved ones), and all of creation into the glory of God the Father. There, we live our consecration to the full, particularly at the Concluding Doxology, which is the perfect Trinitarian prayer at the source and summit of the whole Christian life. Again, it's the priest's prayer at the altar, the prayer that takes us through Christ, with Christ, and in Christ in the unity of the Holy Spirit back to the glory of God our Father.

Now, as we prepare ourselves to make our consecration to the Father at Mass, as we prepare to unite ourselves to the perfect consecration of Jesus on the Cross as he offers himself to the Father for the life of the world, we'd do well to reflect on the words of the Concluding Doxology. Doing so will help us to enter into that powerful prayer of the Mass more fully and consciously as we actively offer ourselves and the rest of creation back to the Father. And we'd also do well to reflect on what we wish to ask from the Father in the name of the Son at that moment of the Mass. For, again, as we know from John's Gospel, whatever we ask the Father in the name of Jesus he will give to us (16:23). Of course, the first gift, the greatest gift, is to receive He who is Gift: the Holy Spirit. And perhaps the greatest petition would be to ask the Father in the name of the Son to send the Spirit of Love, the Spirit of Mercy, into the world that it may be set free from the grip of sin, violence, and war. In short, we could ask the Father to have mercy on us and on the whole world, that all may be one.

Today's Prayer:

> *Eternal Father, I offer you the Body and Blood, Soul and Divinity of your dearly beloved Son, our Lord Jesus Christ, in atonement for our sins and those of the whole world. Loving Father, have mercy on us and on the whole world.*

FIVE FINAL DAYS
Synthesis and Review

*Jesus said, "He who has seen me has seen the Father" (14:19).
Throughout our retreat, as we've followed the Gospel of John,
Jesus has been showing us the Father. But now, as we prepare for
our total consecration to the Father through Jesus, we'll want to
gather into our minds and hearts everything we've covered. Two
things will help us to do just that.*

*First, let's turn to the Holy Spirit, for he's the one who can
remind us of all that the Lord has told us (see 14:26). He's the one
who can impress the Gospel so firmly on our minds and hearts that
we'll overcome our hypocrisy and truly live the Word. Indeed, he's
the one who can make the Word become flesh in us. So let's turn
to him now in prayer:*

> *Come Holy Spirit, Spirit of Truth, move so powerfully
> in me these next five days that I may be consecrated in
> the Truth, live the Truth, and enter more deeply into
> the perfect consecration of Jesus as he offers himself, in
> union with you, to the glory of God the Father. Amen*

*Second, let's reflect on three words from each week that sum-
marize what Jesus reveals about the Father. The readings for these
days will be shorter than usual so as to give us more time to ponder
and reflect on our answers to the questions at the end of each day.*

DAY 29
Opening Characters 4|

Three words summarize what we learned about the Father
through the Opening Characters: (1) Zeal, (2) Humility, and
(3) Mercy.

ZEAL

The Father himself is not zeal, but Jesus reveals to us that
when we truly know the Father, we'll be filled with zeal. Why?
Because the Father is so good. Jesus sees the Father, and he
knows that if only others could see him, too, then they'd be set
on fire with love for the Father. So, for those who are willing,
Jesus says, "Come and see." In other words, "Come and see

how good the Father is. Come and see the love that is in the bosom of the Father." The first disciples came and saw the goodness and love of the Father in Jesus, and then, like Jesus, they had to tell others.

Now, the Father's house in Jerusalem, the Temple, was meant to be a place where all people could "come and see" the goodness of the Father. But when Jesus noticed that vendors and money changers were preventing people from knowing the Father, he made a whip of cords and drove them all out. Through that episode, Jesus' disciples came to understand that zeal for the Father *consumed* Jesus. Does zeal for the Father consume us? Is the passion of our lives to make the Father known and loved? Have we come to know and love the Father by drawing close to Jesus and seeing where he abides?

HUMILITY

Is the Father humble? Of course he is. Just look at the Son. The Son is everything that the Father is. And if we look at the Son, if we behold the Son, we see that he is the Lamb of God. Yes, a lamb. God identifies himself with the most lowly of animals. Now listen to John the Baptist. If we listen to that man, who points to the Son by the will of the Father, we learn the secret of humility: that everything we have comes from the Father, is a gift from the Father. As the Baptist puts it, "No one can receive anything except what is given him from heaven" (3:26). This the Son knows also, for the Son has received everything from the Father. And while everything comes from the Father, we see the Father's humility in that he gives everything he has and is to the Son, so that the Son is totally equal to the Father. Thus, both Father and Son are utterly humble. And what about us? Like the Father, do we give ourselves to raise up others? Like the Son, do we realize that everything good that we are and do comes from the Father?

MERCY

Is the Father merciful? Yes! Even before the Word became flesh, Moses had revealed the mercy of the Father. And Moses could reveal such a mystery because he alone spoke with God face to face, as with a friend. Although he didn't actually see God's face, what he did see was enough to announce that the Father is "merciful and gracious, slow to anger, and abounding in mercy and faithfulness ..." (Ex 34:6).

Jesus is the Prophet like Moses who actually sees the face of the Father, and then he reveals that face as one of most tender mercy. We glimpsed that face, through Jesus, in his interaction with the woman at the well. Recall that her life was a shameful mess. Yet the Lord approached her not from a high pedestal, dispensing grace from above but, rather, from below like a fountain welling up. In that way, Jesus restored her dignity, and he even went so far as to address her from his own need, saying, "Give me a drink." Jesus showed similar mercy to the woman caught in adultery. He looked at her not condescendingly from above but restored her dignity by humbly and mercifully addressing her from below — literally from below, because he spoke to her while bending down to the ground.

In Jesus Christ, the Father has bent down to the ground to show us mercy and restore the dignity that we've all lost due to sin. But not just that. God's mercy also raises us up to his own divine life. It does this not only by making us children of God the Father, but it reminds us of the Father's unending love for us, his children, as we learned in Week Three. So, will we give Jesus a drink, the drink of our brokenness, so he and the Father may fill us with mercy and raise us up?

Today's Meditation:
(1) Zeal: Like Jesus, do I really desire above all to make the Father known and loved? (2) Humility: Like Jesus, do I realize that everything I have — my life, my faith, my good deeds — comes as a gift from the Father? (3) Mercy: Give Jesus a drink now by telling him you are sorry for not being more zealous for the Father and

that you're sorry for the times you've forgotten to see the Father as the source of all your goodness and of any good that you do.

Today, reflect on this: The Father is so good, humble, and merciful that we should be filled with zeal to make him known, especially by our own example of humility and mercy.

DAY 30
The Seven Signs

Three words summarize what we learned about the Father through the Seven Signs: (1) Caring, (2) Life-Giving, and (3) Tender.

CARING

Is the Father caring? Of course he is. And while women are better known for being caring than men, God the Father is not a man. He is most certainly the Father, but he also has maternal characteristics, as we learn from Sacred Scripture.[66] To help reveal this side of himself, God the Father gave us a mother in Mary, and at the Wedding at Cana, we see through her how caring the Father is. For Mary spared the new husband and wife great embarrassment by noticing the wine ran out and moving her Son to help them. We also saw how caring the Father is by the way he strove to console his Son when the royal official's son was ill. During that day's reflection, we also read about how the Father cares not only for the needs of the birds of the air and the lilies of the field but for our needs as well, just like Mary at the Wedding at Cana. We further saw an example of this care when Jesus fed the multitude, who were tired and hungry. In so many ways, the Father lovingly cares for us daily, even though we often don't recognize it. And when Jesus walked on the stormy Sea of Galilee, he revealed that the Father can care for all our needs because he is the Almighty, the one whom the winds and seas obey. Now, do we see the Father as not only all-powerful but as one who uses that power to provide for us and care for us in all our needs, like a loving mother does for her children?

LIFE-GIVING

Is the Father life-giving? Well, consider Jesus' words: "For as the Father has life in himself, so he has granted the Son also to have life in himself" (5:26). And likewise, "The living Father sent me, and I live because of the Father" (6:57). Jesus has life because of the Father. The world teems with life because the Father-Creator is life-giving and said from the beginning, "Be fruitful and multiply" (1:22, 28). And while none of us asked to be born, the Father wanted us to have life. Also, while the paralytic by the pool may not have wanted to be healed, the Father wanted him and all of us to have new life in him through healing. This living Father is the source not only of all temporal life but of eternal life, and he sent the Son that we might have it — even now. He also gave us his Son as the Bread of Life that whoever eats him might live forever. And as for death, that came not from the Father, who has life in himself, but from sin. So, when we grieve, the Father grieves with us, just as Jesus wept over Lazarus. And the Father doesn't just grieve in the Son, but in the Son he is even "fiercely angry" at death. He sent his Son to die for us that he might overcome death and give us eternal life. Do we thank the living Father for the gift of our lives and the gift of eternal life? Do we seek to be life-giving by making the Father known?

TENDER

Is the Father tender? Well, just think of the house of Martha, Mary, and Lazarus. If Jean Vanier is correct, then Lazarus had a severe handicap, and Martha and Mary remained unmarried to care for him. That is the home where Jesus and the Father wanted to rest, which tells us so much about the Heart of the Father. We saw the same tenderness of the Father, through Jesus, when he cured the man born blind. Apparently, touch is very important to those who cannot see, and so when Jesus healed the man born blind, unlike the other miracles in John's Gospel, he did so by touching him. And for us, who hunger and thirst in the desert of this life, the Father feeds us not only with our daily bread but with the Body and Blood of his own Son, which is a divine invention of the deepest intimacy and tenderness. For we also need to be touched, and the Father touches us through the Eucharistic Body and Blood of his Son. And as for the judgment, the Father has given all judgment to the Son such that the only judgment is those who refuse to receive the tenderness of the Father through the gift of the Son.

Today's Meditation:

> *(1) Caring: Do I take time each day, at the end of the day, to recognize the many ways the Father has cared for me and to thank him for his gifts?*
> *(2) Life-Giving: When was the last time I thanked the Father for the gift of my life, and have I sought to show my gratitude by glorifying the Father with my life?*
> *(3) Tender: Do I bring my suffering before the Father with the expectation of receiving his tenderness and encouragement?*
>
> *Today, reflect on this: The Father is Caring, Life-Giving, and Tender.*

DAY 31
The Upper Room

Three words summarize what we learned about the Father in the Upper Room: (1) Love, (2) Truth, and (3) Father.

LOVE

Is the Father love? Yes, because God is Love. And as we ascended the steps of the Upper Room, we learned from the *Catechism* that "God's very being is love" and that "by sending his only Son and the Spirit of Love in the fullness of time," God the Father has revealed "his innermost secret" that God himself is "an eternal exchange of love, Father, Son, and Holy Spirit." We also learned that, in his love, God "has destined us to share in that exchange." We further saw that the Father lovingly looks at us as a father does his newborn infant and that he calls us to his house, where there is a room just for us, where the Father wants to say to us: "You are my beloved." That is the place, even now, where we can find our true peace and joy. But the Father doesn't want us just to remain in our room in his house because, as the Incarnate Son teaches, we are to love others as we ourselves have been loved. This is how we abide in the Father's love because to abide in the Father's love is to love. But again, to love, we must first receive the Father's love. In that case, do we hear the Father say to us, "You are my beloved"? Hear it now.

TRUTH

Is the Father Truth? Yes. But isn't Jesus the Truth? Yes, that's also true. Jesus is the Truth because he's the Son. "Son" implies "Father," and the Son points to the Father. The Father is the Truth, because everything comes from the Father, including the Son. The Father is everything. He is reality, the source of all that is.

The Spirit of Truth makes us sons and daughters of the Father in the Divine Son. We become consecrated in the truth of sonship when we live as sons and daughters of the Father. The truth is that we're God's children, thanks to the eternal Son, and God is our Father. That is the great truth of Divine Revelation, the *name* that Jesus wanted to reveal: Father. The Spirit of Truth gets us to live this truth and to proclaim it with Christ when we call God "Abba, Father." This is a most beautiful truth! Do we realize that we proclaim the truth, the truth that sets us free, the truth of God's love for us, when we call out to God as "Abba, Father"?

FATHER

Is the Father our Father? Of course he is. As we've just read, that's the truth. But do we live that truth? Or do we live as if our father were the father of lies? We live in the truth when we live as children of God our Father, which is the life of love, because God is Love. But the father of lies wants us to think that *he* is our father. When we listen to him, he tells us we must earn love, be "somebody," and go out there and win the love of others through power, wealth, and accomplishments. And it's never enough with the father of lies. There's always more we must do to earn love. But with God as our Father, we're already loved. And it's not because of what we do but because of who we are: his sons and daughters in the Son. That love is enough. We have everything we need in the Father's house when we know that we are his beloved. But do we live as if the father of lies were our father and believe his lies and try to find the fullness of love outside the Father's house?

Today's Meditation:

> *(1) Love: Do I hear the Father say, "You are my beloved"? Hear it now. Rest in that love for a moment. (2) Truth: In my daily life, do I look up to Heaven, as Jesus did, and say from my heart, "Abba, Father"? Can I start living that truth by offering that prayer today? (3) Father: Do I live the truth that God is my Father such that his love is enough for me right here and now? Or do I believe the father of lies, who tells me I must get out there and earn love?*
>
> *Today, reflect on this: The Truth is that God is our Father, and he already loves us with all the love that we could possibly desire.*

DAY 32
Greater Glory

Three words summarize what we learned about the Father through Greater Glory: (1) Glory, (2) Peace, and (3) Communion.

GLORY

Is the Father glory? The Father is all glory and beauty, the beauty of love. However, we cannot see the Father himself with our physical eyes. In that case, God made his glory visible in his dearly beloved Son, incarnate in Jesus Christ. And while every part of Jesus' life reveals the Father's glory, he reveals the *fullness* of the Father's glory through his rejection, suffering, and death. That greater glory is made visible on the Cross through the self-giving love of the Son, a love that holds nothing back. And what we see Jesus doing on the Cross reveals what the Father does for all eternity: He gives himself totally to the Son without holding anything back. That is the Father's glory, and Jesus thirsts that we would come to the Cross and see it. He wants us to behold that glory that we might also become the same glory, that we also might be divinized by giving of ourselves without holding anything back, that we might truly be children of God not only in name but in deed and truth. Of course, we cannot love like that on our own, and so the glory of the Father is poured into our hearts as the blood and water that gush forth from the pierced Heart of Jesus, that blood and water that is the Eucharist and Baptism, that blood and water that is the grace and mercy of the Holy Spirit. Do we drink in that glory? Do we meditate on Jesus' suffering on the Cross and reflect that there we behold the invisible glory and love of God made visible, the glory of the Father in his self-giving love?

PEACE

Is the Father our Peace? Well, let's listen. Not only does the Father say to us, "You are my beloved," but in the Upper Room, through his resurrected Son, he says to us, "Peace be with you." The Father gives us his peace by forgiving us. He invites us to turn away from darkness and return to him so we may hear him say, "Peace be with you. I forgive you." But then Jesus sends us out: "As the Father has sent me, so I send you." He wants us to give peace. The apostles had the power to forgive sin. You may not have that power, but he gives us the power to love and to forgive our enemies, to forgive those who hurt us. When we do, it not only gives them peace, but it allows peace into our hearts as well. But it all starts with letting the Father come to us, through his Son, to give us his peace, his forgiveness. But maybe like Thomas, we're stuck in doubt and discouragement and great woundedness and need to touch the Heart of Jesus to find peace. Well, then do it. His Heart is always there, opened with a wound so we may enter into his love, mercy, and peace. Or maybe, like Peter, we're having a hard time forgiving ourselves and need to hear ourselves say to Jesus and to the Father, "I love you. Despite all my sins, I do love you. I want to love you." Well, say it now. Turn to the Father with your sins. Tell him you're sorry for wounding his Heart. Tell him you love him, and hear him say to you, "Peace be with you. You are my beloved, and I have forgiven you."

COMMUNION

Is the Father Communion? He is the source of all communion. We are one as Christians because we have the same Father. And the Father's delight is when we live that truth, not only when we love one another and forgive each other but also when we come together to celebrate the truth that God is our Father and we are his children. To celebrate that truth, we can show hospitality by creating spaces for the Trinity to become flesh in Christian community. Such community becomes a source of joy and peace, and is itself something to contemplate with wonder. But the Father also draws us to the communion of the Mass, where he invites us to go through Christ, with Christ, and in Christ, in the unity of the Holy Spirit, back to him as an experience of heavenly glory. At Mass, especially during the Concluding Doxology, he invites us not only to go to him ourselves but to bring to him everything in our hearts: our hopes and joys, sorrows and sufferings, friends and family, the sick and the poor, and the beauty of creation. He also wants to put into our hearts his own desire that all may be one, and he wants us to ask for that unity. He wants us to ask that the Holy Spirit come down and renew the face of the earth and make us all one in the Father, Son, and Holy Spirit by calling God "Father" and truly being his children. Now, is that our desire, that all may be one? Do we prepare for Mass and the Concluding Doxology by prayerfully bringing ourselves and our full hearts to offer to the Father through Christ in the Holy Spirit?

Today's Meditation:

(1) Glory: Do I take time to reflect on Jesus' suffering on the Cross and see the invisible glory and love of God made visible, the glory of the Father that is self-giving love? (2) Peace: As I turn to the Father with my sins, are there any particular sins that weigh on my heart? Do I tell him I'm sorry for having hurt him and letting him down? Now let him say to you, "Peace be with you. You are my beloved, and I have forgiven you." (3) Communion: Do I desire that all may be one? Do I see others as my brothers and sisters because we have one Father? Do I prepare for the Concluding Doxology of the Mass, that I may bring myself and a full heart to the Father through Christ in the Holy Spirit?

Today, reflect on this: There on the Cross is the Father's great glory, the glory of love in the sacrifice of his Son. Drink from the blood and water that gush from his pierced side, that you may receive the peace and joy of the Holy Spirit, and then go and love others as you have been loved — that all may be one.

DAY 33
Look Up   4/5

Tomorrow (or soon) is the big day when we'll consecrate ourselves to the Father through Jesus, right? Actually, as we've learned during this retreat, we already are consecrated to the Father (if we're baptized). So, strictly speaking, tomorrow is going to be a more formal *renewal* of our consecration to the Father through Jesus. Specifically, it's an opportunity to recall what we've already been given through the Sacrament of Baptism. It's an occasion to enter more fully, consciously, and actively into Jesus' self-offering to the Father at Mass, particularly during the Concluding Doxology. To get us ready for that moment of renewal and self-offering tomorrow, we'd do well to review what it means to be consecrated to the Father through Jesus by the power of the Holy Spirit.

First, it means to be *set apart from the world*. What world? The world of sin. It's the world that's marked by greed, gluttony, anger, envy, pride, lust, laziness, and fear. It's the world that's dominated by the works of the flesh, such as "immortality, impurity, licentiousness, idolatry, sorcery, enmity, strife, jealousy, anger, selfishness, dissension, party spirit, envy, drunkenness, carousing, and the like" (Gal 5:19-21). It's the threefold way of the world that's obsessed with riches, honors, and ego.

Second, it means to be *set apart in the truth.* What truth? The truth that the suffering, death, and resurrection of Jesus Christ, through the power of the Holy Spirit, has made us sons and daughters of God our Father. It's the truth that God is our Father, the truth of the Father's love, the truth that the Father loves us with the same love with which he loves his eternal Son. It's the truth that the Father always wants to say to us, "*You are my beloved.*" It's the truth that the Father's love is enough, that it doesn't change, and that it's still there, calling out to us, even when we go astray. It's the truth that the Father's love is not based on what we do but on who we are: his dearly beloved children.

Third, it means to be *set apart in love*. What love? The love of the new commandment: "Love one another as I have loved you." And how has God loved us? He has given himself to us without holding anything back. He has come to us in poverty, meekness, humility, and service. He has poured himself out in total self-giving love. To be set apart in such love, to commit to such love, is to be a light amid the darkness of this present world of selfishness and sin.

In summary, the renewal of our baptismal consecration is the renewal of our firm commitment to turn away from sin, accept the truth of who we are in Christ (sons and daughters in the Son), and give ourselves in love as true children of God our Father. That's our consecration. In short, it's to set ourselves apart from the world of selfishness because we belong to the God of self-giving love. Shorter still, it's *to look up.*

What? Let me explain with a story.

I'm one of those people who can't stand needles. Of course, it's not the needles themselves I don't like. It's just when they puncture my body at the doctor's office.

Yesterday, I had to get my blood drawn. As I often do before a date with a needle, I psyched myself up on the way by thinking of all the people for whom I'd like to offer my minuscule suffering. Once in the waiting room, I turned to Mary and courageously offered the whole ordeal to her as part of my Marian consecration. Then, when the receptionist called my name, I made my way to the back office. With a swagger in my step, I thought to myself, "No big deal. I got this." The nurse who would soon poke my arm greeted me with a smile. I confidently smiled back, and with that smile still on my face, I suddenly I spotted an open pack of needles on the nearby counter. With that, my courage left me, my heart began to race, and I thought to myself, "Get ahold of yourself, man!" Next, I slumped down into the blood draw chair, put out my arm, and watched the nurse apply a tourniquet. At that point, I closed my eyes, heard the sound of paper tearing, immediately got a whiff of the sharp smell of rubbing alcohol, and soon felt the coolness of it evaporating on my arm. In the few moments of heightened anticipation before the inevitable jab, while trying to pray and find some courage, the image on the cover of this book suddenly came to mind. With that, I opened my eyes, looked up, and found great peace even as the needle pierced my vein. I thought to myself, "This is *so awesome.*"

What was awesome? What I found in that upward look. Through that look, I was able to say everything that was in my heart. I didn't need to compose a long prayer. I didn't need to name every person I was carrying in my heart and for whom I was offering my suffering. I didn't need to say anything, because I knew that the Father already understood. He could see me, his son, taking my very little suffering and offering it to him with love. He could see me looking at him with love, and I could sense him looking back at me with love. Even though it was just a few moments, I was right there with Jesus and Mary, expressing everything in my heart to the Father in a simple gaze of love.

Now, as I'm proofreading this story two weeks later, I can testify that that experience at the hospital still holds true, an experience that has convinced me of this: It's easy to make the consecration to the Father. We simply need to do what Jesus so often did as he prayed to the Father: *look up* (see 11:41; 17:1).

Of course, by "looking up" I don't mean just the physical action of turning our eyes heavenward, although it includes that. It's the spiritual looking up to our Father of mercy and love whom we've encountered in the Gospel of John. Specifically, it's to see your Father seeing you. It's to behold your Father beholding you. It's to speak to him from your heart, through the Son and in the Spirit, without using words (see Rom 8:26). That's the consecration to the Father through Jesus.[67]

Unlike my other consecration books — *33 Days to Morning Glory* and *33 Days to Merciful Love* — this book does not include a written out "Prayer of Consecration." Instead, the prayer of consecration I propose is simply *to look up*. Of course, we can "look up" to the Father at any time, but I want to encourage you to look up during the Concluding Doxology (and the Our Father) at Mass tomorrow. But to help make that look arise from a heart that is as full as possible, I encourage you to take this day's meditation deeply to heart. I encourage you to reflect on what it means to be consecrated to the Father in the three points described above.

Still, because specific prayers can help to fill our hearts, I will offer not a prayer of consecration but a *Prayer of Preparation for Consecration*. I hope this prayer will help prepare you for the look you will give to the Father at Mass tomorrow as you go to him through Christ, with Christ, and in Christ, in the unity of the Holy Spirit.

PRAYER OF PREPARATION
FOR CONSECRATION TO THE FATHER

*Father, I am sorry for my sins, and I recommit to liv-
ing as a true Christian, not just in name but in deed.
I firmly reject Satan and all his pomps, works, and
empty promises. I renounce the way of the world
with its selfishness and pride. I reaffirm the truth that
you, God, are my Father and that I am your dearly
beloved child. I believe in your love for me. I declare
that your love is enough. And I commit to loving
others as you have so mercifully loved me. I offer this
prayer, Father, through the power of the Holy Spirit
and in the name of Jesus Christ, your Son, my Savior.*

Amen.[68]

Perhaps you can pray this prayer right before Mass
tomorrow or during the Offertory as you prepare to renew
your consecration to the Father during the Concluding Doxology of the Mass. Again, you can renew your consecration
simply by looking up to our Heavenly Father with a gaze that
says so much more than words can express. Or maybe words
can express it. Maybe the Spirit will inspire you to make the cry
that really does say it all: "*Abba! Father!*"

Today's Meditation:

> *Reflect on the three points from this day's reading about
> what it means to be consecrated to the Father. Then,
> ponder the cover of this book. Finally, throughout the day,
> look up to the Father, and pray from your heart, "Abba!
> Father!" Let all this be your preparation to consecrate
> yourself to the Father through Jesus in the unity of the
> Holy Spirit by looking up at him during the Concluding
> Doxology at Mass tomorrow. (Don't forget to bring this
> book with you so you can pray the Prayer of Preparation.)*

By the way, if the Mass when you renew your consecration is still a few days off and you'd like to continue preparing
for that moment (or if you'd simply like to do some more

related reading), see Chapter Three: "The Priestly Mission of Communion" in the book *The 'One Thing' Is Three*, pages 255-283, which may help you to better offer the Lord your praise and thanksgiving, sufferings, worries, and your very self with Mary at the Concluding Doxology of the Mass. Better yet, why not just go and read the entire Gospel of John?

Whatever you do, following your Day of Consecration, don't forget to read the next section, "After Consecration." It will help you to better live what you've learned during this retreat. (Any yes, if you want, feel free to read it beforehand.)

AFTER CONSECRATION
How to Live It

Important: Read this section sometime
after your consecration.

Congratulations! I hope your day of consecration was beautiful and filled with the experience of the Father's love for you, his dearly beloved child. But now that the day is past, how can we continue to live our consecration? I have three suggestions that will help us become even more authentic Christians who live in the world but not of it, who live the truth that God is our Father, and who live the life of loving others as God has loved us.

1. Keep Looking Up (and Listening).

After I finished writing the retreat portion of this book, I noticed a change in my daily life: *I often look up.* In other words, I often seek the Father amid the various circumstances of my day. For instance, when I'm feeling discouraged, I look up and remember the Father's words, "You are my beloved." When I'm suffering some trial or pain, I look up and so "offer it up" to the Father as Jesus did on the Cross. When I see the beauty of nature, such as the verdant Berkshire Hills here in western Massachusetts, I look up and so offer up the beauty of creation with praise to the Father. When I'm in need of light on some problem, I look up and so ask the Father to send the Spirit of Truth. When I hear of some tragedy, I look up and so ask the Father to send the Spirit of Merciful Love.

Now, my offering up and asking the Father in such cases is usually not done with words, and that's okay. I say that because the Father can read our hearts and knows what we want even before we ask it.

Alright, then why even bother to look up if the Father already knows what we want? Because it's not all about what we want. It's about what the Father wants. And what does he want? He wants us to turn to him. He wants us to follow the example of his Incarnate Son, who was always turned toward the Father, thinking of the Father, and often conversing with the Father through a simple look of love, a look *up*.

I just said that the Father wants us to follow the example of the Son, but it's actually more than that. The Father doesn't just want us to imitate the Son. He wants us, so to speak, *to be* the Son. In other words, he wants our look of love and that of the Son's to be totally united as one. The Father wants us to look up to him through the Son, with the Son, and in the Son. And how is that possible? It's possible through the Mass.

As we've learned, the source and summit of the Christian life is the Mass, particularly the Concluding Doxology. That specific moment is a special time to look up to the Father through the eyes of the Son. It's the moment when we can live our consecration to the Father most fully as we gather all of our joys and sorrows, hopes and fears, and go through Christ, with Christ, and in Christ, in the unity of the Holy Spirit, *up* to the glory of God our Father in Heaven, the one who is "above" (Jn 8:23). It's the moment that's meant to become the pattern of our whole lives. It's the moment that should change our lives more and more into one sustained look of love *up* to God our Father.[69]

Now, before moving on to the next point, I'd like to highlight something very important: When we look up to our Father in Heaven, we should also strive *to listen*. Listen to what? Listen to the words the Father is always wanting to say to each one of us, his children: "*You are my beloved*." Alright, but what might that voice sound like, and how do we hear it? Father Henri Nouwen offers an answer in the context of his reflection on the merciful Father in the parable of the Prodigal Son:

> The true voice of love is a very soft and gentle voice speaking to me in the most hidden places of my being. It is not a boisterous voice, forcing itself upon me and demanding attention. It is the voice of a nearly blind father who has cried much and died many deaths. It is a voice that can only be heard by those who allow themselves to be touched.[70]

2. Delve More Deeply into the Gospel of John.

In the Introduction, I recommended that you listen to the Gospel of John download from Leonardo and Patti Defilippis throughout your 33 days of preparation. Well, I hope you were able to do it. And now, why not continue to read or listen to the Gospel of John and go even deeper?

I'd like to begin to explain how we can go even deeper by telling a story.

While writing this book, I spoke with a Catholic Scripture Scholar and asked him if he could recommend any modern commentaries on the Gospel of John. He surprised me by saying that most modern Scripture Scholars avoid this Gospel. He explained that such scholars like things to be clear and that the Gospel of John is not always clear. He also said that St. John was a mystic and scholars are often uncomfortable with the teaching of mystics.

Well, that last statement opened my eyes to a deeper appreciation for one particular lover of the Gospel of John, a modern mystic: Jean Vanier, the founder of L'Arche, whom we met on Day 14 of our retreat.

While preparing to write this book, I watched a video series Vanier had done on the Gospel of John, and it totally blew me away.[71] He spoke about the Gospel of John not as a scholar — although he had certainly done his homework — but as a mystic, as someone who, like John himself, had seen the Lord. In this sense, his presentation was not so much a teaching as *a witness*, a witness to the love and tenderness of the Father that he himself had experienced through Jesus in the Gospel of John. And Vanier's witness was clearly the fruit not just of his experience but of what that experience had done to him. By that, I mean Vanier came across not just as someone who had experienced the Lord's love but as someone in whom the Lord's love had become incarnate.

That, then, is what I mean by going deeper into the Gospel of John. It's not just to study it or listen to it but to behold the love of God that it reveals. It's to believe in that love, abide in it, and so become it. It's to incarnate love by loving others as we ourselves have been loved through the revelation of God's Merciful Love for us in the Gospel of John.

Now, this "going deeper" into the Gospel of John invites us to something more. It invites us to follow the Beloved

Disciple's path of Divine Love and Mercy as a concrete plan of life. We'll learn more about that in the next section.

3. Become a Marian Missionary of Divine Mercy.

Often, when we discover something good, true, or beautiful, we're certainly inspired, enlightened, and touched — but then we move on. We forget about it. Our discovery ends up being a passing grace that entered our lives, consoled us, and then got washed away by the noisy waves of the tumultuous modern world. Sometimes, however, we encounter something so good, so true, and so beautiful that we never want to let it go. We want it to remain with us. We want it to abide in us. You might call it the pearl of great price that motivates us to go, sell everything, and buy it.

For me, that pearl is the Gospel of John. It's the most beautiful revelation of the Father's love through our Merciful Savior. It's that in which I long to abide for the rest of my life. And so, as I mentioned in the Introduction, I wrote this book to own what I myself want to become: an authentic Christian right at a time when the Church and the world need the witness of authentic Christianity, perhaps more than ever. Put differently, I want to become the love that I've discovered in the Gospel of John. Of course, I'm a long, long way off. But my joy is finally to have the goal, finally to see through all the distractions and get right to the heart of it: love. It really is all about love because, as St. John tells us, "God is Love." It really is all about love because, as Jesus commands us, we're to love one another as he has loved us.

But how do we love? How do we grow in love? How do we, so to speak, become love? Again, the example of Jean Vanier sheds light for us.

After first seeing Jean Vanier's video presentation on the Gospel of John, I was so moved by his witness that I read a short biography about him and spoke with people who knew him. (I would have contacted him directly, but he died nine days before I began writing this book.) Anyway, one of the most striking things I learned was that Vanier made the New

Commandment of the Gospel of John a kind of rule of life for L'Arche. But it wasn't just the New Commandment. He also would give an annual retreat to the new community leaders in L'Arche based on the entire Gospel of John. You might say, then, that the Gospel of John became incarnate not only in Vanier but also in the community he founded, a community based on love.

Now, can one make the Gospel of John one's rule of life? Can one make the heart of the Gospel of John the rule of life of a community so as to become love? Vanier did it. So, why can't we?

While most of us can't leave everything to serve the poor or people with disabilities, we can still be in a specific community (within the larger community of our local parish and the Catholic Church) by living a common spirituality and commitment to loving our immediate family and society. Some communities such as these are called "ecclesial movements," and in this era of Vatican II, they can help us live the universal call to holiness, the call we all have to radically follow the Gospel, the call we all have to become saints, to become love.

In the Introduction, I shared an experience I once had with a newly formed ecclesial movement called the Marian Missionaries of Divine Mercy, an experience that has changed my life. Well, as their director of formation, I have tried to understand the spirit of what they are and what God is doing through them so as to communicate it in books that help form future Missionaries. At this point, after five years of discernment, I think that spirit has become quite clear, and so I'd like to give to you what I myself have received. I'd like to share a way that may help you to incarnate the love of the Gospel of John as a way of life in communion with others.

By the way, before I begin, I have one word for those who have already become Marian Missionaries of Divine Mercy or who are in the midst of the formation: What follows is a streamlining of the formation requirements to become a Marian Missionary. In other words, as the director of formation for the Missionaries, after much prayer and counsel, I decided to make it easier than ever to become a Marian Missionary. Why? Because I believe Jesus, the Divine Mercy, and Mary, our Immaculate Mother, want the spirituality to be as accessible as possible. I'll now explain how.

Essentially, the Marian Missionaries of Divine Mercy is a budding ecclesial movement with a spirituality that focuses on the merciful love that we've discovered in the Gospel of John, so we might become that love (or, as the Missionaries describe it, so we might become "living images of Divine Mercy"). To enter fully into this spirituality requires making four retreats, of which this one, *33 Days to Greater Glory*, is the third. Now, if you haven't yet done the other retreats, there's no need to worry. They don't have to be done in order. However, it's important to understand the logical structure of the retreats, which we'll turn to now.

The intended order of the retreats can be summed up like this: Mary, Mercy, and Community. That's the objective structure of how we enter into the love of the Trinity. It begins with *Mary* and her Spouse the Holy Spirit, who lead us to Jesus, the Divine *Mercy*, who then brings us home to the Father in the *Community* of the Trinity.

Let's now unpack that threefold path through the first three retreats.

Mary. The first retreat is *33 Days to Morning Glory*, which is a do-it-yourself retreat in preparation for consecration to Jesus through Mary. We begin with Mary, because she is the Spouse of the Holy Spirit, who is the one who works with Mary to open our eyes to see Jesus, our ears to hear the Gospel, and our hearts to receive Divine Mercy. He's also the one who convicts us of sin and convinces us of our need for a Savior.

Mercy. The second retreat is *33 Days to Merciful Love*, which is a do-it-yourself retreat in preparation for a consecration to Jesus, the Divine Mercy. This retreat comes after the consecration to Mary because Mary always leads us, with her Spouse the Spirit, to an encounter with Jesus, the Divine Mercy. The guide in this retreat is St. Thérèse of Lisieux, Doctor of the Church, who helps us to rediscover and encounter the mercy of God and to believe in God's love for us, and she does this perhaps better than any other modern saint.

Community. The third retreat is this one, *33 Days to Greater Glory.* Its focus is on the Gospel of John, which beautifully reveals the love and mercy of God our Father. This revelation helps us to better go through Christ, with Christ, and in Christ, in the unity of the Holy Spirit, to the glory of God the Father at Mass. In short, the devotional retreats of Marian consecration and Divine Mercy lead us to the fullness of Catholic faith and life that's found in Scripture and Liturgy, in the Father and the Trinity, in love and community.

Those three retreats — *33 Days to Morning Glory, 33 Days to Merciful Love,* and *33 Days to Greater Glory* — bring us, step-by-step, into the spirituality of the Marian Missionaries of Divine Mercy. But to fully own that spirituality, to become initiated into it, to discover how, precisely, to live Mary, Mercy, and Community in our daily lives requires one last retreat, which is forthcoming. The working title is *33 Days to Mary, Mercy, and Community: A Do-It-Yourself Retreat to Become a Marian Missionary of Divine Mercy.* With that retreat, we'll be able to become Marian Missionaries and so find the support of a new ecclesial movement that helps us live what we've learned during the three preceding retreats. (To go deeper into the spirituality, each of the four retreats also has an associated book or books that are shown at the bottom of the back cover.)

By the way, the support you'd find as a Marian Missionary comes not only from the spirituality but also from the living community of a growing number of Marian Missionaries throughout the world. That support comes specifically through the Marian Missionary website (MarianMissionaries.org), retreats at Fire Mountain Retreat Center, and by staying at the Federal Inn Guest House, where you can enjoy prayer, meals, and fellowship with the young people who live near the National Shrine of Divine Mercy and who have given themselves to living out the Marian Missionary spirituality in a concrete community. To learn more about that support, see the Resource Pages and color insert at the end of this book. Before you go, however,

there's one last thing you might want to consider as an aid
to delving more deeply into the truth about the Father that
we've learned in the Gospel of John. It's the consecration to
St. Joseph, which now follows with Appendix One.

In conclusion, I'd like to thank you for journeying with me on
this retreat to the Father through Jesus, based the Gospel of
John. I hope you'll now join me in striving to "look up" to
the Father, experience his love, and make it incarnate through
a concrete plan of life. God bless you, and please pray for me
that I myself might live what I have written.

With prayers also for you,

Fr. Mike

Nine Days to Joseph
(A Consecration)

This consecration to St. Joseph first appeared as an appendix to a book on St. Joseph called Meet Your Spiritual Father. *What follows is the original Introduction I wrote in 2014 and then the nine days of the consecration.*

I just sat down to write this preparation for consecration to St. Joseph and realized an amazing coincidence: *Today is my last day as "Fr. Joseph, MIC."*

That title, "Fr. Joseph," is an honorary designation for the grueling office job I've held for the last three-and-a-half years, namely, the director of the Association of Marian Helpers. I say "grueling," because ... Well, let me put it this way: Shortly before my priestly ordination, my provincial superior called me into his office and said, "Brother Michael, how would you feel about being the next Fr. Joseph?" I replied, "What's that?" He continued, "Well, if I told you, you'd say no ... *So just say yes.*"

Now I know what he meant! The job was *not* easy — but thankfully, St. Joseph helped me in a big way, a way that's related to the preparation for consecration you're about to read. Let me tell you what happened.

After two years on the job as "Fr. Joseph," I was feeling broken down and burned out. I spoke with my superior to see if another priest could fill the position or come help me in the office. Unfortunately, nobody was available, at least not for another year. So, with my health declining, spirit failing, and the work piling up, a hopeful thought suddenly occurred to me on the feast of St. Joseph: "Give it all to Joseph. He'll take care of it."

I knew exactly what to do. I got on my computer and typed out a consecration or "entrustment" to St. Joseph. I brought it to Mass at the office where I worked, and following Mass, I solemnly and publicly put everything — myself, my staff, the office, and our work — into the strong, caring hands of St. Joseph. And then, all *Heaven* broke loose. Let me just say that from our Marian Helpers Center in Stockbridge, Massachusetts, our evangelization works rapidly multiplied, and we were able to bring the message of God's mercy and devotion to Mary to millions more people. Looking back now on that day of entrustment, I firmly believe that St. Joseph was behind this new and dramatic growth.

So, in gratitude to St. Joseph, on this my last day as "Fr. Joseph," I'm writing this brief, heartfelt preparation for consecrating oneself to St. Joseph. I say "brief," because St. Joseph was a man of few words — not one of them is recorded in Scripture — and my guess is that he probably appreciates brevity. I say "heartfelt" because this preparation really comes from my heart, especially as I look back and clearly see how St. Joseph came through for me during my time of need as "Fr. Joseph." But before we get to these "nine days to Joseph," let me briefly explain how this preparation works.

Basically, you pray the specified prayer to St. Joseph each day, from the heart, for nine days. Then, on the last day (the 10th day), the Day of Consecration, you'll pray the prayer of consecration from the heart. It's that simple.

Of course, you'll probably want to time the days so the Day of Consecration falls on a feast of St. Joseph or on a Marian feast (because of St. Joseph's closeness to Mary). In that case, I recommend that you begin the consecration as a novena-style preparation nine days before any Marian feast or feast of St. Joseph, the main ones being March 19 (Solemnity of St. Joseph), May 1 (Memorial of St. Joseph the Worker), and the Second Sunday after Christmas (Feast of the Holy Family).[72] Also, since Wednesdays are traditionally dedicated to St. Joseph, you could also make your consecration to him on any Wednesday of the year. I also recommend that on the day of your consecration, you write it out in your own hand-writing, date it, and then renew it each year. And by the way, this is a perfect complement to Marian consecration, again, because of St. Joseph's closeness to and love for Mary. (If you haven't yet made your Marian consecration, see the Resource Pages at the end of this book.)

DAY 1
St. Joseph, Powerful Intercessor

Dear St. Joseph,

After Mary, you're the most powerful intercessor before God. In a sense, Jesus remains obedient to you and will listen to you as you bring my intentions to him. Because of this, I especially want to entrust myself to your fatherly care, just as Jesus himself did. And while in the past, I may have brought to you one of my intentions here or there, this time I want to do something new. This time, I want to give you *all*. In other words, St. Joseph, I'm not here to offer you a regular "novena" for just one of my intentions. Rather, I want to forever entrust to you *all* of my needs and cares, trusting that you will bring them, with Mary, to your son, Jesus.

Dear St. Joseph, as the best of fathers, as the one God chose to be the virginal father of Jesus, I believe that you know what I need better than I do myself. So go ahead, St. Joseph. I give you permission to care for me as your child. In doing so, I trust that you will do everything in your power to make my life into something beautiful for God. I trust that you will watch over me and that your prayers will guide me, bless me, and protect me. I trust that you will now care for me with the same love and tenderness with which you cared for Jesus. I'll confirm this special relationship with you in nine days, when I make my prayer of consecration.

St. Joseph, Powerful Intercessor,
please pray for me and all of my intentions.

DAY 2
St. Joseph, Loving Spouse of Mary

Dear St. Joseph,

I'm thinking about the angel's words to you, "Do not be afraid to take Mary for your wife" (Matt 1:20). St. Joseph, you weren't afraid. You trusted God. And now you truly are the husband of Mary. After Jesus, you are the dearest person to her heart! Well, St. Joseph, as my spiritual father, I now ask you to speak to Mary about me, about my life. If you kindly adopt me as your spiritual child, then I know all the more that Mary will take me to her heart as well. Both of you truly are my spiritual parents. And just as any good father wants to see his children love their mother, I know that you will help me to know and love my spiritual mother more. By your powerful prayers, I ask you to help me realize what a gift I have in Mary. Pray for me that I will better appreciate her motherly role in my life. St. Joseph, I know that you love her. I know it makes you happy to see her children love her with all their hearts. Therefore, as I prepare to consecrate myself totally to your fatherly care, I give you permission — in fact, I'm pleading with you: Help me to appreciate my Mother Mary even more.

St. Joseph, Loving Spouse of Mary,
   please help me to love my spiritual mother
   even more.

DAY 3
St. Joseph, Good Provider

Dear St. Joseph,

As the foster father of Jesus, you provided for his human needs. Through the work of your hands, he had food to strengthen him, a house to give him shelter, and clothes to keep him warm. Now, from heaven, you're still working, St. Joseph. Indeed, the loving labor of your prayers provide for all the members of the Body of your Son. But as I'm preparing to consecrate myself completely to you, I ask you to please provide for me and for my loved ones in a special way. Through your prayers, please make sure that we always have food to eat, a roof over our heads, and clothes to wear. Also, please pray for us that in times of abundance, we will never forget God. Pray for us that we will always be grateful for God's gifts and that we will never be a slave to things like food or money, pleasure or power. Finally, help us always to remember and be generous with the poor.

St. Joseph, with you as my spiritual father, I will do my best not to give in to useless anxiety about my job, money, or material things. I believe you will always make sure I have what I need, and as a good father, I ask that you indulge me a bit by even providing for my material wants, provided they don't take me away from Jesus.

St. Joseph, Good Provider,
    please provide for my needs through
    your powerful prayers.

DAY 4
St. Joseph, Strong Guardian

Dear St. Joseph,

When I think that God gave me my guardian angel and St. Michael to daily watch over me and defend me, I'm not afraid. But then, when I think that you, you who are even more powerful before God, are my spiritual father, when I think that you are the "terror of demons," when I think of how you protected the baby Jesus from Herod, then I am completely at peace (or, at least I know I should be).

St. Joseph, please pray that I will have the peace that comes from trusting in your fatherly protection. St. Joseph, I believe that you will protect me from my enemies, seen and unseen. I believe that you will protect me from bodily and spiritual harm. I trust in your fatherly care. St. Joseph, I will do my best not to give in to fear, knowing that you are praying for me in a special way as a child who has formally consecrated himself to your fatherly care.

St. Joseph, Strong Guardian,
*   please defend me with your prayers.*

DAY 5
St. Joseph, Who Did God's Will

Dear St. Joseph,

You did God's will. Dare I say you did it perfectly? St. Joseph, I also want to do God's most perfect will. But on my own, I will fail. I need your help. I trust that with you as my spiritual father, you will guide me to always do God's most perfect will. Truly, St. Joseph, I want to reach the degree of glory that God has prepared for me in heaven. I want to bear fruit that will last. I don't want to let God down. I want to be a saint. Help me, St. Joseph. You see how weak and sinful I am. But teach me, good father. Help me to follow the commandments and please make my heart sensitive to the inspirations of the Holy Spirit. I know that as I entrust myself to your care, you will guide me and show me how to always do God's will. I give you permission to redirect the stream of my life if it ever departs from God's most perfect will.

St. Joseph, who did God's will,
    please always keep me in God's most
    perfect will.

DAY 6
St. Joseph, Who Suffered with Love

Dear St. Joseph,

As the day draws closer when I will fully consecrate myself to you, as I draw closer to you, I can't help but notice the scars on your heart, how you suffered with love. You suffered darkness and confusion when Mary was found with child. You suffered the sacrifice of your flesh as you lovingly offered up the absence of bodily intimacy in marriage. You suffered a sword in your heart, with Mary, when Simeon foretold the Passion of your Son. You suffered stress and uncertainty when you had to escape with your family to Egypt and live as an immigrant. You suffered crushing anxiety when your 12-year-old Son was lost for three days. You daily suffered fatigue and bodily aches from your manual labor. Worst of all, your fatherly heart grieved at knowing that you could not be there for Jesus and Mary when their darkest hour would one day come.

St. Joseph, thank you for what you suffered in God's service, in union with your Son, for my salvation. I love you, St. Joseph. Thank you for your yes. Now, please help me to suffer with love as you did. When I suffer, help me not to complain. Help me not to forget love. Help me not to forget others. Dear St. Joseph, through my suffering, watch over my poor heart: May it not harden but rather become more merciful. Help me to remember all God's children who are suffering in the world, and help me to offer my suffering for them and for the good of the Church. I am counting on you, St. Joseph. I know you will be with me, helping me to suffer with love.

St. Joseph, who suffered with love,
please help me also to suffer with a love like yours.

DAY 7
St. Joseph, Pure of Heart

Dear St. Joseph,

I said I want to be a saint, and saints need to be pure not only of body but of soul. Regarding purity of body, St. Joseph, guard me, protect me, and defend me from temptations against purity. I rely on you, St. Joseph. Don't let me fall. Don't let my eyes or thoughts wander. If they do, please bring them back to Jesus. I trust in you, St. Joseph. You lived purely with Mary in the midst of her beauty. Help me to see the beauty of others with your own pure vision. If I fall, help me to find God's mercy and free me from any bondage to such sin. Regarding purity of intentions, help me do everything not to please myself or others but to please God alone. Give me this grace as my dear spiritual father. I trust in you, St. Joseph.

St. Joseph, Pure of Heart,
please lend me your own purity of heart.

DAY 8
St. Joseph, Man of Peace and Joy

Dear St. Joseph,

I know the Bible doesn't speak directly of your joy, but how could you not have been full of joy? I'm sure you were. You lived in the presence of Jesus and Mary. Well, St. Joseph, please pray for me that I will also find my joy by also living in their presence. And having yourself lived in their presence, you must have been a man of such peace. St. Joseph, please pray for me that I keep my joy and not give in to sadness, laziness, or discouragement. Also, pray that I keep my peace of soul and not hold on to anger and bitterness in my heart. Help me to be merciful to everyone by offering forgiveness that I might also, like you, be a man of true peace and joy.

St. Joseph, Man of Peace and Joy,
please put me at peace and help me find joy.

DAY 9
St. Joseph, Who Died So Beautifully

Dear St. Joseph,

I know I am going to die. When I do, I trust that you will be there to greet me with Jesus and Mary in a special way. Promise me this? I trust you. I believe that you will be there for me. For my part, I will try not to be afraid of my death, and I will live my life in preparation for it. I will maybe even look forward to it as the time when I will get to meet you face to face. Prepare me for my death, whenever it may be. If it is sudden, please make sure that my soul is prepared and please make sure I will not be lost! Dear St. Joseph, obtain this grace for me as I consecrate myself to your fatherly care. Tomorrow, I am fully yours. Probably someday after that, I will die, and I give you permission to take me home to my Father's house when that day comes.

St. Joseph, who died so beautifully,
  please prepare my soul for death.

Day of Consecration to St. Joseph

Dear St. Joseph,

On this day, before God and your Immaculate Spouse, Mary, I _____ choose you as my spiritual father forever. I formally entrust myself to your fatherly care. I love you, and I trust in your prayers for my life. As your spiritual child, I give you full permission (and in fact, I'm begging you) to please act in my life, especially by...

> Praying for me constantly in a special way,
>
> Bringing me even deeper into the hearts of Jesus and Mary,
>
> Providing for me and all my loved ones,
>
> Guarding and protecting me from bodily and spiritual evil,
>
> Guiding me to always do God's most perfect will,
>
> Helping me to suffer with love and without complaint,
>
> Giving me purity of body and of soul,
>
> Forming me into a person of peace and joy,
>
> Preparing me for a beautiful and happy death.

From this day forward, St. Joseph, you are my spiritual father, and I am your child. I trust you and love you, and I look forward to meeting you one day in Heaven. I ask all this in Jesus' name and for the glory of God, who is Father, Son, and Holy Spirit. Amen.

The Gospel of John

The Word Became Flesh

1 In the beginning was the Word, and the Word [2]was with God, and the Word was God. He was in the beginning with God; [3]all things were made through him, and without him was not anything made that was made. [4]In him was life, and the life was the light of men. [5]The light shines in the darkness, and the darkness has not overcome it.

6 There was a man sent from God, whose name was John. [7]He came for testimony, to bear witness to the light, that all might believe through him. [8]He was not the light, but came to bear witness to the light.

9 The true light that enlightens every man was coming into the world. [10]He was in the world, and the world was made through him, yet the world knew him not. [11]He came to his own home, and his own people received him not. [12]But to all who received him, who believed in his name, he gave power to become children of God; [13]who were born, not of blood nor of the will of the flesh nor of the will of man, but of God.

14 And the Word became flesh and dwelt among us, full of grace and truth; we have beheld his glory, glory as of the only-begotten Son from the Father. [15](John bore witness to him, and cried, "This was he of whom I said, 'He who comes after me ranks before me, for he was before me.'") [16]And from his fulness have we all received, grace upon grace. [17]For the law was given through Moses; grace and truth came through Jesus Christ. [18]No one has ever seen God; the only-begotten Son, who is in the bosom of the Father, he has made him known.

The Testimony of John the Baptist

19 And this is the testimony of John, when the Jews sent priests and Levites from Jerusalem to ask him, "Who are you?" [20]He confessed, he did not deny, but confessed, "I am not the Christ." [21]And they asked him, "What then? Are you Eli'jah?" He said, "I am not." "Are you the prophet?" And he an-swered, "No." [22]They said to him then, "Who are you? Let us have an answer for those who sent us. What do you say about yourself?" [23]He said, "I am the voice of one crying in the wilderness, 'Make straight the way of the Lord,' as the prophet Isaiah said."

24 Now they had been sent from the Pharisees. [25]They asked him, "Then why are you baptizing, if you are neither the Christ, nor Eli'jah, nor the prophet?" [26]John answered them, "I baptize with water; but among you stands one whom you do not know, [27]even he who comes after me, the thong of whose sandal I am not worthy to untie." [28]This took place in Beth'any beyond the Jordan, where John was baptizing.

The Lamb of God

29 The next day he saw Jesus coming toward him, and said, "Behold, the Lamb of God, who takes away the sin of the world! [30]This is he of whom I said, 'After me comes a man who ranks before me, for he was before me.' [31]I myself did not know him; but for this I came baptizing with water, that he might be revealed to Israel." [32]And John bore witness, "I saw the Spirit descend as a dove from heaven and remain on him. [33]I myself did not know him; but he who sent me to baptize with water said to me, 'He on whom you see the Spirit descend and remain, this is he who baptizes with the Holy Spirit.' [34]And I have seen and have borne witness that this is the Son of God."

The First Disciples of Jesus

35 The next day again John was standing with two of his disciples; [36]and he looked at Jesus as he walked, and said, "Behold, the Lamb of God!" [37]The two disciples heard him say this, and they followed Jesus. [38]Jesus turned, and saw them following, and said to them, "What do you seek?" And they said to him, "Rabbi" (which means Teacher), "where are you staying?" [39]He said to them, "Come and see." They came and saw where he was staying; and they stayed with him that day, for it was about the tenth hour.

⁴⁰One of the two who heard John speak, and followed him, was Andrew, Simon Peter's brother. ⁴¹He first found his brother Simon, and said to him, "We have found the Messiah" (which means Christ). ⁴²He brought him to Jesus. Jesus looked at him, and said, "So you are Simon the son of John? You shall be called Ce'phas" (which means Peter).

Jesus Calls Philip and Nathanael

43 The next day Jesus decided to go to Galilee. And he found Philip and said to him, "Follow me." ⁴⁴Now Philip was from Beth-sa'ida, the city of Andrew and Peter. ⁴⁵Philip found Nathan'a-el, and said to him, "We have found him of whom Moses in the law and also the prophets wrote, Jesus of Nazareth, the son of Joseph." ⁴⁶Nathan'a-el said to him, "Can anything good come out of Nazareth?" Philip said to him, "Come and see." ⁴⁷Jesus saw Nathan'a-el coming to him, and said of him, "Behold, an Israelite indeed, in whom is no guile!" ⁴⁸Nathan'a-el said to him, "How do you know me?" Jesus answered him, "Before Philip called you, when you were under the fig tree, I saw you." ⁴⁹Nathan'a-el answered him, "Rabbi, you are the Son of God! You are the King of Israel!" ⁵⁰Jesus answered him, "Because I said to you, I saw you under the fig tree, do you believe? You shall see greater things than these." ⁵¹And he said to him, "Truly, truly, I say to you, you will see heaven opened, and the angels of God ascending and descending upon the Son of man."

The Marriage at Cana

2 On the third day there was a marriage at Cana in Galilee, and the mother of Jesus was there; ²Jesus also was invited to the marriage, ³with his disciples. When the wine failed, the mother of Jesus said to him, "They have no wine." ⁴And Jesus said to her, "O woman, what have you to do with me? My hour has not yet come." ⁵His mother said to the servants, "Do what-

ever he tells you." ⁶Now six stone jars were standing there, for the Jewish rites of purification, each holding twenty or thirty gallons. ⁷Jesus said to them, "Fill the jars with water." And they filled them up to the brim. ⁸He said to them, "Now draw some out, and take it to the steward of the feast." So they took it. ⁹When the steward of the feast tasted the water now become wine, and did not know where it came from (though the servants who had drawn the water knew), the steward of the feast called the bridegroom ¹⁰and said to him, "Every man serves the good wine first; and when men have drunk freely, then the poor wine; but you have kept the good wine until now." ¹¹This, the first of his signs, Jesus did at Cana in Galilee, and manifested his glory; and his disciples believed in him.

12 After this he went down to Caper'na-um, with his mother and his brethren and his disciples; and there they stayed for a few days.

The Cleansing of the Temple

13 The Passover of the Jews was at hand, and Jesus went up to Jerusalem. ¹⁴In the temple he found those who were selling oxen and sheep and pigeons, and the money-changers at their business. ¹⁵And making a whip of cords, he drove them all, with the sheep and oxen, out of the temple; and he poured out the coins of the money-changers and overturned their tables. ¹⁶And he told those who sold the pigeons, "Take these things away; you shall not make my Father's house a house of trade." ¹⁷His disciples remembered that it was written, "Zeal for your house will consume me." ¹⁸The Jews then said to him, "What sign have you to show us for doing this?" ¹⁹Jesus answered them, "Destroy this temple, and in three days I will raise it up." ²⁰The Jews then said, "It has taken forty-six years to build this temple, and will you raise it up in three days?" ²¹But he spoke of the temple of his body. ²²When therefore he was raised from the dead,

his disciples remembered that he had said this; and they believed the Scripture and the word which Jesus had spoken.

23 Now when he was in Jerusalem at the Passover feast, many believed in his name when they saw the signs which he did; ²⁴but Jesus did not trust himself to them, ²⁵because he knew all men and needed no one to bear witness of man; for he himself knew what was in man.

Nicodemus Visits Jesus

3 Now there was a man of the Pharisees, named Nicode′mus, a ruler of the Jews. ²This man came to Jesus by night and said to him, "Rabbi, we know that you are a teacher come from God; for no one can do these signs that you do, unless God is with him." ³Jesus answered him, "Truly, truly, I say to you, unless one is born anew, he cannot see the kingdom of God." ⁴Nicode′mus said to him, "How can a man be born when he is old? Can he enter a second time into his mother's womb and be born?" ⁵Jesus answered, "Truly, truly, I say to you, unless one is born of water and the Spirit, he cannot enter the kingdom of God. ⁶That which is born of the flesh is flesh, and that which is born of the Spirit is spirit. ⁷Do not marvel that I said to you, 'You must be born anew.' ⁸The wind blows where it wills, and you hear the sound of it, but you do not know where it comes from or where it goes; so it is with every one who is born of the Spirit." ⁹Nicode′mus said to him, "How can this be?" ¹⁰Jesus answered him, "Are you a teacher of Israel, and yet you do not understand this? ¹¹Truly, truly, I say to you, we speak of what we know, and bear witness to what we have seen; but you do not receive our testimony. ¹²If I have told you earthly things and you do not believe, how can you believe if I tell you heavenly things? ¹³No one has ascended into heaven but he who descended from heaven, the Son of man. ¹⁴And as Moses lifted up the serpent in the wilderness, so must the Son of man be lifted up, ¹⁵that whoever believes in him may have eternal life."

16 For God so loved the world that he gave his only-begotten Son, that whoever believes in him should not perish but have eternal life. ¹⁷For God sent the Son into the world, not to condemn the world, but that the world might be saved through him. ¹⁸He who believes in him is not condemned; he who does not believe is condemned already, because he has not believed in the name of the only-begotten Son of God. ¹⁹And this is the judgment, that the light has come into the world, and men loved darkness rather than light, because their deeds were evil. ²⁰For every one who does evil hates the light, and does not come to the light, lest his deeds should be exposed. ²¹But he who does what is true comes to the light, that it may be clearly seen that his deeds have been wrought in God.

Jesus and John the Baptist

22 After this Jesus and his disciples went into the land of Judea; there he remained with them and baptized. ²³John also was baptizing at Ae′non near Sa′lim, because there was much water there; and people came and were baptized. ²⁴For John had not yet been put in prison.

25 Now a discussion arose between John's disciples and a Jew over purifying. ²⁶And they came to John, and said to him, "Rabbi, he who was with you beyond the Jordan, to whom you bore witness, here he is, baptizing, and all are going to him." ²⁷John answered, "No one can receive anything except what is given him from heaven. ²⁸You yourselves bear me witness, that I said, I am not the Christ, but I have been sent before him. ²⁹He who has the bride is the bridegroom; the friend of the bridegroom, who stands and hears him, rejoices greatly at the bridegroom's voice; therefore this joy of mine is now full. ³⁰He must increase, but I must decrease."

He Who Comes from Heaven

31 He who comes from above is above all; he who is of the earth belongs to the earth, and of the earth he speaks; he who comes from heaven is above all. ³²He bears witness to what he has seen and heard, yet no one receives his testimony; ³³he who receives his testimony sets his seal to this, that God is true. ³⁴For he whom God has sent utters the words of God, for it is not by measure that he gives the Spirit; ³⁵the Father loves the Son, and has given all things into his hand. ³⁶He who believes in the Son has eternal life; he who does not obey the Son shall not see life, but the wrath of God rests upon him.

Jesus and the Woman of Samaria

4 Now when the Lord knew that the Pharisees had heard that Jesus was making and baptizing more disciples than John ²(although Jesus himself did not baptize, but only his disciples), ³he left Judea and departed again to Galilee. ⁴He had to pass through Samar′ia. ⁵So he came to a city of Samar′ia, called Sy′char, near the field that Jacob gave to his son Joseph. ⁶Jacob's well was there, and so Jesus, wearied as he was with his journey, sat down beside the well. It was about the sixth hour.

7 There came a woman of Samar′ia to draw water. Jesus said to her, "Give me a drink." ⁸For his disciples had gone away into the city to buy food. ⁹The Samaritan woman said to him, "How is it that you, a Jew, ask a drink of me, a woman of Samar′ia?" For Jews have no dealings with Samaritans. ¹⁰Jesus answered her, "If you knew the gift of God, and who it is that is saying to you, 'Give me a drink,' you would have asked him and he would have given you living water." ¹¹The woman said to him, "Sir, you have nothing to draw with, and the well is deep; where do you get that living water? ¹²Are you greater than our father Jacob, who gave us the well, and drank from it himself, and his sons, and his cattle?" ¹³Jesus said to her, "Every one who drinks of this water will thirst again, ¹⁴but whoever drinks of the water that I shall give him will never thirst; the water that I shall give him will become in him a spring of water welling up to eternal life." ¹⁵The woman said to him, "Sir, give me this water, that I may not thirst, nor come here to draw."

16 Jesus said to her, "Go, call your husband, and come here." ¹⁷The woman answered him, "I have no husband." Jesus said to her, "You are right in saying, 'I have no husband'; ¹⁸for you have had five husbands, and he whom you now have is not your husband; this you said truly." ¹⁹The woman said to him, "Sir, I perceive that you are a prophet. ²⁰Our fathers worshiped on this mountain; and you say that in Jerusalem is the place where men ought to worship." ²¹Jesus said to her, "Woman, believe me, the hour is coming when neither on this mountain nor in Jerusalem will you worship the Father. ²²You worship what you do not know; we worship what we know, for salvation is from the Jews. ²³But the hour is coming, and now is, when the true worshipers will worship the Father in spirit and truth, for such the Father seeks to worship him. ²⁴God is spirit, and those who worship him must worship in spirit and truth." ²⁵The woman said to him, "I know that Messiah is coming (he who is called Christ); when he comes, he will show us all things." ²⁶Jesus said to her, "I who speak to you am he."

27 Just then his disciples came. They marveled that he was talking with a woman, but none said, "What do you wish?" or, "Why are you talking with her?" ²⁸So the woman left her water jar, and went away into the city, and said to the people, ²⁹"Come, see a man who told me all that I ever did. Can this be the Christ?" ³⁰They went out of the city and were coming to him.

31 Meanwhile the disciples begged him, saying, "Rabbi, eat." ³²But he said to them, "I have food to eat of which you do not know." ³³So the disciples said to one another, "Has any one

brought him food?" ³⁴Jesus said to them, "My food is to do the will of him who sent me, and to accomplish his work. ³⁵Do you not say, 'There are yet four months, then comes the harvest'? I tell you, lift up your eyes, and see how the fields are already white for harvest. ³⁶He who reaps receives wages, and gathers fruit for eternal life, so that sower and reaper may rejoice together. ³⁷For here the saying holds true, 'One sows and another reaps.' ³⁸I sent you to reap that for which you did not labor; others have labored, and you have entered into their labor."

39 Many Samaritans from that city believed in him because of the woman's testimony, "He told me all that I ever did." ⁴⁰So when the Samaritans came to him, they asked him to stay with them; and he stayed there two days. ⁴¹And many more believed because of his word. ⁴²They said to the woman, "It is no longer because of your words that we believe, for we have heard for ourselves, and we know that this is indeed the Savior of the world."

Jesus Departs for Galilee

43 After the two days he departed to Galilee. ⁴⁴For Jesus himself testified that a prophet has no honor in his own country. ⁴⁵So when he came to Galilee, the Galileans welcomed him, having seen all that he had done in Jerusalem at the feast, for they too had gone to the feast.

Jesus Heals an Official's Son

46 So he came again to Cana in Galilee, where he had made the water wine. And at Caper'na-um there was an official whose son was ill. ⁴⁷When he heard that Jesus had come from Judea to Galilee, he went and begged him to come down and heal his son, for he was at the point of death. ⁴⁸Jesus therefore said to him, "Unless you see signs and wonders you will not believe." ⁴⁹The official said to him, "Sir, come down before my child dies." ⁵⁰Jesus said to him, "Go; your son will live." The man believed the word that Jesus spoke to him and went his way. ⁵¹As he was going down, his servants met him and told him that his son was living. ⁵²So he asked them the hour when he began to mend, and they said to him, "Yesterday at the seventh hour the fever left him." ⁵³The father knew that was the hour when Jesus had said to him, "Your son will live"; and he himself believed, and all his household. ⁵⁴This was now the second sign that Jesus did when he had come from Judea to Galilee.

Jesus Heals on the Sabbath

5 After this there was a feast of the Jews, and Jesus went up to Jerusalem.

2 Now there is in Jerusalem by the Sheep Gate a pool, in Hebrew called Beth-za'tha, which has five porticoes. ³In these lay a multitude of invalids, blind, lame, paralyzed. ⁵One man was there, who had been ill for thirty-eight years. ⁶When Jesus saw him and knew that he had been lying there a long time, he said to him, "Do you want to be healed?" ⁷The sick man answered him, "Sir, I have no man to put me into the pool when the water is troubled, and while I am going another steps down before me." ⁸Jesus said to him, "Rise, take up your pallet, and walk." ⁹And at once the man was healed, and he took up his pallet and walked.

Now that day was the sabbath. ¹⁰So the Jews said to the man who was cured, "It is the sabbath, it is not lawful for you to carry your pallet." ¹¹But he answered them, "The man who healed me said to me, 'Take up your pallet, and walk.' " ¹²They asked him, "Who is the man who said to you, 'Take up your pallet, and walk'?" ¹³Now the man who had been healed did not know who it was, for Jesus had withdrawn, as there was a crowd in the place. ¹⁴Afterward, Jesus found him in the temple, and said to him, "See, you are well! Sin no more, that nothing worse befall you." ¹⁵The man went away and told the Jews that it was Jesus who had healed him. ¹⁶And this was why the Jews persecuted Jesus, because he did this on the sabbath. [17]But Jesus answered them, "My Father is working still, and I am working." [18]This was why the Jews sought all the more to kill him, because he not only broke the sabbath but also called God his Father, making himself equal with God.

The Authority of the Son

19 Jesus said to them, "Truly, truly, I say to you, the Son can do nothing of his own accord, but only what he sees the Father doing; for whatever he does, that the Son does likewise. [20]For the Father loves the Son, and shows him all that he himself is doing; and greater works than these will he show him, that you may marvel. [21]For as the Father raises the dead and gives them life, so also the Son gives life to whom he will. [22]The Father judges no one, but has given all judgment to the Son, [23]that all may honor the Son, even as they honor the Father. He who does not honor the Son does not honor the Father who sent him. [24]Truly, truly, I say to you, he who hears my word and believes him who sent me, has eternal life; he does not come into judgment, but has passed from death to life.

25 "Truly, truly, I say to you, the hour is coming, and now is, when the dead will hear the voice of the Son of God, and those who hear will live. [26]For as the Father has life in himself, so he has granted the Son also to have life in himself, [27]and has given him authority to execute judgment, because he is the Son of man. [28]Do not marvel at this; for the hour is coming when all who are in the tombs will hear his voice [29]and come forth, those who have done good, to the resurrection of life, and those who have done evil, to the resurrection of judgment.

The Testimony to Jesus

30 "I can do nothing on my own authority; as I hear, I judge; and my judgment is just, because I seek not my own will but the will of him who sent me. [31]If I bear witness to myself, my testimony is not true; [32]there is another who

bears witness to me, and I know that the testimony which he bears to me is true. [33]You sent to John, and he has borne witness to the truth. [34]Not that the testimony which I receive is from man; but I say this that you may be saved. [35]He was a burning and shining lamp, and you were willing to rejoice for a while in his light. [36]But the testimony which I have is greater than that of John; for the works which the Father has granted me to accomplish, these very works which I am doing, bear me witness that the Father has sent me. [37]And the Father who sent me has himself borne witness to me. His voice you have never heard, his form you have never seen; [38]and you do not have his word abiding in you, for you do not believe him whom he has sent. [39]You search the Scriptures, because you think that in them you have eternal life; and it is they that bear witness to me; [40]yet you refuse to come to me that you may have life. [41]I do not receive glory from men. [42]But I know that you have not the love of God within you. [43]I have come in my Father's name, and you do not receive me; if another comes in his own name, him you will receive. [44]How can you believe, who receive glory from one another and do not seek the glory that comes from the only God? [45]Do not think that I shall accuse you to the Father; it is Moses who accuses you, on whom you set your hope. [46]If you believed Moses, you would believe me, for he wrote of me. [47]But if you do not believe his writings, how will you believe my words?"

Feeding the Five Thousand

6After this Jesus went to the other side of the Sea of Galilee, which is the Sea of Tibe′ri-as. [2]And a multitude followed him, because they saw the signs which he did on those who were diseased. [3]Jesus went up into the hills, and there sat down with his disciples. [4]Now the Passover, the feast of the Jews, was at hand. [5]Lifting up his eyes, then, and seeing that a multitude was coming to him, Jesus said to Philip,

"How are we to buy bread, so that these people may eat?" [6]This he said to test him, for he himself knew what he would do. [7]Philip answered him, "Two hundred denarii would not buy enough bread for each of them to get a little." [8]One of his disciples, Andrew, Simon Peter's brother, said to him, [9]"There is a lad here who has five barley loaves and two fish; but what are they among so many?" [10]Jesus said, "Make the people sit down." Now there was much grass in the place; so the men sat down, in number about five thousand. [11]Jesus then took the loaves, and when he had given thanks, he distributed them to those who were seated; so also the fish, as much as they wanted. [12]And when they had eaten their fill, he told his disciples, "Gather up the fragments left over, that nothing may be lost." [13]So they gathered them up and filled twelve baskets with fragments from the five barley loaves, left by those who had eaten. [14]When the people saw the sign which he had done, they said, "This is indeed the prophet who is to come into the world!"

15 Perceiving then that they were about to come and take him by force to make him king, Jesus withdrew again to the hills by himself.

Jesus Walks on the Sea

16 When evening came, his disciples went down to the sea, [17]got into a boat, and started across the sea to Caper'na-um. It was now dark, and Jesus had not yet come to them. [18]The sea rose because a strong wind was blowing. [19]When they had rowed about three or four miles, they saw Jesus walking on the sea and drawing near to the boat. They were frightened, [20]but he said to them, "It is I; do not be afraid." [21]Then they were glad to take him into the boat, and immediately the boat was at the land to which they were going.

The Bread from Heaven

22 On the next day the people who remained on the other side of the sea saw that there had been only one boat there, and that Jesus had not entered the boat with his disciples, but that his disciples had gone away alone. [23]However, boats from Tibe'ri-as came near the place where they ate the bread after the Lord had given thanks. [24]So when the people saw that Jesus was not there, nor his disciples, they themselves got into the boats and went to Caper'na-um, seeking Jesus.

25 When they found him on the other side of the sea, they said to him, "Rabbi, when did you [26]come here?" Jesus answered them, "Truly, truly, I say to you, you seek me, not because you saw signs, but because you ate your fill of the loaves. [27]Do not labor for the food which perishes, but for the food which endures to eternal life, which the Son of man will give to you; for on him has God the Father set his seal." [28]Then they said to him, "What must we do, to be doing the works of God?" [29]Jesus answered them, "This is the work of God, that you believe in him whom he has sent." [30]So they said to him, "Then what sign do you do, that we may see, and believe you? What work do you perform? [31]Our fathers ate the manna in the wilderness; as it is written, 'He gave them bread from heaven to eat.' " [32]Jesus then said to them, "Truly, truly, I say to you, it was not Moses who gave you the bread from heaven; my Father gives you the true bread from heaven. [33]For the bread of God is that which comes down from heaven, and gives life to the world." [34]They said to him, "Lord, give us this bread always."

35 Jesus said to them, "I am the bread of life; he who comes to me shall not hunger, and he who believes in me shall never thirst. [36]But I said to you that you have seen me and yet do not believe. [37]All that the Father gives me will come to me; and him who comes to me I will not cast out. [38]For I have come down from heaven, not to do my own will, but the will of him who sent me; [39]and this is the will of him who sent me,

that I should lose nothing of all that he has given me, but raise it up at the last day. ⁴⁰For this is the will of my Father, that every one who sees the Son and believes in him should have eternal life; and I will raise him up at the last day."

41 The Jews then murmured at him, because he said, "I am the bread which came down from heaven." ⁴²They said, "Is not this Jesus, the son of Joseph, whose father and mother we know? How does he now say, 'I have come down from heaven'?" ⁴³Jesus answered them, "Do not murmur among yourselves. ⁴⁴No one can come to me unless the Father who sent me draws him; and I will raise him up at the last day. ⁴⁵It is written in the prophets, 'And they shall all be taught by God.' Every one who has heard and learned from the Father comes to me. ⁴⁶Not that any one has seen the Father except him who is from God; he has seen the Father. ⁴⁷Truly, truly, I say to you, he who believes has eternal life. ⁴⁸I am the bread of life. ⁴⁹Your fathers ate the manna in the wilderness, and they died. ⁵⁰This is the bread which comes down from heaven, that a man may eat of it and not die. ⁵¹I am the living bread which came down from heaven; if any one eats of this bread, he will live for ever; and the bread which I shall give for the life of the world is my flesh."

52 The Jews then disputed among themselves, saying, "How can this man give us his flesh to eat?" ⁵³So Jesus said to them, "Truly, truly, I say to you, unless you eat the flesh of the Son of man and drink his blood, you have no life in you; ⁵⁴he who eats my flesh and drinks my blood has eternal life, and I will raise him up at the last day. ⁵⁵For my flesh is food indeed, and my blood is drink indeed. ⁵⁶He who eats my flesh and drinks my blood abides in me, and I in him. ⁵⁷As the living Father sent me, and I live because of the Father, so he who eats me will live because of me. ⁵⁸This is the bread which came down from heaven, not such as the fathers ate and died; he

who eats this bread will live for ever." ⁵⁹This he said in the synagogue, as he taught at Caper'na-um.

The Words of Eternal Life

60 Many of his disciples, when they heard it, said, "This is a hard saying; who can listen to it?" ⁶¹But Jesus, knowing in himself that his disciples murmured at it, said to them, "Do you take offense at this? ⁶²Then what if you were to see the Son of man ascending where he was before? ⁶³It is the Spirit that gives life, the flesh is of no avail; the words that I have spoken to you are Spirit and life. ⁶⁴But there are some of you that do not believe." For Jesus knew from the first who those were that did not believe, and who it was that would betray him. ⁶⁵And he said, "This is why I told you that no one can come to me unless it is granted him by the Father."

66 After this many of his disciples drew back and no longer walked with him. ⁶⁷Jesus said to the Twelve, "Will you also go away?" ⁶⁸Simon Peter answered him, "Lord, to whom shall we go? You have the words of eternal life; ⁶⁹and we have believed, and have come to know, that you are the Holy One of God." ⁷⁰Jesus answered them, "Did I not choose you, the Twelve, and one of you is a devil?" ⁷¹He spoke of Judas the son of Simon Iscariot, for he, one of the Twelve, was to betray him.

The Unbelief of Jesus' Brethren

7After this Jesus went about in Galilee; he would not go about in Judea, because the Jews sought to kill him. ²Now the Jews' feast of Tabernacles was at hand. ³So his brethren said to him, "Leave here and go to Judea, that your disciples may see the works you are doing. ⁴For no man works in secret if he seeks to be known openly. If you do these things, show yourself to the world." ⁵For even his brethren did not believe in him. ⁶Jesus said to them, "My time has not yet come, but your time is always here. ⁷The world cannot hate you, but it hates me because I testify of it that its works are evil. ⁸Go to the feast yourselves; I am not going up to this feast, for my time has not yet fully come." ⁹So saying, he remained in Galilee.

Jesus at the Feast of Tabernacles

10 But after his brethren had gone up to the feast, then he also went up, not publicly but in private. ¹¹The Jews were looking for him at the feast, and saying, "Where is he?" ¹²And there was much muttering about him among the people. While some said, "He is a good man," others said, "No, he is leading the people astray." ¹³Yet for fear of the Jews no one spoke openly of him.

14 About the middle of the feast Jesus went up into the temple and taught. ¹⁵The Jews marveled at it, saying, "How is it that this man has learning, when he has never studied?" ¹⁶So Jesus answered them, "My teaching is not mine, but his who sent me; ¹⁷if any man's will is to do his will, he shall know whether the teaching is from God or whether I am speaking on my own authority. ¹⁸He who speaks on his own authority seeks his own glory; but he who seeks the glory of him who sent him is true, and in him there is no falsehood. ¹⁹Did not Moses give you the law? Yet none of you keeps the law. Why do you seek to kill me?" ²⁰The people answered, "You have a demon! Who is seeking to kill you?" ²¹Jesus answered them, "I did one deed, and you all marvel at it. ²²Moses gave you circumcision (not that it is from Moses, but from the fathers), and you circumcise a man upon the sabbath. ²³If on the sabbath a man receives circumcision, so that the law of Moses may not be broken, are you angry with me because on the sabbath I made a man's whole body well? ²⁴Do not judge by appearances, but judge with right judgment."

Is This the Christ?

25 Some of the people of Jerusalem therefore said, "Is not this the man whom they seek to kill? ²⁶And here he is, speaking openly, and they say nothing to him! Can it be that the authorities really know that this is the Christ? ²⁷Yet we know where this man comes from; and when the Christ appears, no one will know where he comes from." ²⁸So Jesus proclaimed, as he taught in the temple, "You know me, and you know where I come from? But I have not come of my own accord; he who sent me is true, and him you do not know. ²⁹I know him, for I come from him, and he sent me." ³⁰So they sought to arrest him; but no one laid hands on him, because his hour had not yet come. ³¹Yet many of the people believed in him; they said, "When the Christ appears, will he do more signs than this man has done?"

Officers Are Sent to Arrest Jesus

32 The Pharisees heard the crowd thus muttering about him, and the chief priests and Pharisees sent officers to arrest him. ³³Jesus then said, "I shall be with you a little longer, and then I go to him who sent me; ³⁴you will seek me and you will not find me; where I am you cannot come." ³⁵The Jews said to one another, "Where does this man intend to go that we shall not find him? Does he intend to go to the Dispersion among the Greeks and teach the Greeks? ³⁶What does he mean by saying, 'You will seek me and you will not find me,' and, 'Where I am you cannot come'?"

Rivers of Living Water

37 On the last day of the feast, the great day, Jesus stood up and proclaimed, "If any one thirst, let him come to me and drink. ³⁸He who believes in me, as the Scripture has said, 'Out of his heart shall flow rivers of living water.' " ³⁹Now this he said about the Spirit, which those who believed in him were to receive; for as yet the Spirit had not been given, because Jesus was not yet glorified.

Division among the People

40 When they heard these words, some of the people said, "This is really the prophet." ⁴¹Others said, "This is the Christ." But some said, "Is the Christ to come from Galilee? ⁴²Has not the Scripture said that the Christ is descended from David, and comes from Bethle-

hem, the village where David was?" [43]So there was a division among the people over him. [44]Some of them wanted to arrest him, but no one laid hands on him.

The Authorities and the Woman Caught in Adultery

45 The officers then went back to the chief priests and Pharisees, who said to them, "Why did you not bring him?" [46]The officers answered, "No man ever spoke like this man!" [47]The Pharisees answered them, "Are you led astray, you also? [48]Have any of the authorities or of the Pharisees believed in him? [49]But this crowd, who do not know the law, are accursed." [50]Nicode′mus, who had gone to him before, and who was one of them, said to them, [51]"Does our law judge a man without first giving him a hearing and learning what he does?" [52]They replied, "Are you from Galilee too? Search and you will see that no prophet is to rise from Galilee." [53]They went each to his own house,

8but Jesus went to the Mount of Olives. [2]Early in the morning he came again to the temple; all the people came to him, and he sat down and taught them. [3]The scribes and the Pharisees brought a woman who had been caught in adultery, and placing her in their midst [4]they said to him, "Teacher, this woman has been caught in the act of adultery. [5]Now in the law Moses commanded us to stone such. What do you say about her?" [6]This they said to test him, that they might have some charge to bring against him. Jesus bent down and wrote with his finger on the ground. [7]And as they continued to ask him, he stood up and said to them, "Let him who is without sin among you be the first to throw a stone at her." [8]And once more he bent down and wrote with his finger on the ground. [9]But when they heard it, they went away, one by one, beginning with the eldest, and Jesus was left alone with the woman standing before him. [10]Jesus looked up and said to her, "Woman, where are they? Has no one con-

demned you?" [11]She said, "No one, Lord." And Jesus said, "Neither do I condemn you; go, and do not sin again."

Jesus and the Light of the World

12 Again Jesus spoke to them, saying, "I am the light of the world; he who follows me will not walk in darkness, but will have the light of life." [13]The Pharisees then said to him, "You are bearing witness to yourself; your testimony is not true." [14]Jesus answered, "Even if I do bear witness to myself, my testimony is true, for I know where I have come from and where I am going, but you do not know where I come from or where I am going. [15]You judge according to the flesh, I judge no one. [16]Yet even if I do judge, my judgment is true, for it is not I alone that judge, but I [17]and he who sent me. In your law it is written that the testimony of two men is true; [18]I bear witness to myself, and the Father who sent me bears witness to me." [19]They said to him therefore, "Where is your Father?" Jesus answered, "You know neither me nor my Father; if you knew me, you would know my Father also." [20]These words he spoke in the treasury, as he taught in the temple; but no one arrested him, because his hour had not yet come.

Jesus Alludes to His Death

21 Again he said to them, "I go away, and you will seek me and die in your sin; where I am going, you cannot come." [22]Then said the Jews, "Will he kill himself, since he says, 'Where I am going, you cannot come'?" [23]He said to them, "You are from below, I am from above; you are of this world, I am not of this world. [24]I told you that you would die in your sins, for you will die in your sins unless you believe that I am he." [25]They said to him, "Who are you?" Jesus said to them, "Even what I have told you from the beginning. [26]I have much to say about you and much to judge; but he who sent me is true, and I declare to the world what I have heard from him." [27]They did not understand that he spoke to them of the Father.

[28]So Jesus said, "When you have lifted up the Son of man, then you will know that I am he, and that I do nothing on my own authority but speak thus as the Father taught me. [29]And he who sent me is with me; he has not left me alone, for I always do what is pleasing to him." [30]As he spoke thus, many believed in him.

True Disciples of Jesus

31 Jesus then said to the Jews who had believed in him, "If you continue in my word, you are truly my disciples, [32]and you will know the truth, and the truth will make you free." [33]They answered him, "We are descendants of Abraham, and have never been in bondage to any one. How is it that you say, 'You will be made free'?"

34 Jesus answered them, "Truly, truly, I say to you, every one who commits sin is a slave to sin. [35]The slave does not continue in the house for ever; the son continues for ever. [36]So if the Son makes you free, you will be free indeed. [37]I know that you are descendants of Abraham; yet you seek to kill me, because my word finds no place in you. [38]I speak of what I have seen with my Father, and you do what you have heard from your father."

Jesus and Abraham

39 They answered him, "Abraham is our father." Jesus said to them, "If you were Abraham's children, you would do what Abraham did, [40]but now you seek to kill me, a man who has told you the truth which I heard from God; this is not what Abraham did. [41]You do the works of your father." They said to him, "We were not born of fornication; we have one Father, even God." [42]Jesus said to them, "If God were your Father, you would love me, for I proceeded and came forth from God; I came not of my own accord, but he sent me. [43]Why do you not understand what I say? It is because you cannot bear to hear my word. [44]You are of your father the devil, and your will is to do your father's desires. He was a murderer from the beginning, and has nothing to do with the truth, because there is no truth in him. When he lies, he speaks according to his own nature, for he is a liar and the father of lies. [45]But, because I tell the truth, you do not believe me. [46]Which of you convicts me of sin? If I tell the truth, why do you not believe me? [47]He who is of God hears the words of God; the reason why you do not hear them is that you are not of God."

48 The Jews answered him, "Are we not right in saying that you are a Samaritan and have a demon?" [49]Jesus answered, "I have not a demon; but I honor my Father, and you dishonor me. [50]Yet I do not seek my own glory; there is One who seeks it and he will be the judge. [51]Truly, truly, I say to you, if any one keeps my word, he will never see death." [52]The Jews said to him, "Now we know that you have a demon. Abraham died, as did the prophets; and you say, 'If any one keeps my word, he will never taste death.' [53]Are you greater than our father Abraham, who died? And the prophets died! Who do you claim to be?" [54]Jesus answered, "If I glorify myself, my glory is nothing; it is my Father who glorifies me, of whom you say that he is your God. [55]But you have not known him; I know him. If I said, I do not know him, I should be a liar like you; but I do know him and I keep his word. [56]Your father Abraham rejoiced that he was to see my day; he saw it and was glad." [57]The Jews then said to him, "You are not yet fifty years old, and have you seen Abraham?" [58]Jesus said to them, "Truly, truly, I say to you, before Abraham was, I am." [59]So they took up stones to throw at him; but Jesus hid himself, and went out of the temple.

Healing of the Blind Man

9 As he passed by, he saw a man blind from his birth. [2]And his disciples asked him, "Rabbi, who sinned, this man or his parents, that he was born blind?" [3]Jesus answered, "It was not that this man sinned, or his parents, but that the works of God might be made manifest in him. [4]We must work

the works of him who sent me, while it is day; night comes, when no one can work. [5]As long as I am in the world, I am the light of the world." [6]As he said this, he spat on the ground and made clay of the spittle and anointed the man's eyes with the clay, [7]saying to him, "Go, wash in the pool of Silo′am" (which means Sent). So he went and washed and came back seeing. [8]The neighbors and those who had seen him before as a beggar, said, "Is not this the man who used to sit and beg?" [9]Some said, "It is he"; others said, "No, but he is like him." He said, "I am the man." [10]They said to him, "Then how were your eyes opened?" [11]He answered, "The man called Jesus made clay and anointed my eyes and said to me, 'Go to Silo′am and wash'; so I went and washed and received my sight." [12]They said to him, "Where is he?" He said, "I do not know."

The Pharisees Investigate the Healing

13 They brought to the Pharisees the man who had formerly been blind. [14]Now it was a sabbath day when Jesus made the clay and opened his eyes. [15]The Pharisees again asked him how he had received his sight. And he said to them, "He put clay on my eyes, and I washed, and I see." [16]Some of the Pharisees said, "This man is not from God, for he does not keep the sabbath." But others said, "How can a man who is a sinner do such signs?" There was a division among them. [17]So they again said to the blind man, "What do you say about him, since he has opened your eyes?" He said, "He is a prophet."

18 The Jews did not believe that he had been blind and had received his sight, until they called the parents of the man who had received his sight, [19]and asked them, "Is this your son, who you say was born blind? How then does he now see?" [20]His parents answered, "We know that this is our son, and that he was born blind; [21]but how he now sees we do not know, nor do we know who opened his eyes. Ask him; he is of age, he will speak for himself." [22]His parents said this because they feared the Jews, for the Jews had already agreed that if any one should confess him to be Christ, he was to be put out of the synagogue. [23]Therefore his parents said, "He is of age, ask him."

24 So for the second time they called the man who had been blind, and said to him, "Give God the praise; we know that this man is a sinner." [25]He answered, "Whether he is a sinner, I do not know; one thing I know, that though I was blind, now I see." [26]They said to him, "What did he do to you? How did he open your eyes?" [27]He answered them, "I have told you already, and you would not listen. Why do you want to hear it again? Do you too want to become his disciples?" [28]And they reviled him, saying, "You are his disciple, but we are disciples of Moses. [29]We know that God has spoken to Moses, but as for this man, we do not know where he comes from." [30]The man answered, "Why, this is a marvel! You do not know where he comes from, and yet he opened my eyes. [31]We know that God does not listen to sinners, but if any one is a worshiper of God and does his will, God listens to him. [32]Never since the world began has it been heard that any one opened the eyes of a man born blind. [33]If this man were not from God, he could do nothing." [34]They answered him, "You were born in utter sin, and would you teach us?" And they cast him out.

Spiritual Blindness

35 Jesus heard that they had cast him out, and having found him he said, "Do you believe in the Son of man?" [36]He answered, "And who is he, sir, that I may believe in him?" [37]Jesus said to him, "You have seen him, and it is he who speaks to you." [38]He said, "Lord, I believe"; and he worshiped him. [39]Jesus said, "For judgment I came into this world, that those who do not see may see, and that those who see may become blind." [40]Some of the Pharisees near him heard this, and they said to him, "Are we also blind?" [41]Jesus

said to them, "If you were blind, you would have no guilt; but now that you say, 'We see,' your guilt remains.

Jesus the Good Shepherd

10 "Truly, truly, I say to you, he who does not enter the sheepfold by the door but climbs in by another way, that man is a thief and a robber; ²but he who enters by the door is the shepherd of the sheep. ³To him the gatekeeper opens; the sheep hear his voice, and he calls his own sheep by name and leads them out. ⁴When he has brought out all his own, he goes before them, and the sheep follow him, for they know his voice. ⁵A stranger they will not follow, but they will flee from him, for they do not know the voice of strangers." ⁶This figure Jesus used with them, but they did not understand what he was saying to them.

7 So Jesus again said to them, "Truly, truly, I say to you, I am the door of the sheep. ⁸All who came before me are thieves and robbers; but the sheep did not heed them. ⁹I am the door; if any one enters by me, he will be saved, and will go in and out and find pasture. ¹⁰The thief comes only to steal and kill and destroy; I came that they may have life, and have it abundantly. ¹¹I am the good shepherd. The good shepherd lays down his life for the sheep. ¹²He who is a hireling and not a shepherd, whose own the sheep are not, sees the wolf coming and leaves the sheep and flees; and the wolf snatches them and scatters them. ¹³He flees because he is a hireling and cares nothing for the sheep. ¹⁴I am the good shepherd; I know my own and my own know me, ¹⁵as the Father knows me and I know the Father; and I lay down my life for the sheep. ¹⁶And I have other sheep, that are not of this fold; I must bring them also, and they will heed my voice. So there shall be one flock, one shepherd. ¹⁷For this reason the Father loves me, because I lay down my life, that I may take it again. ¹⁸No one takes it from me, but I lay it down of my own accord. I have power to lay it down, and I have power to take it again; this charge I have received from my Father."

19 There was again a division among the Jews because of these words. ²⁰Many of them said, "He has a demon, and he is mad; why listen to him?" ²¹Others said, "These are not the sayings of one who has a demon. Can a demon open the eyes of the blind?"

Jesus Is Rejected by the Jews

22 It was the feast of the Dedication at Jerusalem; ²³it was winter, and Jesus was walking in the temple, in the portico of Solomon. ²⁴So the Jews gathered round him and said to him, "How long will you keep us in suspense? If you are the Christ, tell us plainly." ²⁵Jesus answered them, "I told you, and you do not believe. The works that I do in my Father's name, they bear witness to me; ²⁶but you do not believe, because you do not belong to my sheep. ²⁷My sheep hear my voice, and I know them, and they follow me; ²⁸and I give them eternal life, and they shall never perish, and no one shall snatch them out of my hand. ²⁹My Father, who has given them to me, is greater than all, and no one is able to snatch them out of the Father's hand. ³⁰I and the Father are one."

31 The Jews took up stones again to stone him. ³²Jesus answered them, "I have shown you many good works from the Father; for which of these do you stone me?" ³³The Jews answered him, "We stone you for no good work but for blasphemy; because you, being a man, make yourself God." ³⁴Jesus answered them, "Is it not written in your law, 'I said, you are gods'? ³⁵If he called them gods to whom the word of God came (and Scripture cannot be nullified), ³⁶do you say of him whom the Father consecrated and sent into the world, 'You are blaspheming,' because I said, 'I am the Son of God'? ³⁷If I am not doing the works of my Father, then do not believe me; ³⁸but if I do them, even though you do not believe me, believe the works, that you may know and understand that the Father is in me

and I am in the Father." ³⁹Again they tried to arrest him, but he escaped from their hands.

40 He went away again across the Jordan to the place where John at first baptized, and there he remained. ⁴¹And many came to him; and they said, "John did no sign, but everything that John said about this man was true." ⁴²And many believed in him there.

The Death of Lazarus

11 Now a certain man was ill, Laz'arus of Beth'any, the village of Mary and her sister Martha. ²It was Mary who anointed the Lord with ointment and wiped his feet with her hair, whose brother Laz'arus was ill. ³So the sisters sent to him, saying, "Lord, he whom you love is ill." ⁴But when Jesus heard it he said, "This illness is not unto death; it is for the glory of God, so that the Son of God may be glorified by means of it."

5 Now Jesus loved Martha and her sister and Laz'arus. ⁶So when he heard that he was ill, he stayed two days longer in the place where he was. ⁷Then after this he said to the disciples, "Let us go into Judea again." ⁸The disciples said to him, "Rabbi, the Jews were but now seeking to stone you, and are you going there again?" ⁹Jesus answered, "Are there not twelve hours in the day? If any one walks in the day, he does not stumble, because he sees the light of this world. ¹⁰But if any one walks in the night, he stumbles, because the light is not in him." ¹¹Thus he spoke, and then he said to them, "Our friend Laz'arus has fallen asleep, but I go to awake him out of sleep." ¹²The disciples said to him, "Lord, if he has fallen asleep, he will recover." ¹³Now Jesus had spoken of his death, but they thought that he meant taking rest in sleep. ¹⁴Then Jesus told them plainly, "Laz'arus is dead; ¹⁵and for your sake I am glad that I was not there, so that you may believe. But let us go to him." ¹⁶Thomas, called the Twin, said to his fellow disciples, "Let us also go, that we may die with him."

Jesus the Resurrection and the Life

17 Now when Jesus came, he found that Laz'arus had already been in the tomb four days. ¹⁸Beth'any was near Jerusalem, about two miles off, ¹⁹and many of the Jews had come to Martha and Mary to console them concerning their brother. ²⁰When Martha heard that Jesus was coming, she went and met him, while Mary sat in the house. ²¹Martha said to Jesus, "Lord, if you had been here, my brother would not have died. ²²And even now I know that whatever you ask from God, God will give you." ²³Jesus said to her, "Your brother will rise again." ²⁴Martha said to him, "I know that he will rise again in the resurrection at the last day." ²⁵Jesus said to her, "I am the resurrection and the life; he who believes in me, though he die, yet shall he live, ²⁶and whoever lives and believes in me shall never die. Do you believe this?" ²⁷She said to him, "Yes, Lord; I believe that you are the Christ, the Son of God, he who is coming into the world."

Jesus Weeps

28 When she had said this, she went and called her sister Mary, saying quietly, "The Teacher is here and is calling for you." ²⁹And when she heard it, she rose quickly and went to him. ³⁰Now Jesus had not yet come to the village, but was still in the place where Martha had met him. ³¹When the Jews who were with her in the house, consoling her, saw Mary rise quickly and go out, they followed her, supposing that she was going to the tomb to weep there. ³²Then Mary, when she came where Jesus was and saw him, fell at his feet, saying to him, "Lord, if you had been here, my brother would not have died." ³³When Jesus saw her weeping, and the Jews who came with her also weeping, he was deeply moved in spirit and troubled; ³⁴and he said, "Where have you laid him?" They said to him, "Lord, come and see." ³⁵Jesus wept. ³⁶So the Jews said, "See how he loved him!" ³⁷But some of them said, "Could not he who opened the eyes of the blind

man have kept this man from dying?"

Jesus Raises Lazarus to Life

38 Then Jesus, deeply moved again, came to the tomb; it was a cave, and a stone lay upon it. ³⁹Jesus said, "Take away the stone." Martha, the sister of the dead man, said to him, "Lord, by this time there will be an odor, for he has been dead four days." ⁴⁰Jesus said to her, "Did I not tell you that if you would believe you would see the glory of God?" ⁴¹So they took away the stone. And Jesus lifted up his eyes and said, "Father, I thank you that you have heard me. ⁴²I knew that you always hear me, but I have said this on account of the people standing by, that they may believe that you sent me." ⁴³When he had said this, he cried with a loud voice, "Laz'arus, come out." ⁴⁴The dead man came out, his hands and feet bound with bandages, and his face wrapped with a cloth. Jesus said to them, "Unbind him, and let him go."

The Plot to Put Jesus to Death

45 Many of the Jews therefore, who had come with Mary and had seen what he did, believed in him; ⁴⁶but some of them went to the Pharisees and told them what Jesus had done. ⁴⁷So the chief priests and the Pharisees gathered the council, and said, "What are we to do? For this man performs many signs. ⁴⁸If we let him go on like this, every one will believe in him, and the Romans will come and destroy both our holy place and our nation." ⁴⁹But one of them, Cai'aphas, who was high priest that year, said to them, "You know nothing at all; ⁵⁰you do not understand that it is expedient for you that one man should die for the people, and that the whole nation should not perish." ⁵¹He did not say this of his own accord, but being high priest that year he prophesied that Jesus should die for the nation, ⁵²and not for the nation only, but to gather into one the children of God who are scattered abroad. ⁵³So from that day on they took counsel about how to put him to death.

54 Jesus therefore no longer went about openly among the Jews, but went from there to the country near the wilderness, to a town called E'phraim; and there he stayed with the disciples.

55 Now the Passover of the Jews was at hand, and many went up from the country to Jerusalem before the Passover, to purify themselves. ⁵⁶They were looking for Jesus and saying to one another as they stood in the temple, "What do you think? That he will not come to the feast?" ⁵⁷Now the chief priests and the Pharisees had given orders that if any one knew where he was, he should let them know, so that they might arrest him.

Mary of Bethany Anoints Jesus

12 Six days before the Passover, Jesus came to Beth'any, where Laz'arus was, whom Jesus had raised from the dead. ²There they made him a supper; Martha served, and Laz'arus was one of those at table with him. ³Mary took a pound of costly ointment of pure nard and anointed the feet of Jesus and wiped his feet with her hair; and the house was filled with the fragrance of the ointment. ⁴But Judas Iscariot, one of his disciples (he who was to betray him), said, ⁵"Why was this ointment not sold for three hundred denarii and given to the poor?" ⁶This he said, not that he cared for the poor but because he was a thief, and as he had the money box he used to take what was put into it. ⁷Jesus said, "Let her alone, let her keep it for the day of my burial. ⁸The poor you always have with you, but you do not always have me."

The Plot to Put Lazarus to Death

9 When the great crowd of the Jews learned that he was there, they came, not only on account of Jesus but also to see Laz'arus, whom he had raised from the dead. ¹⁰So the chief priests planned to put Laz'arus also to death, ¹¹because on account of him many of the Jews were going away and believing in Jesus.

Jesus' Triumphal Entry into Jerusalem

12 The next day a great crowd who had come to the feast heard that

Jesus was coming to Jerusalem. [13]So they took branches of palm trees and went out to meet him, crying, "Hosanna! Blessed is he who comes in the name of the Lord, even the King of Israel!" [14]And Jesus found a young donkey and sat upon it; as it is written, [15]"Fear not, daughter of Zion; behold, your king is coming, sitting on a donkey's colt!"

[16]His disciples did not understand this at first; but when Jesus was glorified, then they remembered that this had been written of him and had been done to him. [17]The crowd that had been with him when he called Laz'arus out of the tomb and raised him from the dead bore witness. [18]The reason why the crowd went to meet him was that they heard he had done this sign. [19]The Pharisees then said to one another, "You see that you can do nothing; look, the world has gone after him."

Some Greeks Wish to See Jesus

20 Now among those who went up to worship at the feast were some Greeks. [21]So these came to Philip, who was from Beth-sa'ida in Galilee, and said to him, "Sir, we wish to see Jesus." [22]Philip went and told Andrew; Andrew went with Philip and they told Jesus. [23]And Jesus answered them, "The hour has come for the Son of man to be glorified. [24]Truly, truly, I say to you, unless a grain of wheat falls into the earth and dies, it remains alone; but if it dies, it bears much fruit. [25]He who loves his life loses it, and he who hates his life in this world will keep it for eternal life. [26]If any one serves me, he must follow me; and where I am, there shall my servant be also; if any one serves me, the Father will honor him.

Jesus Speaks about His Death

27 "Now is my soul troubled. And what shall I say? 'Father, save me from this hour'? No, for this purpose I have come to this hour. [28]Father, glorify your name." Then a voice came from heaven, "I have glorified it, and I will glorify it again." [29]The crowd standing by heard it and said that it had thundered. Others said, "An angel has spoken to him."

[30]Jesus answered, "This voice has come for your sake, not for mine. [31]Now is the judgment of this world, now shall the ruler of this world be cast out; [32]and I, when I am lifted up from the earth, will draw all men to myself." [33]He said this to show by what death he was to die. [34]The crowd answered him, "We have heard from the law that the Christ remains for ever. How can you say that the Son of man must be lifted up? Who is this Son of man?" [35]Jesus said to them, "The light is with you for a little longer. Walk while you have the light, lest the darkness overtake you; he who walks in the darkness does not know where he goes. [36]While you have the light, believe in the light, that you may become sons of light."

The Unbelief of the People

When Jesus had said this, he departed and hid himself from them. [37]Though he had done so many signs before them, yet they did not believe in him; [38]it was that the word spoken by the prophet Isaiah might be fulfilled:

"Lord, who has believed our report,
and to whom has the arm of the Lord
been revealed?"

[39]Therefore they could not believe. For Isaiah again said,

[40]"He has blinded their eyes and
hardened their heart, lest they
should see with their eyes and perceive with their heart, and turn for me
to heal them."

[41]Isaiah said this because he saw his glory and spoke of him. [42]Nevertheless many even of the authorities believed in him, but for fear of the Pharisees they did not confess it, lest they should be put out of the synagogue: [43]for they loved the praise of men more than the praise of God.

Summary of Jesus' Teaching

44 And Jesus cried out and said, "He who believes in me, believes not in me but in him who sent me. [45]And he who sees me sees him who sent me. [46]I have come as light into the world, that whoever believes in me may not remain in darkness. [47]If any one hears my

sayings and does not keep them, I do not judge him; for I did not come to judge the world but to save the world. [48]He who rejects me and does not receive my sayings has a judge; the word that I have spoken will be his judge on the last day. [49]For I have not spoken on my own authority; the Father who sent me has himself given me commandment what to say and what to speak. [50]And I know that his commandment is eternal life. What I say, therefore, I say as the Father has bidden me."

Jesus Washes the Disciples' Feet

13Now before the feast of the Passover, when Jesus knew that his hour had come to depart out of this world to the Father, having loved his own who were in the world, he loved them to the end. [2]And during supper, when the devil had already put it into the heart of Judas Iscariot, Simon's son, to betray him, [3]Jesus, knowing that the Father had given all things into his hands, and that he had come from God and was going to God, [4]rose from supper, laid aside his garments, and tied a towel around himself. [5]Then he poured water into a basin, and began to wash the disciples' feet, and to wipe them with the towel that was tied around him. [6]He came to Simon Peter; and Peter said to him, "Lord, do you wash my feet?" [7]Jesus answered him, "What I am doing you do not know now, but afterward you will understand." [8]Peter said to him, "You shall never wash my feet." Jesus answered him, "If I do not wash you, you have no part in me." [9]Simon Peter said to him, "Lord, not my feet only but also my hands and my head!" [10]Jesus said to him, "He who has bathed does not need to wash, except for his feet, but he is clean all over; and you are clean, but not all of you." [11]For he knew who was to betray him; that was why he said, "You are not all clean."

[12] When he had washed their feet, and taken his garments, and resumed his place, he said to them, "Do you know what I have done to you? [13]You call me Teacher and Lord; and you are right, for so I am. [14]If I then, your Lord and Teacher, have washed your feet, you also ought to wash one another's feet. [15]For I have given you an example, that you also should do as I have done to you. [16]Truly, truly, I say to you, a servant is not greater than his master; nor is he who is sent greater than he who sent him. [17]If you know these things, blessed are you if you do them. [18]I am not speaking of you all; I know whom I have chosen; it is that the Scripture may be fulfilled, 'He who ate my bread has lifted his heel against me.' [19]I tell you this now, before it takes place, that when it does take place you may believe that I am he. [20]Truly, truly, I say to you, he who receives any one whom I send receives me; and he who receives me receives him who sent me."

Jesus Foretells His Betrayal

[21] When Jesus had thus spoken, he was troubled in spirit, and testified, "Truly, truly, I say to you, one of you will betray me." [22]The disciples looked at one another, uncertain of whom he spoke. [23]One of his disciples, whom Jesus loved, was lying close to the breast of Jesus; [24]so Simon Peter beckoned to him and said, "Tell us who it is of whom he speaks." [25]So lying thus, close to the breast of Jesus, he said to him, "Lord, who is it?" [26]Jesus answered, "It is he to whom I shall give this morsel when I have dipped it." So when he had dipped the morsel, he gave it to Judas, the son of Simon Iscariot. [27]Then after the morsel, Satan entered into him. Jesus said to him, "What you are going to do, do quickly." [28]Now no one at the table knew why he said this to him. [29]Some thought that, because Judas had the money box, Jesus was telling him, "Buy what we need for the feast"; or, that he should give something to the poor. [30]So, after receiving the morsel, he immediately went out; and it was night.

The New Commandment

[31] When he had gone out, Jesus said, "Now is the Son of man glorified, and in him God is glorified; [32]if God is

glorified in him, God will also glorify him in himself, and glorify him at once. ³³Little children, yet a little while I am with you. You will seek me; and as I said to the Jews so now I say to you, 'Where I am going you cannot come.' ³⁴A new commandment I give to you, that you love one another; even as I have loved you, that you also love one another. ³⁵By this all men will know that you are my disciples, if you have love for one another."

Jesus Foretells Peter's Denial

36 Simon Peter said to him, "Lord, where are you going?" Jesus answered, "Where I am going you cannot follow me now; but you shall follow afterward." ³⁷Peter said to him, "Lord, why can I not follow you now? I will lay down my life for you." ³⁸Jesus answered, "Will you lay down your life for me? Truly, truly, I say to you, the cock will not crow, till you have denied me three times.

Jesus the Way, the Truth, and the Life

14 "Let not your hearts be troubled; believe in God, believe also in me. ²In my Father's house are many rooms; if it were not so, would I have told you that I go to prepare a place for you? ³And when I go and prepare a place for you, I will come again and will take you to myself, that where I am you may be also. ⁴And you know the way where I am going." ⁵Thomas said to him, "Lord, we do not know where you are going; how can we know the way?" ⁶Jesus said to him, "I am the way, and the truth, and the life; no one comes to the Father, but by me. ⁷If you had known me, you would have known my Father also; henceforth you know him and have seen him."

8 Philip said to him, "Lord, show us the Father, and we shall be satisfied." ⁹Jesus said to him, "Have I been with you so long, and yet you do not know me, Philip? He who has seen me has seen the Father; how can you say, 'Show us the Father'? ¹⁰Do you not believe that I am in the Father and the Father is in me? The words that I say to you I do not speak on my own authority; but the Father who dwells in me does his works. ¹¹Believe me that I am in the Father and the Father is in me; or else believe me for the sake of the works themselves.

12 "Truly, truly, I say to you, he who believes in me will also do the works that I do; and greater works than these will he do, because I go to the Father. ¹³Whatever you ask in my name, I will do it, that the Father may be glorified in the Son; ¹⁴if you ask anything in my name, I will do it.

The Promise of the Holy Spirit

15 "If you love me, you will keep my commandments. ¹⁶And I will ask the Father, and he will give you another Counselor, to be with you for ever, ¹⁷even the Spirit of truth, whom the world cannot receive, because it neither sees him nor knows him; you know him, for he dwells with you, and will be in you.

18 "I will not leave you desolate; I will come to you. ¹⁹Yet a little while, and the world will see me no more, but you will see me; because I live, you will live also. ²⁰In that day you will know that I am in my Father, and you in me, and I in you. ²¹He who has my commandments and keeps them, he it is who loves me; and he who loves me will be loved by my Father, and I will love him and manifest myself to him." ²²Judas (not Iscariot) said to him, "Lord, how is it that you will manifest yourself to us, and not to the world?" ²³Jesus answered him, "If a man loves me, he will keep my word, and my Father will love him, and we will come to him and make our home with him. ²⁴He who does not love me does not keep my words; and the word which you hear is not mine but the Father's who sent me.

25 "These things I have spoken to you, while I am still with you. ²⁶But the Counselor, the Holy Spirit, whom the Father will send in my name, he will teach you all things, and bring to your remembrance all that I have said to you. ²⁷Peace I leave with you; my peace I give to you; not as the world gives do I

give to you. Let not your hearts be troubled, neither let them be afraid. ²⁸You heard me say to you, 'I go away, and I will come to you.' If you loved me, you would have rejoiced, because I go to the Father; for the Father is greater than I. ²⁹And now I have told you before it takes place, so that when it does take place, you may believe. ³⁰I will no longer talk much with you, for the ruler of this world is coming. He has no power over me; ³¹but I do as the Father has commanded me, so that the world may know that I love the Father. Rise, let us go from here.

Jesus the True Vine

15"I am the true vine, and my Father is the vinedresser. ²Every branch of mine that bears no fruit, he takes away, and every branch that does bear fruit he prunes, that it may bear more fruit. ³You are already made clean by the word which I have spoken to you. ⁴Abide in me, and I in you. As the branch cannot bear fruit by itself, unless it abides in the vine, neither can you, unless you abide in me. ⁵I am the vine, you are the branches. He who abides in me, and I in him, he it is that bears much fruit, for apart from me you can do nothing. ⁶If a man does not abide in me, he is cast forth as a branch and withers; and the branches are gathered, thrown into the fire and burned. ⁷If you abide in me, and my words abide in you, ask whatever you will, and it shall be done for you. ⁸By this my Father is glorified, that you bear much fruit, and so prove to be my disciples. ⁹As the Father has loved me, so have I loved you; abide in my love. ¹⁰If you keep my commandments, you will abide in my love, just as I have kept my Father's commandments and abide in his love. ¹¹These things I have spoken to you, that my joy may be in you, and that your joy may be full.

12 "This is my commandment, that you love one another as I have loved you. ¹³Greater love has no man than this, that a man lay down his life for his friends. ¹⁴You are my friends if you do what I command you. ¹⁵No longer do I call you servants, for the servant does not know what his master is doing; but I have called you friends, for all that I have heard from my Father I have made known to you. ¹⁶You did not choose me, but I chose you and appointed you that you should go and bear fruit and that your fruit should abide; so that whatever you ask the Father in my name, he may give it to you. ¹⁷This I command you, to love one another.

The World's Hatred

18 "If the world hates you, know that it has hated me before it hated you. ¹⁹If you were of the world, the world would love its own; but because you are not of the world, but I chose you out of the world, therefore the world hates you. ²⁰Remember the word that I said to you, 'A servant is not greater than his master.' If they persecuted me, they will persecute you; if they kept my word, they will keep yours also. ²¹But all this they will do to you on my account, because they do not know him who sent me. ²²If I had not come and spoken to them, they would not have sin; but now they have no excuse for their sin. ²³He who hates me hates my Father also. ²⁴If I had not done among them the works which no one else did, they would not have sin; but now they have seen and hated both me and my Father. ²⁵It is to fulfil the word that is written in their law, 'They hated me without a cause.' ²⁶But when the Counselor comes, whom I shall send to you from the Father, even the Spirit of truth, who proceeds from the Father, he will bear witness to me; ²⁷and you also are witnesses, because you have been with me from the beginning.

16"I have said all this to you to keep you from falling away. ²They will put you out of the synagogues; indeed, the hour is coming when whoever kills you will think he is offering service to God. ³And they will do this because they have not known the Father, nor me. ⁴But I have said these things to you, that when their hour comes you may remember that I told you of them.

The Work of the Spirit

"I did not say these things to you from the beginning, because I was with you. [5]But now I am going to him who sent me; yet none of you asks me, 'Where are you going?' [6]But because I have said these things to you, sorrow has filled your hearts. [7]Nevertheless I tell you the truth: it is to your advantage that I go away, for if I do not go away, the Counselor will not come to you; but if I go, I will send him to you. [8]And when he comes, he will convince the world of sin and of righteousness and of judgment: [9]of sin, because they do not believe in me; [10]of righteousness, because I go to the Father, and you will see me no more; [11]of judgment, because the ruler of this world is judged.

[12] "I have yet many things to say to you, but you cannot bear them now. [13]When the Spirit of truth comes, he will guide you into all the truth; for he will not speak on his own authority, but whatever he hears he will speak, and he will declare to you the things that are to come. [14]He will glorify me, for he will take what is mine and declare it to you. [15]All that the Father has is mine; therefore I said that he will take what is mine and declare it to you.

Sorrow Will Turn into Joy

[16] "A little while, and you will see me no more; again a little while, and you will see me." [17]Some of his disciples said to one another, "What is this that he says to us, 'A little while, and you will not see me, and again a little while, and you will see me'; and, 'because I go to the Father'?" [18]They said, "What does he mean by 'a little while'? We do not know what he means." [19]Jesus knew that they wanted to ask him; so he said to them, "Is this what you are asking yourselves, what I meant by saying, 'A little while, and you will not see me, and again a little while, and you will see me'? [20]Truly, truly, I say to you, you will weep and lament, but the world will rejoice; you will be sorrowful, but your sorrow will turn into joy. [21]When a woman is in labor, she has pain, because her hour has come; but when she is delivered of the child, she no longer remembers the anguish, for joy that a child is born into the world. [22]So you have sorrow now, but I will see you again and your hearts will rejoice, and no one will take your joy from you. [23]In that day you will ask nothing of me. Truly, truly, I say to you, if you ask anything of the Father, he will give it to you in my name. [24]Until now you have asked nothing in my name; ask, and you will receive, that your joy may be full.

Peace for the Disciples

[25] "I have said this to you in figures; the hour is coming when I shall no longer speak to you in figures but tell you plainly of the Father. [26]In that day you will ask in my name; and I do not say to you that I shall ask the Father for you; [27]for the Father himself loves you, because you have loved me and have believed that I came from the Father. [28]I came from the Father and have come into the world; again, I am leaving the world and going to the Father."

[29] His disciples said, "Ah, now you are speaking plainly, not in any figure! [30]Now we know that you know all things, and need none to question you; by this we believe that you came from God." [31]Jesus answered them, "Do you now believe? [32]The hour is coming, indeed it has come, when you will be scattered, every man to his home, and will leave me alone; yet I am not alone, for the Father is with me. [33]I have said this to you, that in me you may have peace. In the world you have tribulation; but be of good cheer, I have overcome the world."

Jesus Prays for the Church

17 When Jesus had spoken these words, he lifted up his eyes to heaven and said, "Father, the hour has come; glorify your Son that the Son may glorify you, [2]since you have given him power over all flesh, to give eternal life to all whom you have given him. [3]And this is eternal life, that they know you the only true God, and Jesus Christ whom you have sent. ⁴I glorified you on earth, having accomplished the work which you gave me to do; ⁵and now, Father, glorify me in your own presence with the glory which I had with you before the world was made.

6 "I have manifested your name to the men whom you gave me out of the world; they were yours, and you gave them to me, and they have kept your word. ⁷Now they know that everything that you have given me is from you; ⁸for I have given them the words which you gave me, and they have received them and know in truth that I came from you; and they have believed that you sent me. ⁹I am praying for them; I am not praying for the world but for those whom you have given me, for they are yours; ¹⁰all mine are yours, and yours are mine, and I am glorified in them. ¹¹And now I am no more in the world, but they are in the world, and I am coming to you. Holy Father, keep them in your name, which you have given me, that they may be one, even as we are one. ¹²While I was with them, I kept them in your name, which you have given me; I have guarded them, and none of them is lost but the son of perdition, that the Scripture might be fulfilled. ¹³But now I am coming to you; and these things I speak in the world, that they may have my joy fulfilled in themselves. ¹⁴I have given them your word; and the world has hated them because they are not of the world, even as I am not of the world. ¹⁵I do not pray that you should take them out of the world, but that you should keep them from the evil one. ¹⁶They are not of the world, even as I am not of the world. ¹⁷Sanctify them in the truth; your word is truth. ¹⁸As you sent me into the world, so I have sent them into the world. ¹⁹And for their sake I consecrate myself, that they also may be consecrated in truth.

20 I do not pray for these only, but also for those who believe in me through their word, ²¹that they may all be one; even as you, Father, are in me, and I in you, that they also may be in us, so that the world may believe that you have sent me. ²²The glory which you have given me I have given to them, that they may be one even as we are one, ²³I in them and you in me, that they may become perfectly one, so that the world may know that you have sent me and have loved them even as you have loved me. ²⁴Father, I desire that they also, whom you have given me, may be with me where I am, to behold my glory which you have given me in your love for me before the foundation of the world. ²⁵O righteous Father, the world has not known you, but I have known you; and these know that you have sent me. ²⁶I made known to them your name, and I will make it known, that the love with which you have loved me may be in them, and I in them."

The Arrest of Jesus

18 When Jesus had spoken these words, he went forth with his disciples across the Kidron valley, where there was a garden, which he and his disciples entered. ²Now Judas, who betrayed him, also knew the place; for Jesus often met there with his disciples. ³So Judas, procuring a band of soldiers and some officers from the chief priests and the Pharisees, went there with lanterns and torches and weapons. ⁴Then Jesus, knowing all that was to befall him, came forward and said to them, "Whom do you seek?" ⁵They answered him, "Jesus of Nazareth." Jesus said to them, "I am he." Judas, who betrayed him, was standing with them. ⁶When he said to them, "I am he," they drew back and fell to the ground. ⁷Again he asked them, "Whom do you seek?" And they said, "Jesus of Nazareth." ⁸Jesus answered, "I told you that I am he; so, if you seek me, let these men go." ⁹This was to fulfil the word which he had spoken, "Of those whom you gave me I lost not one." ¹⁰Then Simon Peter, having a sword, drew it and struck the high priest's slave and cut off his right ear. The slave's name was Malchus. ¹¹Jesus said to Peter, "Put your sword into its sheath; shall I not drink the chalice which the Father has given me?"

Jesus before the High Priest

12 So the band of soldiers and their captain and the officers of the Jews seized Jesus and bound him. [13]First they led him to Annas; for he was the father-in-law of Cai'aphas, who was high priest that year. [14]It was Cai'aphas who had given counsel to the Jews that it was expedient that one man should die for the people.

Peter Denies Jesus

15 Simon Peter followed Jesus, and so did another disciple. As this disciple was known to the high priest, he entered the court of the high priest along with Jesus, [16]while Peter stood outside at the door. So the other disciple, who was known to the high priest, went out and spoke to the maid who kept the door, and brought Peter in. [17]The maid who kept the door said to Peter, "Are not you also one of this man's disciples?" He said, "I am not." [18]Now the servants and officers had made a charcoal fire, because it was cold, and they were standing and warming themselves; Peter also was with them, standing and warming himself.

The High Priest Questions Jesus

19 The high priest then questioned Jesus about his disciples and his teaching. [20]Jesus answered him, "I have spoken openly to the world; I have always taught in synagogues and in the temple, where all Jews come together; I have said nothing secretly. [21]Why do you ask me? Ask those who have heard me, what I said to them; they know what I said." [22]When he had said this, one of the officers standing by struck Jesus with his hand, saying, "Is that how you answer the high priest?" [23]Jesus answered him, "If I have spoken wrongly, bear witness to the wrong; but if I have spoken rightly, why do you strike me?" [24]Annas then sent him bound to Cai'aphas the high priest.

Peter Denies Jesus Again

25 Now Simon Peter was standing and warming himself. They said to him, "Are not you also one of his disciples?" He denied it and said, "I am not." [26]One of the servants of the high priest, a kinsman of the man whose ear Peter had cut off, asked, "Did I not see you in the garden with him?" [27]Peter again denied it; and at once the cock crowed.

Jesus before Pilate

28 Then they led Jesus from the house of Cai'aphas to the praetorium. It was early. They themselves did not enter the praetorium, so that they might not be defiled, but might eat the Passover. [29]So Pilate went out to them and said, "What accusation do you bring against this man?" [30]They answered him, "If this man were not an evildoer, we would not have handed him over." [31]Pilate said to them, "Take him yourselves and judge him by your own law." The Jews said to him, "It is not lawful for us to put any man to death." [32]This was to fulfil the word which Jesus had spoken to show by what death he was to die.

Jesus Sentenced to Death

33 Pilate entered the praetorium again and called Jesus, and said to him, "Are you the King of the Jews?" [34]Jesus answered, "Do you say this of your own accord, or did others say it to you about me?" [35]Pilate answered, "Am I a Jew? Your own nation and the chief priests have handed you over to me; what have you done?" [36]Jesus answered, "My kingship is not of this world; if my kingship were of this world, my servants would fight, that I might not be handed over to the Jews; but my kingship is not from the world." [37]Pilate said to him, "So you are a king?" Jesus answered, "You say that I am a king. For this I was born, and for this I have come into the world, to bear witness to the truth. Every one who is of the truth hears my voice." [38]Pilate said to him, "What is truth?"

After he had said this, he went out to the Jews again, and told them, "I find no crime in him. ³⁹But you have a custom that I should release one man for you at the Passover; will you have me release for you the King of the Jews?" ⁴⁰They cried out again, "Not this man, but Barab'bas!" Now Barab'bas was a robber.

19 Then Pilate took Jesus and scourged him. ²And the soldiers plaited a crown of thorns, and put it on his head, and clothed him in a purple robe; ³they came up to him, saying, "Hail, King of the Jews!" and struck him with their hands. ⁴Pilate went out again, and said to them, "Behold, I am bringing him out to you, that you may know that I find no crime in him." ⁵So Jesus came out, wearing the crown of thorns and the purple robe. Pilate said to them, "Here is the man!" ⁶When the chief priests and the officers saw him, they cried out, "Crucify him, crucify him!" Pilate said to them, "Take him yourselves and crucify him, for I find no crime in him." ⁷The Jews answered him, "We have a law, and by that law he ought to die, because he has made himself the Son of God." ⁸When Pilate heard these words, he was even more afraid; ⁹he entered the praetorium again and said to Jesus, "Where are you from?" But Jesus gave no answer. ¹⁰Pilate therefore said to him, "You will not speak to me? Do you not know that I have power to release you, and power to crucify you?" ¹¹Jesus answered him, "You would have no power over me unless it had been given you from above; therefore he who delivered me to you has the greater sin."

12 Upon this Pilate sought to release him, but the Jews cried out, "If you release this man, you are not Caesar's friend; every one who makes himself a king sets himself against Caesar." ¹³When Pilate heard these words, he brought Jesus out and sat down on the judgment seat at a place called The Pavement, and in Hebrew, Gab'batha. ¹⁴Now it was the day of Preparation of the Passover; it was about the sixth hour. He said to the Jews, "Here is your King!" ¹⁵They cried out, "Away with him, away with him, crucify him!" Pilate said to them, "Shall I crucify your King?" The chief priests answered, "We have no king but Caesar." ¹⁶Then he handed him over to them to be crucified.

The Crucifixion

17 So they took Jesus, and he went out, bearing his own cross, to the place called the place of a skull, which is called in Hebrew Gol'gotha. ¹⁸There they crucified him, and with him two others, one on either side, and Jesus between them. ¹⁹Pilate also wrote a title and put it on the cross; it read, "Jesus of Nazareth, the King of the Jews." ²⁰Many of the Jews read this title, for the place where Jesus was crucified was near the city; and it was written in Hebrew, in Latin, and in Greek. ²¹The chief priests of the Jews then said to Pilate, "Do not write, 'The King of the Jews,' but, 'This man said, I am King of the Jews.' " ²²Pilate answered, "What I have written I have written."

23 When the soldiers had crucified Jesus they took his garments and made four parts, one for each soldier; also his tunic. But the tunic was without seam, woven from top to bottom; ²⁴so they said to one another, "Let us not tear it, but cast lots for it to see whose it shall be." This was to fulfil the Scripture, "They parted my garments among them, and for my clothing they cast lots."

25 So the soldiers did this. But standing by the cross of Jesus were his mother, and his mother's sister, Mary the wife of Clopas, and Mary Mag'dalene. ²⁶When Jesus saw his mother, and the disciple whom he loved standing near, he said to his mother, "Woman, behold, your son!" ²⁷Then he said to the disciple, "Behold, your mother!" And from that hour the disciple took her to his own home.

28 After this Jesus, knowing that all was now finished, said (to fulfil the Scripture), "I thirst." ²⁹A bowl full of vinegar stood there; so they put a sponge full of the vinegar on hyssop and held it

to his mouth. ³⁰When Jesus had received the vinegar, he said, "It is finished"; and he bowed his head and gave up his spirit.

Jesus' Side Is Pierced

31 Since it was the day of Preparation, in order to prevent the bodies from remaining on the cross on the sabbath (for that sabbath was a high day), the Jews asked Pilate that their legs might be broken, and that they might be taken away. ³²So the soldiers came and broke the legs of the first, and of the other who had been crucified with him; ³³but when they came to Jesus and saw that he was already dead, they did not break his legs. ³⁴But one of the soldiers pierced his side with a spear, and at once there came out blood and water. ³⁵He who saw it has borne witness — his testimony is true, and he knows that he tells the truth — that you also may believe. ³⁶For these things took place that the Scripture might be fulfilled, "Not a bone of him shall be broken." ³⁷And again another Scripture says, "They shall look on him whom they have pierced."

The Burial of Jesus

38 After this Joseph of Arimathe′a, who was a disciple of Jesus, but secretly, for fear of the Jews, asked Pilate that he might take away the body of Jesus, and Pilate gave him leave. So he came and took away his body. ³⁹Nicode′mus also, who had at first come to him by night, came bringing a mixture of myrrh and aloes, about a hundred pounds' weight. ⁴⁰They took the body of Jesus, and bound it in linen cloths with the spices, as is the burial custom of the Jews. ⁴¹Now in the place where he was crucified there was a garden, and in the garden a new tomb where no one had ever been laid. ⁴²So because of the Jewish day of Preparation, as the tomb was close at hand, they laid Jesus there.

The Resurrection of Jesus

20 Now on the first day of the week, Mary Mag′dalene came to the tomb early, while it was still dark, and saw that the stone had been taken away from the tomb. ²So she ran, and went to Simon Peter and the other disciple, the one whom Jesus loved, and said to them, "They have taken the Lord out of the tomb, and we do not know where they have laid him." ³Peter then came out with the other disciple, and they went toward the tomb. ⁴They both ran, but the other disciple outran Peter and reached the tomb first; ⁵and stooping to look in, he saw the linen cloths lying there, but he did not go in. ⁶Then Simon Peter came, following him, and went into the tomb; he saw the linen cloths lying, ⁷and the napkin, which had been on his head, not lying with the linen cloths but rolled up in a place by itself. ⁸Then the other disciple, who reached the tomb first, also went in, and he saw and believed; ⁹for as yet they did not know the Scripture, that he must rise from the dead. ¹⁰Then the disciples went back to their homes.

Jesus Appears to Mary Magdalene

11 But Mary stood weeping outside the tomb, and as she wept she stooped to look into the tomb; ¹²and she saw two angels in white, sitting where the body of Jesus had lain, one at the head and one at the feet. ¹³They said to her, "Woman, why are you weeping?" She said to them, "Because they have taken away my Lord, and I do not know where they have laid him." ¹⁴Saying this, she turned round and saw Jesus standing, but she did not know that it was Jesus. ¹⁵Jesus said to her, "Woman, why are you weeping? Whom do you seek?" Supposing him to be the gardener, she said to him, "Sir, if you have carried him away, tell me where you have laid him, and I will take him away." ¹⁶Jesus said to her, "Mary." She turned and said to him in Hebrew, "Rab-bo′ni!" (which means Teacher). ¹⁷Jesus said to her, "Do not hold me, for I have not yet ascended to the Father; but go to my brethren and say to them, I am ascending to my Father and your Father, to my God and your God." ¹⁸Mary Mag′dalene went

and said to the disciples, "I have seen the Lord"; and she told them that he had said these things to her.

Jesus Gives the Disciples the Power to Forgive Sins

19 On the evening of that day, the first day of the week, the doors being shut where the disciples were, for fear of the Jews, Jesus came and stood among them and said to them, "Peace be with you." ²⁰When he had said this, he showed them his hands and his side. Then the disciples were glad when they saw the Lord. ²¹Jesus said to them again, "Peace be with you. As the Father has sent me, even so I send you." ²²And when he had said this, he breathed on them, and said to them, "Receive the Holy Spirit. ²³If you forgive the sins of any, they are forgiven; if you retain the sins of any, they are retained."

Jesus and Thomas

24 Now Thomas, one of the Twelve, called the Twin, was not with them when Jesus came. ²⁵So the other disciples told him, "We have seen the Lord." But he said to them, "Unless I see in his hands the print of the nails, and place my finger in the mark of the nails, and place my hand in his side, I will not believe."

26 Eight days later, his disciples were again in the house, and Thomas was with them. The doors were shut, but Jesus came and stood among them, and said, "Peace be with you." ²⁷Then he said to Thomas, "Put your finger here, and see my hands; and put out your hand, and place it in my side; do not be faithless, but believing." ²⁸Thomas answered him, "My Lord and my God!" ²⁹Jesus said to him, "You have believed because you have seen me. Blessed are those who have not seen and yet believe."

The Purpose of This Book

30 Now Jesus did many other signs in the presence of the disciples, which are not written in this book; ³¹but these are written that you may believe that Jesus is the Christ, the Son of God, and that believing you may have life in his name.

Jesus Appears to Disciples by the Sea of Tiberias

21 After this Jesus revealed himself again to the disciples by the Sea of Tibe′ri-as; and he revealed himself in this way. ²Simon Peter, Thomas called the Twin, Nathan′a-el of Cana in Galilee, the sons of Zeb′edee, and two others of his disciples were together. ³Simon Peter said to them, "I am going fishing." They said to him, "We will go with you." They went out and got into the boat; but that night they caught nothing.

4 Just as day was breaking, Jesus stood on the beach; yet the disciples did not know that it was Jesus. ⁵Jesus said to them, "Children, have you any fish?" They answered him, "No." ⁶He said to them, "Cast the net on the right side of the boat, and you will find some." So they cast it, and now they were not able to haul it in, for the quantity of fish. ⁷That disciple whom Jesus loved said to Peter, "It is the Lord!" When Simon Peter heard that it was the Lord, he put on his clothes, for he was stripped for work, and sprang into the sea. ⁸But the other disciples came in the boat, dragging the net full of fish, for they were not far from the land, but about a hundred yards off.

9 When they got out on land, they saw a charcoal fire there, with fish lying on it, and bread. ¹⁰Jesus said to them, "Bring some of the fish that you have just caught." ¹¹So Simon Peter went aboard and hauled the net ashore, full of large fish, a hundred and fifty-three of them; and although there were so many, the net was not torn. ¹²Jesus said to them, "Come and have breakfast." Now none of the disciples dared ask him, "Who are you?" They knew it was the Lord. ¹³Jesus came and took the bread and gave it to them, and so with the fish. ¹⁴This was now the third time that Jesus was revealed to the disciples after he was raised from the dead.

Peter Is Given a Command

15 When they had finished breakfast, Jesus said to Simon Peter, "Simon, son of John, do you love me more than these?" He said to him, "Yes, Lord; you know that I love you." He said to him, "Feed my lambs." [16]A second time he said to him, "Simon, son of John, do you love me?" He said to him, "Yes, Lord; you know that I love you." He said to him, "Tend my sheep." [17]He said to him the third time, "Simon, son of John, do you love me?" Peter was grieved because he said to him the third time, "Do you love me?" And he said to him, "Lord, you know everything; you know that I love you." Jesus said to him, "Feed my sheep. [18]Truly, truly, I say to you, when you were young, you fastened your own belt and walked where you would; but when you are old, you will stretch out your hands, and another will fasten your belt for you and carry you where you do not wish to go." [19](This he said to show by what death he was to glorify God.) And after this he said to him, "Follow me."

Jesus and the Beloved Disciple

20 Peter turned and saw following them the disciple whom Jesus loved, who had lain close to his breast at the supper and had said, "Lord, who is it that is going to betray you?" [21]When Peter saw him, he said to Jesus, "Lord, what about this man?" [22]Jesus said to him, "If it is my will that he remain until I come, what is that to you? Follow me!" [23]The saying spread abroad among the brethren that this disciple was not to die; yet Jesus did not say to him that he was not to die, but, "If it is my will that he remain until I come, what is that to you?"

24 This is the disciple who is bearing witness to these things, and who has written these things; and we know that his testimony is true.

25 But there are also many other things which Jesus did; were every one of them to be written, I suppose that the world itself could not contain the books that would be written.

Endnotes

[1] This phrase was coined by Fr. Richard John Neuhaus to describe the public disclosure by *The Boston Globe* beginning in January of 2002 of clergy sex abuse and cover-up by the Boston Archdiocese.

[2] This is not to say that the Church wasn't at times treated unfairly by the media, civil leaders, and people greedy for money. In fact, sometimes it was. Moreover, in some sense the Church *was* held to a higher standard by the larger society in terms of the scrutiny that it received. All that aside, my experience in the seminary environment and the clerical culture that sometimes comes with it was that a number of us may not have wanted to accept anything that might have challenged our assumption that, institutionally speaking, our house was in order. As it turned out, it was not, and we needed to take an honest look at our assumptions, which I eventually did, as we'll see.

[3] That Cardinal Law was considered by some as one of the "good guys" is based on the following: He was appointed archbishop of Boston by Pope John Paul II, was made a cardinal by the same pope, was well known as a leader of the pro-life movement in the United States, and initiated the *Catechism of the Catholic Church*.

[4] The book *Consoling the Heart of Jesus* actually predated the scandals of 2002 but has a backstory that's related to them.

Although the book was not published until 2010, I actually finished the first draft in the last days of 2001. After finishing it, I wanted to follow up with my spiritual director to continue sharing with him how consoling spirituality had been impacting me. We scheduled our meeting for Jan. 9, 2002. At the last minute, my director changed the venue from his religious house to the archdiocesan chancery, where he'd be working. Because I was unfamiliar with the chancery, I mistakenly went to Cardinal Law's residence, which was on the same grounds. As I approached the residence, I noticed a news van on the front lawn. I didn't think much of it at the time and proceeded to knock on the building's front door. A member of the cardinal's staff answered, and I told him I had a meeting scheduled there with my spiritual director. Looking very flustered, he abruptly replied, "You've got the wrong place. We're having a press conference right now with the cardinal. You'd better go." As I passed the news van on my way back, I saw a reporter, pressing her earpiece and saying into her microphone, "'*Tragically incorrect.*' *Did you get that? 'Tragically incorrect.*'" Though I didn't know it at the time, those were the words Cardinal Law had used during the press conference to describe his judgment regarding the handling of a priest in his archdiocese who had serially abused children. When I finally found the chancery, I asked my spiritual director what was going on. He told me that a story had recently broken of a big scandal in the archdiocese and that if ever Jesus' Heart needed to be consoled, it was now.

[5] The Marian Missionaries of Divine Mercy started out simply as a service and spiritual formation program for young people. It still is that — called the "M-1 Program" — but it has also expanded into an ecclesial

movement that provides a spirituality for priests, religious, and lay people throughout the world. See photo insert for more information.

[6] See *The Second Greatest Story Ever Told: Now Is the Time of Mercy* (Stockbridge: Marian Press, 2015).

[7] John Paul II, apostolic letter, *Novo Millennio Ineunte*, 57.

[8] John XXIII, opening address at the Second Eccumenical Council of the Vatican, Oct. 11, 1962.

[9] See *The 'One Thing' Is Three: How the Most Holy Trinity Explains Everything* (Stockbridge: Marian Press, 2012), pp. 101-128.

[10] Second Vatican Council, Dogmatic Constitution on the Church, *Lumen Gentium*, Nov. 21, 1964, 36.

[11] Ibid., Constitution on the Sacred Liturgy, *Sacrosanctum Concilium*, Dec. 4, 1963, 14.

[12] See *Lumen Gentium*, Chapter 5.

[13] See John Paul II, encyclical letter, *Dives in Misericorida*, November 13, 1980, 15.

[14] See Second Vatican Council, Dogmatic Constitution on Divine Revelation, *Dei Verbum*, Nov. 18, 1965, 25.

[15] In support of this point, for instance, see the following assessment of the intentions of the bishops regarding the drafting of the documents of the Second Vatican Council by one of the Council's most notable historians, Fr. Joseph A. Komonchak:

> The orientations of the Council were now set. The vote on the liturgical schema revealed the pastoral concerns of the bishops; the vote on the doctrinal text revealed that they did not wish to produce texts that simply repeated in neo-scholastic language the teachings of recent popes. Over the next three years the bishops would elaborate texts that departed from the traditional language and choose instead a rhetoric closer to the Bible, the Fathers of the Church, and the liturgy to express a far more positive, organic, and ecumenically sensitive statement of the faith. ... This transformation of purpose and of language greatly reduced the presence of St. Thomas [Aquinas] in the doctrinal texts ... .
> ["Thomism and the Second Vatican Council" in *Continuity and Plurality in Catholic Theology: Essays in Honor of Gerald A. McCool, S.J.*, ed. Anthony J. Cernera (Fairfield, CT: Sacred Heart University Press, 1998), pp. 58-59.]

[16] For instance, in the prologue to his *Commentary on the Gospel of John*, St. Thomas Aquinas writes: "Because secrets are revealed to friends ... Jesus confided his secrets in a special way to that disciple who was specially loved. ... [I]t is John who sees the light of the Incarnate Word more excellently and expresses it to us" (trans. James A. Weisheipl, OP [Albany: Magi Books, Inc., 1998]). It's for this reason that a tradition of the Church marks the Gospel of John with the symbol of an eagle,

indicating that it is the Gospel that soars. See St. Augustine, *The Homilies on John*, trans. C.C. Starbuck, Tractate XV.

[17] I'm going to assume, following the Tradition of the Church, that the author is the Apostle John, the Beloved Disciple, the apostle who was "loved by the Lord above the others." (Ant. 1, Morning Prayer, Feast of St. John, Apostle and Evangelist, Dec. 27)

[18] There's also the Presentation of the Lord on Feb. 2 and the Solemnity of All Saints on Nov. 1.

[19] There's an apparent contradiction in Exodus regarding the question of whether Moses actually saw God's face. In Exodus 33:11, it seems that he did: "Thus the Lord used to speak to Moses face to face, as a man speaks to his friend." But then in Exodus 33:20, it seems that he didn't: "You cannot see my face; for man shall not see me and live." So, did he or didn't he? Well, here's one interpretation. In the first instance, speaking to God "face to face, as a man speaks to his friend" simply indicates the familiarity with and closeness to God that Moses enjoyed. In the second instance, it's referring to something that goes beyond mere closeness and familiarity, namely, an intimacy that is reserved for the beatitude of Heaven, where we will see God "face to face" (the Beatific Vision) in the fullness of his divine glory. A couple verses before 33:20, we find the crucial context for understanding "seeing God's face" as the deeper intimacy that's reserved for Heaven. Specifically, Moses asks God for what cannot be fully experienced in this life: "I beg you, show me your glory" (Ex 33:18). By "glory," as this interpretation holds, he means the fullness of God's divine beauty, which again, goes beyond mere familiarity and closeness. One could say the latter is more akin to friendship while the former would be closer to spousal love. Moreover, the latter is what Moses enjoyed on earth while the former is what he enjoys in Heaven.

[20] Benedict XVI, *Jesus of Nazareth: From the Baptism in the Jordan to the Transfiguration*, trans. Adrian J. Walker (New York: Doubleday, 2007), pp. 5-6.

[21] At the beginning of each day's reading you will find the chapter and sometimes verses from the Gospel of John that indicate what will be covered during the day's reading. These chapters and verses will not be cited within the text itself. The exception is Scripture chapters and/or verses in parentheses, which indicate secondary treatment within the given day's text and will still be cited.

[22] If ever this text is read aloud, please be sure to vocalize the punctuation of "the Jews" by saying "quote, unquote the Jews." These quote marks are very important, as we'll see.

[23] The distinction between Jews and "the Jews" is also clear in John 7:13, where a crowd of Jews is said to have "fear of the Jews," meaning the religious leaders who are hostile to Jesus. Also, one could say that the term "the Jews" is geographical and not racial as it refers to the people in Jerusalem proper, around Judea. In this sense, John and Peter, who are from Galilee, are technically Galileans and not Jews.

[24] See Francis J. Moloney, SDB, *The Gospel of John* (Collegeville: The Liturgical Press, 1998), pp. 9-10.

[25] See Stephen K. Ray, *St. John's Gospel: A Bible Study Guide and Commentary* (San Francisco: Ignatius Press, 2002), pp. 185-186.

[26] *The Navarre Bible: The Gospel of Saint John* (New York: Scepter Press, 1984), p. 100.

[27] Some Scripture commentators speculate that the religious leaders "couldn't care less" about the woman perhaps because, in their own lives, they were used to thinking of and treating women as objects. They would not have considered it a problem, then, to exploit this woman to get at Jesus.

[28] Saint Augustine, *De Doctrina Christiana*, I.35.39-I.36.41.

[29] While Jesus Christ is truly God, who knows everything, it seems that in his human nature, the Incarnate Son allowed himself to be surprised or amazed by the other two divine Persons of the Trinity. For instance, see Luke 7:9 and Matthew 8:10, where the Holy Spirit is clearly working in the centurion, giving him a gift of faith that causes Jesus to marvel and be amazed. Also, apart from the interpretation given in the text to this passage of John, we read from Mark 13:32 and Matthew 24:36 that only the Father knows the day and the hour when Heaven and earth will pass away. Finally, the *Catechism* summarizes for us the theology of the human knowledge of Jesus:

> This human soul that the Son of God assumed is endowed with a true human knowledge. As such, this knowledge could not in itself be unlimited: it was exercised in the historical conditions of his existence in space and time. This is why the Son of God could, when he became man, "increase in wisdom and in stature, and in favour with God and man" (Lk 2:52), and would even have to inquire for himself about what one in the human condition can learn only from experience. This corresponded to the reality of his voluntary emptying of himself, taking "the form of a slave" (Phi 2:7).
>
> But at the same time, this truly human knowledge of God's Son expressed the divine life of his person. "The human nature of God's Son, not by itself but by its union with the Word, knew and showed forth in itself everything that pertains to God." Such is first of all the case with the intimate and immediate knowledge that the Son of God made man has of his Father. The Son in his human knowledge also showed the divine penetration he had into the secret thoughts of human hearts. (English translation of the *Catechism of the Catholic Church: Modifications from the Editio Typica* (Washington, D.C./Vatican: United States Catholic Conference, Inc./Libreria Editrice Vaticana, 1997), 472-473)

[30] It's interesting that the father asks the "hour" when his son began to mend, because it's in the "hour" of the Passion of Jesus that God the Father's future sons and daughters will begin to mend.

[31] The Sabbath was also meant to be a memorial of God's action of freeing Israel from bondage in Egypt (see Deut 5:12-15).

[32] See Francis Martin and William M. Wright IV, *The Gospel of John* (Grand Rapids: Baker Academic, 2015), p. 100.

[33] Ibid, p. 105

[34] *Catechism*, 679.

[35] Saint Augustine, *Confessions*, Book I:1. Also, commenting on this passage from the Gospel of John about the Father who draws us, the saint writes, "Give me a man that loves, and he feels what I say. Give me one that longs, one that hungers, one that is traveling in this wilderness, and thirsting and panting after the fountain of his eternal home; give such, and he knows what I say." (*The Homilies on John*, Tractate XXVI.)

[36] Jean Vanier, *Drawn into the Mystery of Jesus Through the Gospel of John*, (New York/Mahwah, New Jersey: Paulist Press, 2004), p. 196.

[37] See *Paschale Solemnitatis, Circular Letter Concerning the Preparation and Celebration of the Easter Feasts*, Congregation for Divine Worship and the Discipline of the Sacraments, 1988, 56:

> After the Mass of the Lord's Supper the faithful should be encouraged to spend a suitable period of time during the night in the church in adoration before the Blessed Sacrament which has been solemnly reserved. Where appropriate, this prolonged eucharistic adoration may be accompanied by the reading of some part of the Gospel of St. John (chs. 13-17).

[38] *Catechism*, 125.

[39] *The Homilies on John*, Tractate XV.

[40] See *Catechism*, 234: "The mystery of the Most Holy Trinity is the central mystery of Christian faith and life. It is the mystery of God in himself. It is therefore the source of all the other mysteries of faith, the light that enlightens them. It is the most fundamental and essential teaching in the 'hierarchy of the truths of the faith.'"

[41] See 1 Cor 11:23-25.

[42] If the Concluding Doxology is the Consecration's "culmination," one might say that the Consecration's "consumation" is Holy Communion. Holy Communion is the moment of personal intimacy when we receive the Body and Blood of Jesus into our very bodies. Now, in my experience, while people tend to more readily appreciate both the Consecration and Communion as particularly powerful and profound moments of Mass, which they truly are, I believe the Concluding Doxology, which may be even more sublime, is often underappreciated. Why? I wonder if it is because the Concluding Doxology is more explicit about a mystery that, to many, seems esoteric and out of touch: namely, the mystery of the Most Holy Trinity. That the Gospel of John underscores this most important

mystery in the context of the Eucharist is a testament to its greatness. However, as I've pointed out, the Gospel of John is often underappreciated because of its mysticism and mystery. And so, unfortunately, the Concluding Doxology also remains underappreciated.

[43] *Catechism*, 221.

[44] Ibid., 51.

[45] Ibid., 478.

[46] Henri J. Nouwen, *The Return of the Prodigal Son* (New York: Convergent, 1992), pp. 43-45.

[47] Ibid., p. 45.

[48] Saint Thomas Aquinas, *Commentary on the Gospel of John*, 1997.

[49] Francis J. Moloney, SDB, *Love in the Gospel of John: An Exegetical, Theological, and Literary Study* (Grand Rapids: Baker Academic, 2013), p. ix.

[50] Saint Athanasius, *De Incarnatione Verbi Dei*, 54:3.

[51] *Catechism*, 221.

[52] Ibid, 51.

[53] For more on the topic of our "divinization," of our becoming "partakers of the divine nature" (2 Pet 1:4), see *The 'One Thing' Is Three*, p. 39-46.

[54] See *Lumen Gentium*, Chapter 5.

[55] The greatest passage in all of Scripture? Obviously, not everyone will agree with me on this, but I've got a good reason for saying it. Here's how I came to discover this passage and how it's all about communion.

I began by asking myself, "If I could only memorize one great passage in all of the Bible, what would it be?" I didn't know. So, I began a process of elimination. I began with the broadest of choices: Old Testament or New Testament? Surely, "the greatest passage" would be in the New Testament, because that's where Christ is most fully revealed.

Next, I thought, "Okay, so what category of books in the New Testament are likely to contain the passage I seek?" That was also easy. Even though I love the Acts of the Apostles, St. Paul and his letters, and those of St. John, I knew that, as the *Catechism* teaches, "The Gospels are the heart of all the scriptures 'because they are our principal source for the life and teaching'" of Jesus Christ, our Savior (125). So, I figured that the greatest passage must be located in the Gospels. Alright, but which one? Matthew, Mark, Luke, or John?

That was also an easy choice for me: The Gospel of John. The other three Gospels follow more or less the same storyline (hence, they're known collectively as the "synoptic Gospels"). The Gospel of John is different. It blazes its own trail. And what a trail it blazes! A tradition in the Church gives it the symbol of an eagle, because it's the Gospel that soars. It's the last Gospel, written by the apostle who was "loved by the Lord above the others," a Gospel that's the fruit of his lifelong contemplation on the mystery of the Word made flesh. It's the Gospel recommended by great saints and mystics as containing the deepest riches of our faith and mysteries of Christ.

Alright, so that narrowed it down for me. I would find "the greatest passage" in the Gospel of John. But where specifically? John has 21 chapters, and they're all filled to the brim. Well, the Gospel of John is divided into two major sections: the Book of Signs and the Book of Glory. The Book of Signs is about how Jesus reveals himself to the world and to "his own" and how they don't receive him. The Book of Glory is about how Jesus reveals his glory to those who do receive him. Of course, I want to receive him and behold his glory, so I chose the Book of Glory.

Now, the Book of Glory is divided into three sections: The Farewell Discourse, the Passion and Death, and the Resurrection. So, where's the greatest passage? I chose to look in the Farewell Discourse, which spans chapters 13-17. Why? Because that's where all the glory of the suffering, death, and Resurrection is explained. More specifically, it contains Jesus' last words to his disciples on the very night he was betrayed, right before he plunges into the dark "hour" of his suffering and death. In other words, it contains Jesus' precious last words, his "farewell" to his disciples — and he truly saves the best for last. Just as dying people often save their most meaningful declarations of love for the end, so also Jesus reserves his most sublime and intimate teaching for these chapters. For instance, in them, we find "the new commandment" (13:34), "the vine and the branches" (15:5), and "the way, and the truth, and the life" (14:6).

After I had already decided to limit my search for "the greatest passage" to the Farewell Discourse, I read something in the *Diary of Saint Faustina Kowalska* that seemed to confirm for me that this discourse truly hides a mystery that's unsurpassed in beauty. Referring to the place of the last discourse as the "Cenacle" (also known as the "upper room" of the Last Supper), the great mystic of Divine Mercy writes:

> Holy Hour. — Thursday. During this hour of prayer, Jesus allowed me to enter the Cenacle, and I was witness to what happened there. However, I was most deeply moved when, before the Consecration, Jesus raised His eyes to heaven and entered into a mysterious conversation with His Father. It is only in eternity that we shall really understand that moment. His eyes were like two flames; His face was radiant, white as snow; His whole personage full of majesty, His soul full of longing. At the moment of Consecration, love rested satiated — the sacrifice fully consummated. Now only the external ceremony of death will be carried out — external destruction; the essence [of it] is in the Cenacle. Never in my whole life had I understood this mystery so profoundly as during that hour of adoration. Oh, how ardently I desire that the whole world would come to know this unfathomable mystery! [*The Diary of Saint Maria Faustina Kowalska: Divine Mercy in My Soul* (Stockbridge: Marian Press, 1987), 684].

What is this unfathomable mystery? What is the great longing of Jesus? What is his profound conversation with the Father? I believe that this remarkable passage from the *Diary* is referring to the climax of the entire Farewell Discourse: Chapter 17. In my opinion, this chapter is the greatest in all of Sacred Scripture. Why? Because in this chapter, Jesus is no longer speaking his last, glorious words of love to his disciples. Rather, even more glorious still, he's speaking his last, glorious words of love to his heavenly Father. It's in this chapter that the veil is lifted, the veil that covers the eternal exchange of love of the Most Holy Trinity. It's in this chapter that, more than anywhere else, we get a glimpse into the fundamental longing of the Heart of Jesus, precisely as he ardently expresses it to his Father.

And what is it that Jesus longs for? What is his burning desire? *That we all be one.* He wants us all to participate in the communion of love of the Most Holy Trinity. Read Chapter 17. It's all there. Jesus expresses his desire over and over in different ways, poetically weaving a kind of tapestry of communion and love. For instance, he prays to the Father "that they may all be one; even as thou, Father, art in me, and I in thee, that they also may be in us" (v. 21). The beauty of the expression in verse after glorious verse doesn't dilute the clarity of the desire: Jesus wants us to be one with him in the Most Holy Trinity.

But again, remember: My quest was to find one specific passage to memorize, not a whole chapter. No problem. The last verses of the chapter get to the heart of the matter, and they contain what I believe is the most beautiful passage in all of Sacred Scripture, a passage that reveals the mystery at the Heart of the Word made flesh and the deepest expression of communion:

> Father, I desire that they also, whom thou hast given me, may be with me where I am, to behold my glory which thou has given me in thy love for me before the foundation of the world. O righteous Father, the world has not known thee, but I have known thee, and these know that thou hast sent me. I made known to them thy name, and I will make it known, that the love with which thou hast loved me may be in them and I in them (Jn 17:24-26) (*The 'One Thing' Is Three*, pp. 21-23).

[56] For more on the reaction of the angels to God's plan of love for humanity, see *The 'One Thing' Is Three*, pp. 46-49.

[57] Saint Thomas Aquinas, *Summa Theologiae*, I, q. 21, a. 2c.

[58] See Ignace de la Potterie, SJ, *The Hour of Jesus: The Passion and the Resurrection of Jesus According to John* (New York: Alba House, 1989), p. 69: "John has quite a different view [from the western, medieval one]. With him the word 'truth' must be understood in the biblical sense. Already in ancient apocalyptic and wisdom literature 'truth' signifies the revelation of the divine plan of salvation. The 'truth' is not the being of things, but the manifestation, the revealing of God's plan. According to the literary genre where this use is employed, the 'truth' is transmitted

by the word of a prophet, the message of an angel, by a supernatural apparition or by the explanation of an enigma. But it is always a revelation in which a divine secret is revealed."

[59] See *33 Days to Merciful Love: A Do-It-Yourself Retreat in Preparation for Consecration to Divine Mercy,* (Stockbridge: Marian Press, 2016), pp. 153-157.

[60] See Ibid., pp. 160-166.

[61] But what about the fact that it says John saw and believed? According to St. Augustine, he believed that what Mary Magdalene had said was true: His body really was no longer there (*The Homilies on John,* Tratate, CXX). Or if he did believe, it clearly wasn't yet mature faith.

[62] As we read in the Book of Revelation, God the Father and Jesus are both referred to as the Alpha and the Omega, the beginning and the end (1:8; 21:6-7; 22:13). In the Gospel of John, the emphasis is on the Father being the final end, the one to whom Jesus leads us. In this sense, Jesus is not the end but, rather, the Father is the end.

[63] Tertullian, *Apologeticus* ch. 39, sect. 7

[64] *Catechism,* 398.

[65] For more about our role in bringing all of creation back to the Father, see *The 'One Thing' Is Three,* pp. 57-71.

[66] See the following passages from Sacred Scripture that point to the maternal characteristics of God: Is 49:15-16; Is 46:3-4; Is 66:13. Also, see Pope John Paul II's comments on such characteristics in his encyclical letter *Dives in Misericordia* (endnote 52) in the context of his analysis of the concept of mercy in the Old Testament.

[67] I should point out that essential to living the consecration to the Father is not just looking but *listening.* Listening to what? Listening to the Father saying to us what he says to all of his sons and daughters: "*You are my beloved.*"

[68] If you're interested in other prayers of entrustment to the Father, here's a popular one by Blessed Charles de Foucauld:

> Father,
> I abandon myself into your hands; do with me what you will.
> Whatever you may do, I thank you:
> I am ready for all, I accept all.
> Let only your will be done in me, and in all your creatures.
> I wish no more than this, O Lord.
> Into your hands I commend my soul;
> I offer it to you
> with all the love of my heart,
> for I love you, Lord,
> and so need to give myself,
> to surrender myself into your hands,
> without reserve,
> and with boundless confidence,
> for you are my Father.

Here's another one by a friend of mine, Fr. James Devine:

> Father, I give my life into your hands this day. Please help me to trust in your infinite goodness, even in the midst of deepest darkness, after the example of my mother Mary.
>
> May I never doubt that you watch over me every second of every day and may my heart always be turned to you like the heart of your Son, Jesus.
>
> May you always be my source of comfort and consolation in this life, following the example of your Son, and help me to resist the voice of the tempter in his efforts to turn my heart from you.
>
> Father, my Father, help me to believe that I am your beloved child and help me to trust you with all my heart all the days of my life.
>
> Amen.

[69] In the final scene of Mel Gibson's movie *The Passion of the Christ*, Jesus looks up to the Father immediately after the Resurrection. That moment captures the kind of intensity and fullness that a look up to the Father can have. There's another scene from the movie, as Jesus prepares to be horrifically scouraged, where he looks up and prays to the Father. It captures the kind of love that a look up in suffering can express. We, too, can look up to the Father when we're going through darkness or light, desolation or consolation, and the Father is always there.

When I was reading a draft manuscript of this book to the Marian Missionaries of Divine Mercy in Lee, Massachusetts, they told me about a beautiful song by the Christian singer Lauren Daigle called "Look Up Child." I listened to it, and it's a great way to remember the simple summary of our retreat: *Look up.*

[70] *Return of the Prodigal Son*, p. 45.

[71] John Vanier has several video series that cover the Gospel of John, most of which were available as free streaming on Amazon Prime Video at the time of this printing. One is called *Knowing Eternity: A Probing Examination of the Gospel of John Chapters 1-10 with Jean Vanier* and also *Knowing Eternity Volume 2.* A second series, not available for free streaming on Amazon Prime Video, is called *Knowing Ourselves: A Continuing Examination of the Gospel of John Chapters 11-18 with Jean Vanier.* A third series is called *Experiencing the Mystical*, which covers chapter 13 to the end of the Gospel.

[72] There's also the Presentation of the Lord on Feb. 2 and the Solemnity of All Saints on Nov. 1.

Resource Pages

Hearts Afire: Parish-based Programs (HAPP®)
from the Marian Fathers of the Immaculate Conception

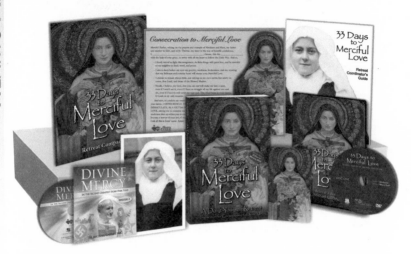

Hearts Afire Parish-based Programs provide dynamic, easy-to-use, and affordable group retreats and studies for the following popular titles from Marian Press:

- *33 Days to Morning Glory*
- *33 Days to Merciful Love*
- *Consoling the Heart of Jesus*
- *The 'One Thing' Is Three/You Did It to Me*
- *The Second Greatest Story Ever Told*

Hearts AFIRE
Parish-based Programs from the
Marian Fathers of the Immaculate Conception

HAPP: 1-844-551-3755
Orders: 1-800-462-7426
AllHeartsAfire.org
HAPP@marian.org

Mercy Through Mary Collegiate Outreach

Be part of the Mercy through Mary national collegiate outreach of the Mary and Mercy Center in Ave Maria, FL, and bring the Marian Missionary of Divine Mercy spirituality to your campus, starting with *33 Days to Morning Glory*. This outreach offers free copies of the four 33-day retreats required to become a Marian Missionary. Visit **MercyThroughMary.com**.

Spiritual Enrollments & Masses

As a work of mercy, you can request a Mass to be offered by the Marian Fathers for your loved ones both living and deceased. Gregorian Masses (30 days of consecutive Masses for the deceased) are also available. Also, if you know someone who has experienced the loss of a loved one or who is need of prayer, a Marian spiritual enrollment allows them to share in the graces from the Masses, prayers, good works, and merits of the Marian priests, brothers, and seminarians throughout the world.

marian.org/enrollments • marian.org/mass
1-800-462-7426

Fire Mountain Retreat Center

Those who'd like to go deeper into the Marian Missionary of Divine Mercy spirituality are invited to come for a retreat at the Fire Mountain Retreat Center in Becket, Massachusetts. This stunning mountaintop facility is just a 30 min drive from the National Shrine of Divine Mercy in Stockbridge. Nestled in the beautiful Berkshire mountains, it a perfect destination for spiritual renewal. Visit FireMountainRetreatCenter.org.

Federal Inn Guest House

This beautiful Guest House is located five minutes from the National Shrine of Divine Mercy and across the street from the Marian Missionaries. Contact us at Info@MarianMissionaries.org.

Marian Missionaries

Want to live in a joyful community, grow in your faith, and live a life of prayer and service? Then maybe the Marian Missionaries of Divine Mercy "M-1 Year" is for you. If you're a single man or woman between the ages of 18-35, send us an email at M1@MarianMissionaries.org.

THE GOSPEL ACCORDING TO JOHN

ENHANCE YOUR RETREAT WITH
THE GOSPEL ACCORDING TO JOHN AUDIO DRAMA!

⬇ DOWNLOAD FOR **FREE** HERE:
WWW.STLUKEPRODUCTIONS.COM/JOHN
USE THE CODE: **GLORY**

MARIAN MISSIONARIES
of
DIVINE MERCY

A Spirituality of Mary, Mercy, and Community

The Marian Missionaries of Divine Mercy provides a spirituality for priests, religious, and most especially, laypeople. Even more specifically, it's geared toward those who want to become saints but who may see themselves as too weak, broken, and sinful to ever hope to achieve great sanctity. Drawing upon the testimony of St. John Paul II that "now is the time of mercy," the Marian Missionaries joyfully embrace this special moment of grace, a grace that accords with Romans 5:20: "where sin abounded, grace abounded all the more." At the heart of this abounding grace is the good news that, in a certain sense, God is making it easier than ever before to become great saints, especially through the teachings of the main patrons of the Missionaries, namely, Saints John Paul II, Thérèse of Lisieux, Faustina Kowalska, Mother Teresa, and Maximilian Kolbe.

Inspired by our patrons, the Marian Missionaries feel called to a great sanctity that is not fundamentally determined by ardent spiritual labors. Rather, first and foremost, this sanctity is the fruit of discovering the incredible tenderness of the Heart of Jesus, a tenderness beautifully depicted in the original Image of Divine Mercy. It's the fruit of a daily encounter with that tenderness, where our great misery meets God's greater mercy. It's the fruit of a firm commitment to love others with the same tenderness that we ourselves have received from the Lord. Finally, it's the fruit of our trust in the power of Divine Mercy to transform us into great saints, into living Images of Divine Mercy.

Of course, as *Marian* Missionaries of Divine Mercy, the Immaculate Mother of God has a special role in all of this. She's the one who, with her Spouse, the Holy Spirit, helps pull aside the veil that prevents us from seeing the goodness and tender mercy of God. She's the one who obtains for us the grace of the Holy Spirit to repent of sin and then to believe, accept, and trust in Divine Mercy. She's the one who, therefore, obtains for us the joy of the Gospel, which is the fundamental spiritual attitude of every Marian Missionary of Divine Mercy.

Now, this summary of the Missionary spirituality gets fleshed out and becomes something concrete and real through the books on the back cover. Because those books are so important for understanding and embracing the spirituality, let's briefly look at what they're all about.

Admittedly, there are a lot of books on the back cover. So where do we begin? Well, while one can read them in any order, here's the ideal sequence. First, start with *33 Days to Morning Glory*. That book is about Mary and, at least implicitly, her Spouse, the Holy Spirit. But it doesn't end with Mary and the Holy Spirit. They bring us to a personal encounter with Jesus in his mercy, which is what *33 Days to Merciful Love* is all about. But it doesn't end with Jesus, either. Jesus brings us home to God, our Father, whom we get to know in *33 Days to Greater Glory*. More specifically, relying on the Gospel of John, that book highlights the greater glory of the Mass that brings us through Christ, with Christ, and in Christ, in the unity of the Holy Spirit, into the communion of love that ends with God our Father and embraces us even now.

In summary (and this is what the forthcoming book *33 Days to Mary, Mercy, and Community* is all about), you might say that the Marian Missionary spirituality really comes down to three things. You guessed it: Mary, Mercy, and Community.

Now, if you want to go deeper into the spirituality, you'll also want to read the books at the bottom of the back cover, the books that correspond to *33 Days to Morning Glory* (Mary), *33 Days to Merciful Love* (Mercy), and *33 Days to Greater Glory* (Community). You may also want to participate in the Hearts Afire Programs, which cover the various books through the experience of small group community. Finally, because a spirituality is best communicated not through books and programs but by those who strive to incarnate its ideals, we invite you to come visit the vibrant community of Marian Missionaries at their headquarters in Lee, Massachusetts, which is just down the street from the National Shrine of Divine Mercy in Stockbridge. Find out how you can come for a visit or make a retreat at the end of these pages. To learn more, please visit our website, **MarianMissionaries.org**.

Marian Missionary Community
Lee, Massachusetts

Just a five minute drive from the National Shrine of Divine Mercy, the Marian Missionaries welcome guests, run a farm, staff a retreat center (in nearby Becket), and serve the poor and lonely in the region.